THE TEN COMMANDMENTS
FOR JEWS, CHRISTIANS, AND OTHERS

The Ten Commandments
for Jews, Christians, and Others

Edited by

ROGER E. VAN HARN

William B. Eerdmans Publishing Company
Grand Rapids, Michigan / Cambridge, U.K.

© 2007 Wm. B. Eerdmans Publishing Co.

Published 2007 by
Wm. B. Eerdmans Publishing Co.
2140 Oak Industrial Drive N.E., Grand Rapids, Michigan 49505 /
P.O. Box 163, Cambridge CB3 9PU U.K.

Printed in the United States of America

12 11 10 09 08 07   7 6 5 4 3 2 1

Library of Congress Cataloging-in-Publication Data

The Ten commandments for Jews, Christians, and others /
edited by Roger E. Van Harn.
p.   cm.
ISBN 978-0-8028-2965-8 (pbk.: alk. paper)
1. Ten commandments — Criticism, interpretation, etc.
I. Van Harn, Roger, 1932-

BS1285.52.T46   2007
222′.1606 — dc22

2007011303

www.eerdmans.com

Contents

Contents

Foreword

Peter W. Ochs

On the North Shore of Long Island in the 1950s, Jewish-Christian relations remained largely at the stage of asking questions about how or whether to integrate "exclusive" neighborhoods and country clubs. At least that is how I remember it. As the only Jewish child in my culturally Protestant grade school, the central question of "Jewish-Christian dialogue" was one I asked myself: "Will her mom let her date a Jew?" The social histories I have since read suggest that my childhood memory may not be far off the mark. In those days in those places, the questions were about social etiquette and, sometimes, ethics.

This very dear and profound volume shows us how far we have come: so far that the book's central dialogue is not between Jews and Christians but between some very fine readers of Scripture — both Jewish and Christian scholars — and the God who declared "You shall have no other gods before me!"

The essays of this volume bear the fruit of many layers of maturation since those early dialogues of the 1950s. First, there is the opening of Christian theologians, in the decades after the Holocaust, to reconsider and then acknowledge the people Israel's enduring covenant with the God of Israel. It then took some decades of care from a widening circle of Christian colleagues before Jewish theologians opened themselves, in response, to address topics of Christian theology without defensiveness.[1] During these

---

1. One mark of this opening was "Dabru Emet: A Jewish Statement on Christians and Christianity," which appeared in 1991 along with the accompanying book, *Christianity in Jewish Terms*, ed. Frymer-Kensky et al. (Boulder, Colo.: Westview, 1991). *The Ten Commandments for Jews, Christians, and Others* deepens, extends, and expands this earlier opening.

decades the topics of Jewish-Christian interaction deepened as well: stimulated first by concerns about civil rights, then by issues of supererogatory ethics, and only recently by fundamental questions of theology. The turn to theology has led, in only the past decade or so, to a turn to Scripture, and with it a return to social ethics — reread, now, as a topic of revealed instruction.

This volume is one of the first and finest fruits of this latest turn. While acknowledging differences and similarities between the two traditions of reading, the essays of this volume devote their greatest attention to the Ten Words (or Commandments) themselves. Each essay reads one of the words on several levels at once: intrascripturally, and through the lens of each distinct tradition of theological commentary, and for the sake of illuminating the everyday lives of believing Jews and Christians today, and, hopefully, to offer scriptural guidelines for our responses to today's societal challenges and crises. This is the singular achievement of this volume: to gather Jewish and Christian scholars, side by side, who are so attentive to Scripture's commanding voice that they cease to be overly self-conscious about the Jewish or Christian interlocutors who sit beside them. One senses that when these authors do comment on one another's reading, both affirmatively and critically, it is for the sake of better hearing what God has to say to us, not for the sake of dialogue itself. This is, I believe, the truest sign of how these authors glorify God — the way the psalmist declares that "one generation will laud your work to another" (Ps. 145), for "YHWH frees the bound, . . . gives sight to the blind, . . . raises those bowed down; he loves the just" (Ps. 146), so that "at his command the ice melts; he stirs the wind and the waters flow" (Ps. 147).

In the process, the words of these authors should turn the attention of all readers — from whatever their traditions of reading and belief — to the issues themselves: the actual human condition today and in what strong and complex ways the Words of the Tablets speak to them. We read of the first word: of the "I am" who is at once the God of all creation beyond the limits of time and the God of Israel in historical time: united in the God who commands each person and nation to care for the *other*. Then the second word: of the One and only One whom we may worship and adore, whatever images and thoughts we may have of him. Then the third word: of the name of God that names both whom we cannot know and whom we know most intimately in the way we become with him. Then the fourth word: of hallowing a day in both cosmic and historical time the way we hallow God, as both separate from us and elevated within us. Then the fifth word: of the limitless and limited obligations of child to parent, complementing those of parent to child and of creature to the Creator who is parent of us all. Then the sixth word — which, for this era of Shoah and genocide, may now be heard as a supererogatory command: to defend the life of the other. Then the seventh word: of hallowing the Creator's love for us by both disciplining and celebrating marital love in this created world. Then the eighth word: which, for a society of such unequal abundance, may now be heard as a supererogatory command to assure the economic well-being of our neighbors. Then the ninth word: to employ words not only not to injure, but also to portray the other and oneself in the best light. Then the tenth word: which, for a society of unequal abundance, may now be heard as a supererogatory command: to employ what we have been given for the sake of service, charity, and holiness.

It is unlikely that the readers of this book will tremble with fear and "stand at a distance," as did the first auditors of the Ten Words (Exod. 20:18). However, with eyes open to the needs of our world, and ears tuned to our covenanting Creator, a slight tremor could be a harbinger of better things to come.

Preface

A recent news brief sidebar in our daily paper boldly reported what appeared to be a revolutionary event: "Ten Commandments OK'd." The event to which the notice referred turned out to be less dramatic than what the headline suggested. In Lincoln, Nebraska, a federal appeals court had reversed an order to remove a Ten Commandments monument from a city park. Removing or approving a monument is considerably less radical than stamping a *nihil obstat* on the ten "words" or "utterances" we know more popularly as the ten "commandments."

The judge who allowed the monument to stand did so because "it acknowledges the role of religion in our nation's heritage." While that may be an honorable basis for a monument on the grounds of the Texas Capitol or a Nebraska city park, it is not an adequate basis for the publication of this book. This book is based on the conviction that the "Decalogue" was given by God to guide the life of God's covenant community.

Since the birth of the Christian church, the covenant community has been known and experienced as two faith communities: Jewish and Christian. Careful attention to the list of Eerdmans publications during the last ten years reveals what was hardly noticeable along the way, namely, the titles that encouraged or expressed partnership between Jewish and Christian theologians. The titles themselves are revealing: *Preaching Biblical Texts: Expositions by Jewish and Christian Scholars,* edited by Fredrick C. Holmgren and Herman E. Schaalman (1995); *Jews and Christians: Rivals or Partners for the Kingdom of God? In Search of an Alternative for the Theology of Substitution,* edited by Didier Pollefeyt (1998); *Jews and Christians: The Parting of the Ways, A.D. 70 to 135,* edited by James D. G. Dunn (1999); *The Old Testament and the Significance of Jesus: Embracing Change — Main-*

taining Christian Identity, by Fredrick C. Holmgren (1999); *Jews and Christians: People of God,* edited by Carl E. Braaten and Robert W. Jenson (2003); *The Jewish-Christian Schism Revisited,* by John Howard Yoder, edited by Michael G. Cartwright and Peter Ochs (2003); *Abraham's Promise: Judaism and Jewish-Christian Relations,* by Michael Wyschogrod, edited and introduced by R. Kendall Soulen (2004); *Talking with Christians: Musings of a Jewish Theologian,* by David Novak (2005).

The Decalogue provides a unique opportunity to practice the partnership that characterizes the above titles. Through the mediation of Moses, the Decalogue was received by Israel at Mount Sinai, and therefore lies at the heart of the Lord's covenant. It has also been firmly lodged in Christian teaching and catechisms. The older covenant and the newer covenant communities, therefore, have both been nurtured by the "ten words" to know the love for God and neighbor that life in covenant with God requires. This volume expresses partnership in each chapter, following the order of the Ten Words.

None of the contributors claims to speak for all Jews or all Christians. The representative contributors express the understandings, insights, and values that derive from the "commandment" being considered. They have made no attempt to homogenize the variety of emphases that characterize thought in Jewish and Christian communities. Nor have they attempted to reduce Jewish and Christian teaching to fit the categories of religion in general. The partnership practiced here has not been purchased at the cost of sacrificing Jewish or Christian identity.

The authors and publisher offer these essays and responses to them in the hope that they will encourage partnership and stimulate conversation. Listening to one another may hold pleasant surprises that open us to new possibilities. What Christian, for example, will not identify with and benefit from the testimony of Elie Wiesel:

> Since my childhood, without ever losing interest, I have continued to study the biblical stories that remain the foundation of Jewish history. Each reading brings with it a new excitement and previously unsuspected meaning.
>
> Adam and Eve, Cain and Abel, Noah and his survival, Abraham and Isaac, Joseph and his brothers, Moses and the tragedy of his destiny: for decades I have tried to understand them, knowing all the while that I will never succeed. . . .

Today, I am far from the child I was, but that child's questions remain open questions — my questions. I learn these texts again, I study the midrashic commentaries on them: their mysterious light fascinates but does not soothe me. What next? I will carry on.[1]

Or what Jew could not appreciate the seriousness with which Calvin Seerveld takes the Torah as he introduces the Torah Psalms:

> *Torah* is the rich biblical term noted Jewish theologian Martin Buber translates *Weisung*, meaning the guidance and leading of the covenantal LORD God. . . .
>
> Simply put, *torah* refers to the underlying provident will of the trustworthy God of the universe and to God's Spirit-leading in the direction of shalom. *Torah* reveals creational laws like gravity to be God's hug for all creatures — not an impediment, but an upholding embrace. God's will reiterated at Sinai is a hedge to protect us from wasting our lifetime by stumbling off the Way of blessing. The LORD's *torah* reposited by Jesus Christ for us humans to follow (Matthew 5–7; Galatians 5:16–6:2) has the liberating effect of asking us to mature in thankfulness for the LORD God's loving hold on our daily lives and to bear each other's burdens. *Torah* is why Jesus taught us to pray, "Your will be done, O God, on earth as it is in heaven."[2]

It may help the reader of these pages, whether Jew, Christian, or other, to remember that the Ten Commandments were given and received on a freedom march of the Lord's redeemed people.

ROGER E. VAN HARN

1. Elie Wiesel, foreword to *Preaching Biblical Texts: Expositions by Jewish and Christian Scholars*, ed. Fredrick C. Holmgren and Herman E. Schaalman (Grand Rapids: Eerdmans, 1995), p. viii.

2. Calvin Seerveld, *Voicing God's Psalms* (Grand Rapids: Eerdmans, 2005), p. 3.

The Ten Words

Exodus 20:2-17
(New Revised Standard Version)

1. I am the LORD your God, who brought you out of the land of Egypt, out of the house of slavery; you shall have no other gods before me.
2. You shall not make for yourself an idol, whether in the form of anything that is in heaven above, or that is on the earth beneath, or that is in the water under the earth. You shall not bow down to them or worship them; for I the LORD your God am a jealous God, punishing children for the iniquity of parents, to the third and fourth generation of those who reject me, but showing steadfast love to the thousandth generation of those who love me and keep my commandments.
3. You shall not make wrongful use of the name of the LORD your God, for the LORD will not acquit anyone who misuses his name.
4. Remember the sabbath day, and keep it holy. Six days you shall labor and do all your work. But the seventh day is a sabbath to the LORD your God; you shall not do any work — you, your son or your daughter, your male or female slave, your livestock, or the alien resident in your towns. For in six days the LORD made heaven and earth, the sea, and all that is in them, but rested the seventh day; therefore the LORD blessed the sabbath day and consecrated it.
5. Honor your father and your mother, so that your days may be long in the land that the LORD your God is giving you.
6. You shall not murder.
7. You shall not commit adultery.
8. You shall not steal.
9. You shall not bear false witness against your neighbor.
10. You shall not covet your neighbor's house; you shall not covet your neighbor's wife, or male or female slave, or ox, or donkey, or anything that belongs to your neighbor.

The Face of Ethical Encounter

James A. Diamond

I am the LORD *your God . . . you shall have no other gods before me.*

The first of the Ten Commandments (or more appropriately the "ten utterances," translated by the Septuagint Greek as *deka logoi*) reads. "I am the
LORD your God, who brought you out of the land of Egypt, out of the
house of slavery; you shall have no other gods before me" (Exod. 20:2-3;
Deut. 5:6-7). One is immediately struck by what does not really amount to
much of a commandment but appears to be more in the nature of an introduction, a legislative preamble, a greeting. Despite variant rabbinic traditions as to whether "I am God . . ." and "You shall have no other gods"
are to be counted as two separate commandments, by all accounts the ten
commence with "I am God," which either stands alone or forms an integral component of the first.[1]

It assumes an encounter with a power, among others, that must identify itself and establish its credentials in order to command authority and
inspire obedience. There is a relational history between this power and the
Israelites it addresses, marked by a collective memory of an event unique
to this addressee's heritage. It is an "I" that recalls a deliverance that would
radically reorient the direction in which this people were headed and re-
ignite a national vitality thought irrecoverable after generations of brutal
repression under the ancient Egyptians. Since the Israelites had been a nation enslaved by another, God's identity as the promulgator of the Ten

1. See Mordechai Breuer, "Dividing the Decalogue into Verses and Commandments," in
The Ten Commandments in History and Tradition, ed. B. Z. Segal and G. Levi (Jerusalem:
Magnes Press, 1990), pp. 291-330.

3

Commandments is vindicated by recalling his liberation of them, what itself amounts to a granting of identity and selfhood.

As a scholar of Jewish studies and as a practicing Jew, I cannot simply encounter the words on the biblical page but must listen to the myriad of voices that emerge from the long interpretive tradition since those initial words were first heard and ultimately transferred to parchment. In this sense, the very first commandment is no different from any other verse (or for that matter, due to the perceived hyper-significance of divine authorship, any word, character, shape, cantillation mark, or indeed the very blank spaces on the page!) in the Hebrew Bible where consensus as to meaning has never been achieved. Unanimity of opinion has never been the goal of the Jewish exegetical enterprise. It is the interpretive process itself that was and remains, in a sense, not a means but an end for the preservation of the ongoing voice of God. When two second-century rabbis, R. Eliezer and R. Yehoshua, struggled together to unlock the meaning of passages in the Hebrew Bible, a heavenly fire encircled them in a virtual reenactment of the Sinaitic theophany (Jerusalem Talmud, *Hagigah* 2:1). The fiery passion of their hermeneutical engagement linked up with the original text of flames at Sinai, drawing it into the presentness of Torah study.

The voice of the Ten Commandments, which literally ceased and was "no more" (Deut. 5:19), has itself been exegetically inverted, taking advantage of Hebrew philological elasticity, to have "never ended."[2] Biblically, because the voice of the commandments at Sinai was a unique sound that ceased, never to be repeated, its content needed to be recorded for posterity. God, therefore, "inscribed them on two tablets of stone and gave them to me [Moses]" (Deut. 5:22). Rabbinically, that pristine voice is retrieved again and again by a reversal of that original sequence. Divine orality becomes text at Sinai, and text transforms itself into divine word as a consequence of the oral debates over the meaning of the text in the halls of the rabbinic academy. What was transcribed and fixed becomes fluid. The "I" continues to address precisely out of the learned disharmony of rabbinic engagement with its foundational text.

The Ten Commandments are the very first divine communications to be transcribed, but with these commandments it is not merely the author

---

2. See the Aramaic *Targum Onqelos* on this verse subscribed to by the eleventh-century exegete Rashi: "because His voice is powerful and indestructible." See also Babylonian Talmud, *Sanhedrin* 17a, and Jerusalem Talmud, *Megillah* 1:5.

that is divine, but also the writing surface, the letters and the transcription itself — "The tablets were God's work, and the writing was God's writing, incised upon the tablets" (Exod. 32:16). However, it would be an error to identify this process with the proverbial "etched in stone" conveying the senses of rigid, fixed, static, and immutable. Though the divine word at Sinai reaches out to eternity, the rabbis never tire of revowelizing the singular word for "incised" *(charut)* to render it "freedom" *(cherut)* to the extent of mandating its lexical reconstitution — "Don't read it *incised* but rather *freedom*, for only he who exerts himself in the study of Torah is truly free."[3] Freedom is attained in the study of God's text precisely because the text itself is not "written in stone" but speaks only through those who engage it and interpret it. The tablets bearing the Ten Commandments are themselves paradigmatic of the entire rabbinic project that, though bound by the text, is not enslaved to it. How appropriate it is then that the tablets, as a microcosmic Torah,[4] whose very substance represents existential freedom, should commence with an "I" who released others from the "house of slavery," who granted political liberty to its subjects.

From whatever perspective I choose to view this primal "I," whether midrashically, normatively, philosophically, mystically, or existentially, I am greeted by an array of identities. Philosophically, for the rationalist, chief and representative among them Moses Maimonides (d. 1204), it is an abstract expression of a universal notion, the existence of a supreme Being, who is the formal (in the Aristotelian sense) ground of all being. A noble attempt to wrench this "I" from its parochial moorings comes at the cost of surrendering its immediate identification as the "I" "who took you out of Egypt." Ultimately it can even dispense with the very speaker "I," because "I" as indicative of the existence of God and "You shall not have any other gods" as that of the unity of God are, according to Maimonides, unique among the commandments in their ability to be cognized by the human intellect — "for these are knowable by human speculation alone."[5]

---

3. *Ethics of the Fathers* 6:2. For other significations of this reading as freedom from death or freedom from foreign subjugation, see Babylonian Talmud, *Eruvin* 54a.

4. There was a prevalent view in Geonic and medieval times that the Decalogue contains within itself all 613 biblical commandments, a prime example of which is Saadiah Gaon's attempt to fit them all in under each of the ten in his *Siddur*, ed. Israel Davidson et al. (Jerusalem, 1941), pp. 191-216.

5. *Guide of the Perplexed*, trans. S. Pines (Chicago: University of Chicago Press, 1963), II:33, p. 364.

Normatively, for some Jewish jurists (halakhists), once more, chief among them Maimonides, the "I" constitutes a formal commandment, a mitzvah incumbent upon every Jew to know that a creator God exists.[6] Again, the second half of the verse, historically contingent and particularistic, must be sacrificed and the intimacy of a relational "I" must accede to an "I" that has been objectified by an implicit command to believe in it. The "I" no longer speaks to me as a subject but as a formulaic object. The opposing school, which does not include this as a formal commandment among the traditional 613 biblical mitzvoth, leaves me equally wanting since it is absurdly feasible, according to this opinion, to be a fully observant Jew without believing in the existence of God!

If I then move toward a proponent of a more mystical, antiphilosophical approach such as the great twelfth-century poet Judah Halevi (d. 1141), who embraced the second half of the verse, "who took you out of Egypt," as this commandment's dominant component, then I find myself in a camp even more troubling than the former. For him, the implication is that we know this God first and foremost through personal experience and subsequently through an uninterrupted flow of tradition. However, as he makes quite clear to the Khazari king who has embarked on a search for *the* true religion, this commandment relates to Jews alone.[7] So chauvinistic does this command become that even the convert to Judaism cannot gain equal access with his new religious compatriots to its message, since he does not hereditarily share their particular historical exodus experience. His ancestry limits his ability to cognize or relate to an "I" that is defined by a shared memory from which he is excluded.

It seems that I am faced with two mutually exclusive choices. Either the God of this first commandment is the universal God of creation, in which case the second half of its formulation must be ignored, or he is the Jewish God of the exodus, in which case universalism loses out to chosenness. However, as I search for a solution, a possibility arises with another of the

6. See Maimonides' *Book of Divine Commandments*, trans. Charles Chavel (London: Soncino Press, 1940), vol. 1, positive commandment #1, p. 79. For other formulations of the same principle, see the first of Maimonides' thirteen principles cited by Chavel in appendix 4, p. 400, and the first chapter of the *Laws of the Foundation of the Torah* in his *Mishneh Torah*.

7. *Kuzari* I:25. That Maimonides shuns this theology is most evident from a letter he addressed to a query from a Muslim convert to Judaism that relates to this very issue. See James A. Diamond, "Maimonides and the Convert: A Juridical and Philosophical Embrace of the Outsider," *Medieval Philosophy and Theology* 11 (2003): 125-46.

great medieval Jewish commentators, Abraham Ibn Ezra (d. 1167), this time in the course of a recollected conversation between him and his contemporary, none other than Judah Halevi. Halevi challenges the rationalist position with a critique that strikes at the very heart of their philosophical universalist reading of the first commandment. If the "I" is as they say, then why does the commandment not define that "I" universally as "the one who created heaven and earth," rather than particularly, as the one who freed the Israelites from Egypt. Ibn Ezra ingeniously offers a compromise response that has the commandment accommodate both Gods. The commandment addresses primarily two audiences — those who are philosophically astute and intellectually capable, and those who lack such sophistication. For the former, the first half of the commandment suffices since they can reason their way to a creator God. However, for the latter, the commandment offers the alluring, and seemingly weightier, evidence of direct experience substantiating a supreme being.[8] Though it is more appealing than its ethnocentric adversary, I am averse to the idea that the very first words uttered by God at Sinai, and that ground the entire Torah, cater to any divisive hierarchy, be it intellectual or otherwise. This reading is self-defeating, for its elitism belies the very universalism it purportedly advocates.

Perhaps the key to this "I" is its introduction to the crowd at the foot of Mount Sinai by two of its divine names — Yahweh (YHWH) and Elohim. The midrashic tradition associates each of these divine epithets with two primary facets of God. "YHWH" (the Tetragrammaton) exemplifies compassion and mercy while "Elohim" manifests justice, law, and truth. Their combination expresses a strict and inflexible providence (Elohim) tempered by the compassion and understanding (YHWH) necessary to accommodate the foibles of human nature. The switch from a world created solely by Elohim in Genesis 1:1 to a joint YHWH/Elohim venture in a recounting of the creation commencing with Genesis 2:4 is accounted for by a divine change of heart. God immediately realized that the world would quickly collapse if his governance operated along the lines of strict justice, without being mediated by extralegal considerations of mercy.[9] By implication, God as creator is drawn into our first commandment to take its place alongside God as historical intervener.

---

8. Ibn Ezra's *Commentary to the Torah* on Exod. 20:2.

9. Among the many variations of this midrash, see for example *Genesis Rabbah* 12 and *Pesiqta Rabbati* 40.

I would draw the analogy that when God makes the transition from creator to legislator at Sinai, he undergoes the same process of experimentation and deliberation as took place at the very origins of the universe. His initial intent is that the Law be grounded in strict justice as indicated by the prologue to the entire list of commandments — "And *Elohim* spoke all these words, saying: . . ." (Exod. 20:1).[10] However ideal truth and justice may be, when God begins his address, his perspective changes by the mere fact of encounter. If the Ten Commandments are considered a "covenant" with Israel, as the tablets are referred to in the Hebrew Bible, then the mutuality that is essential to the viability of "covenant" must inhere in them. That cannot be achieved by a God that reacts solely on the basis of consideration of law and retributive sanction. He must also look beyond the writing to a third factor, the people, and assume the name YHWH, as he did at creation, so that the empathy necessary to maintain a covenant informs his governance. Not to couple with YHWH would be to administer the law without regard for the humanity that stands before him, accentuating power and domination over that of relationship. Without the compassion of YHWH, God would have assumed a posture of Master vis-à-vis a constituency of slaves, exchanging one kind of despotism for another and rendering the "freedom" expressed by he who "took you out of the land of Egypt from the house of slavery" deceptively illusory.

The combined names of God not only reflect the manner in which God interacts with man and the world but are instructive for the reverse direction as well, for how man must in turn envisage and relate to God. One of the overarching motifs of rabbinic interpretation focusing on this commandment is that no matter how fragmented the world appears, all can be traced to the One, the source of all being and existence. Discord, rather than harmony, seems to be the order of the day where the chaos of tsunamis, earthquakes, disease, and drought competes with the majesty of a sunset or a polar glacier for our sense of who is truly in charge. To the question of why the need for this seemingly superfluous introduction, the rabbis respond, "for at the Sea He appeared as a mighty warrior, and at Sinai as a scribe who teaches Torah, and then again in the times of Solomon as a naïve youth, while during the period of Daniel as an old man, therefore God dispels any possible confusion raised by these multiple identities

10. See the *Mekilta* and Rashi's comments on the use of the name *elohim* in this opening verse.

8

with a resounding *I*, I am the same one who appeared at the sea and at Sinai, *I am the Lord your God*."[11] The "I" dispels the appearance of fragmentation raised by multidimensional encounters. Unity does not entail uniformity. The profound superiority of this "I" over its pagan counterparts does not lie in its truer theological representation of God but in its ethical repercussions.

The Hebrew word *Adam* connotes the collective sense of humanity, not the personal name of one individual, and so mankind was created one as God is one. Just as divine diversity does not infringe on his unity, so humanity's complexity need not undermine its essential unity. Unity does not demand the monotony of sameness. Maimonides' great code of law reflects this notion in its very structure, for it begins with a requisite knowledge of a creator God who is one, as the first commandment demands, and ends with a description of the messianic age where all mankind merges in a unity of purpose — knowledge of God. The forward-looking road to that utopian age where conflict is no longer the order of the day because humankind is engaged in a common enterprise is fueled by that first "I," the model of unity as the very ground of all Being. If Maimonides' code purports to be a comprehensive digest of all Jewish law, then the bracketing of this legal system by the first commandment on one end and the messianic age on the other informs every performance of a mitzvah in between. Each and every such act recalls both the unity of God and humankind's ultimate destination toward its own realization of unity at the end of days.

In their microscopic exegesis of this first commandment, the rabbis make the "I" resonate with the means of achieving that utopian universal accord of humanity. The Hebrew term for "I am" *(anochi)* begins with an aleph, the first letter of the Hebrew alphabet. The very first letter of the first word in the Torah, "In the Beginning," commences with a beth, the second letter of the Hebrew alphabet. The rabbis have been immediately afforded an opportunity to mine the treasures of their foundational text before the opening word has even been read. Why, they ask, does not the beginning start with the beginning? What motivated the divine author to pass over the aleph and favor the beth with the commencement of the Torah and the origins of the world?

Before the divine pen was put to parchment, each of the letters of the Hebrew alphabet, beginning with the last, vied for the privilege, and each

---

11. *Mekilta.*

in turn was rebuffed until it was conferred on the second letter, the beth. In return for the aleph's silence throughout the other characters' arrogant jockeying for esteem, and its humble submission to divine preference, God granted it the lead position in the Ten Commandments. Implicit then in the "I" of supremely overwhelming Presence is the humility that allows for acceptance and recognition of the other. *Adam* and "one" *(echad)* also begin with aleph, and so the modesty of the aleph is drawn into these two terms to read that humankind stands or falls on the acknowledgment of another's space while oneness is the inevitable consequence of the individual's ability to limit itself so that others can share the same ground.

Perhaps the aleph modeled its behavior on what the Kabbalah describes as God's own act of self-sacrifice to make way for the creation. How could the creation take place if God's pervasive presence occupies all of space? Sixteenth-century Jewish mystics attributed the possibility of the universe to a primordial act of divine self-contraction and withdrawal leaving space for the world to inhabit. The "I" of the first commandment, which demands belief, loyalty, and obedience, is also the "I" that limits itself so that its subjects can enjoy existential autonomy.[12]

After introducing himself as "I am the LORD your God," God does not, as one might expect, go on to describe himself by the dogmatic theological characterizations that have become so commonplace in our religious language such as omnipotent, omniscient, omnipresent, or even, for that matter, unitary. He reveals himself primarily as the one "who brought you out of the land of Egypt, out of the house of slavery." His existence is tied inextricably to a historical intervention of national liberation. His subsequent commandments are sanctioned not simply by the unfettered power he yields, for that could assert itself in any arbitrary show of brute force, but his authority flows from the moral exercise of that infinite power.

The strength of this deity's moral authority is further deepened by the common rabbinic motif of God actually suffering, going into exile or being imprisoned along with his people, which notably emerges in this first commandment by a philological twist, reading it as "I am the Lord your God who took *myself* out of Egypt" (Jerusalem Talmud, *Sukkah* 4:3). Read in this way, the commandment that commences the collective revelation at Sinai harkens back to the personal revelation granted Moses at the burning bush that portends Sinai, both by its location — "Horeb, the mountain of

---

12. See Joseph B. Soloveitchik, "Majesty and Humility," *Tradition* 17, no. 2 (1978): 35-37.

God" (Exod. 3:1) — and by its linguistic assonance *(Sinai/Seneh)*. Why, R. Joshua asks, does God choose to lower himself from the heavenly heights and appear from within a lowly thornbush? It is to teach us that as long as his people suffer, he suffers, and as long as they are in captivity, he shall likewise remain so (*Midrash Tanhuma*, Exod. 14). What is so provocative, however, about this portrait of an empathetic God is not what it says about God, but what it demands of man. The moral crisis is so desperate that God himself is in need of liberation, urgently calling for human activism rather than prayer, quietism, contemplative asceticism, or any form of retreat from redressing the injustice at hand. Moses merits this spectacular epiphany, not because of his withdrawal to the silence of the desert but because he resorted to the most extreme form of violence — murder — when confronted with the most extreme form of human oppression. This is the man whom God has chosen to release him from his own shackles, and this is what the first commandment's "who took you out of Egypt" recollects in its address to the people as a whole.

God's name revealed to Moses at the bush of "I will be what I will be" (Exod. 3:14) conveys of course not a personal appellation, but a state of being that is ever in flux. One of the greatest of all Jewish exegetes, Rashi (d. 1105) expands this strange formulation to an eternal declaration of allegiance — "As I am with you in this catastrophe I shall be with you in all future times of oppression." The Tetragrammaton (YHWH), then, pronounced in the first commandment, derived from the same verb "to be," sets the standard of what it means to "be," to exist. "To be" is to be outraged by injustice, to join ranks with the oppressed, and ultimately to vanquish the oppressor. In some sense the twentieth-century existentialist axiom "existence precedes essence" may very well capture this God who promulgates the commandments.

The commandment is not satisfied with recalling just "the land of Egypt," the foreign country they were trapped in, but refines it further as "the house of slavery." The Israelites, and all future subjects of this commandment, must be reminded of a state of being they in particular had been reduced to, and that always looms as a danger in any oppressive regime. Release from "the land of Egypt" covers but one stage in the process of liberation — that of rescuing a national identity that has been suppressed and submerged by the dominant culture. God helps Israel emerge from a political demography that consisted only of Egypt and the nameless minions that were compelled to serve Egypt.

But there is another stage to the liberation, represented by "house of slavery," which must remedy the scarred psyche of those who have been subjugated for so long. The term "house" connotes a structure that is fixed and permanent — the Israelites, in other words, were not only enslaved, but were transformed into slaves, which accounts for why there was no substantive resistance or uprising until Moses, a child of the upper class, arrived on the scene. If, according to some Jewish thinkers, what distinguishes humankind from all other species is the ability to exercise freedom of choice (rather than intellect or speech), then the Egyptian straitjacketing of the Israelites inducing a wholly determined existence, was an attack on their very humanity. It was a largely successful concerted effort to remove the *image of God* from others. The claustrophobic hopelessness of this predicament is captured by Gersonides' (d. 1344) explanation of "house of slavery" as a house that has been virtually sealed airtight with no crack or crevice that could offer even a glimmer of escape. Halevi's question of why doesn't the first commandment refer to the God of creation misses the point. Creation is integral to its formulation, for it warns that what God has ideally worked into nature at the beginning, such as the *image of God,* is precariously vulnerable to the actions of men.

The ultimate verse of the first creation account concludes with a syntactically difficult description of God ceasing (or resting) "from all the work of creation that he had done" (Gen. 2:3), which literally translates as "all his work that God created to do." A textual invitation presents itself to an exegete such as Ibn Ezra, who inserts man as the subject of the final verb "to do." God has completed his task, from which point onward it is humanity's responsibility "to do," to create, to preserve the creation God has delivered. The constraint of a "house of slavery," in its restriction of the powers "to do," violates the raison d'être of the creation itself, where there was a changing of the guard from God to humanity, obliging it to exercise its image *of God,* which fuels its power *to do.*

The second half of our first commandment, "you shall have no other gods before me," makes the transition from the conceptual underpinnings we have been discussing to an actual prohibition. What precisely is outlawed, though, by the proscription "you shall have no"? What is the act of having contemplated by this commandment? The expression most often occurs biblically in the context of establishing a spousal relationship.[13]

13. See J. Tigay, *JPS Torah Commentary: Deuteronomy* (Philadelphia: Jewish Publica-

Marriage is in fact a pervasive metaphor in the Hebrew Bible for the people's relationship with God, while, concomitantly, idolatry is often depicted as marital infidelity. If marriage as relational exclusivity is the paradigm for relationship with God, then this commandment also reflects back on the ideal of marriage between a man and a woman. Since the having of this God is a direct consequence of liberation from a master/slave relationship, it cannot replace it with more of the same. Mutuality, as the term "covenant" in the "tablets of the covenant" implies, not domination, is paramount. Once again creation, contra Halevi, is implicit in this commandment, for where else does one look for the ideal than what was established between man and woman at creation. In the first account they are created as one being (Gen. 1:27), while in the second man is commanded to leave his former primal relationship with his parents to "cleave to his wife and become one flesh" (Gen. 2:24). The imbalance of domination would be an insurmountable barrier to both unity with God and unity with another human being since the subordinate partner would be overwhelmed and negated by the other's supremacy.

There may be another reason for the illegitimacy of entering into relationships with foreign gods that is provided by their identification as "other." Heightened rabbinic philological sensitivity hones in on this term as a characteristic that distinguishes them from the God deserving of worship. As cited by Rashi, they are "*other gods* because they are *other* to their devotees, they cry out to them and the gods do not respond, it is as if they are an *other* who have never afforded them recognition." The determining factor that distinguishes false gods from the one true God is an ethical moment of encounter where the Other hears and empathizes with and reacts to my needs.

The highest religious ideal in Judaism and other religious traditions is that of *imitatio Dei*, attaching oneself to and mimicking God, or in rabbinic idiom, "as He is, so shall you be." Just what those traits to be imitated are can be gleaned from the way God interacts with man such as clothing the naked ("And the LORD God made garments of skin for Adam and his wife, and clothed them," Gen. 3:21) or visiting the sick, following his appearance to Abraham, who was recovering from his circumcision (Gen. 18:1), or burying the dead, as he personally attended to when Moses passed away

---

tion Society, 1996), and the verses cited by him in his comments to Deut. 5:7 to illustrate this usage.

(Deut. 34:6). The midrash goes so far as to note that the entire Torah is bracketed by acts of compassion, beginning with clothing the naked and ending with burying the dead, thus pervading everything that lies between.

Here then does the first commandment culminate, not in some abstract tenet of monotheism stipulating the parameters of belief or dogma, but in the ultimate paradigm of *imitatio Dei* — a God that is not oblivious to otherness, but rather who cares. In this way the second clause of the commandment seamlessly follows the first, for liberation does not end in mere self-autonomy but also in the responsibility it carries for a sovereign member of the human race. The two halves of the first commandment interlock in an integral whole whose message is articulated no more eloquently than by Emmanuel Levinas, who asserted that "Israel would teach that the greatest intimacy of me to myself consists in being at every moment responsible for the others, the hostage of others. . . . You are not just free; you are also bound to others beyond your freedom. You are responsible for all. Your liberty is also fraternity."[14]

Finally, the commandment ends with the "face" of God, for the Hebrew "before me" translates literally "before my face." The Ten Commandments are spoken out of the most intimate of relationships: "face to face the LORD spoke to you on the mountain out of the fire" (Deut. 5:4), a collective experience that had been individually reserved exclusively for Moses (Deut. 34:10). As long as the ethical posture that I have argued is mandated by this first commandment is maintained, the divine face, his presence, manifests itself on earth. Conversely, if it is not, if the order of the day is to turn one's back (the Hebrew words for "back," *achor,* and for "other," *acher,* are identical except for a vowel change) on the face of others, then the divine face on earth is occluded. Such a perverse state of affairs is, unfortunately, not uncommon and overturns what the Bible defines as the essence of the face-to-face encounter with God — "as a man speaks with his friend" (Exod. 33:11). The prescribed punishment then for service to "other gods" of a "hiding of the face" (Deut. 31:18), or what Martin Buber has termed an "eclipse of God," is more of a natural consequence of man's egotistical hiding of his own face from other men.

The precedent was set at the foot of Mount Sinai, the very moment Israel was to be granted the legacy of the commandments, when the first

14. Emmanuel Levinas, *Nine Talmudic Readings,* trans. A. Aronowicz (Bloomington: Indiana University Press, 1990), p. 85.

commandment was rejected before even being received. The golden calf stands as an infamous memorial to faith being invested in cold and unfeeling utility over Moses *the person* (Exod. 32:1), in the value of commodity over humanity. The midrash attributes the singling out of Moses as a *person* to convey "perfection and conduct, since he led Israel as a man leads the members of his own family." Moses' leadership exudes the love, care, and altruism associated with family, and the people have rejected it and what it stands for.

Moses' response to this moral outrage is to seize initiative and angrily smash the tablets, but the rabbis offer another reading whereby the people's behavior constitutes a direct assault on the integrity of the tablets as follows: "Moses took the Tablets and descended and the Tablets carried their own weight and Moses with them; but when they saw the calf and the dancing, the writing took flight from the Tablets and they became heavy in his hands and Moses was unable to carry himself and the Tablets, and he cast them away and they shattered beneath the mountain" (Chapters of Rabbi Eliezer, chap. 45). Without hearing the message of the commandments, all that remains is impervious and unbearable stone, mirroring the state of humanity that has turned its back on them.

Response

Calvin P. Van Reken

In his essay Professor Diamond graciously accommodates the numbering of the commandments adopted for this volume; in so doing he includes his reflections on both the Jewish first commandment and the first part of the Jewish second commandment. (The Jewish first commandment is taken by Christians as the prologue to the commandments.) Both the Jewish reading and the Reformed understanding of the prologue take it as providing a contextual foundation for the whole Decalogue. In this brief response I will engage Professor Diamond regarding a few of his lines of inquiry with respect to the prologue and first commandment. My primary intent, however, will be to lay out a Christian and Reformed understanding of the prologue and first commandment.

Professor Diamond's provocative essay is full of imaginative insights as to the conceptual foundations of the Decalogue. Foremost among these are his reflections on the identity of the God whose voice was heard at Sinai. An undeniable link does exist between the prologue and the first commandment since "YHWH" of the prologue is the antecedent of the pronoun "me" in the first commandment. Thus Professor Diamond's focus on the "I am" of the prologue is perfectly fitting. In his reflections he draws upon a long history of rabbinic reflection, a history with which he is very familiar. My own familiarity with this tradition is not great, so it was interesting for me to follow some of the hermeneutic strategies that are used within that tradition. For example, Diamond draws conclusions from the fact that Exodus 20 begins with the first letter of the Hebrew alphabet, an aleph, while Genesis 1 begins with the second letter, a beth. For Diamond this raises the issue whether the law logically precedes the creation. Framing the issue by this consideration proceeds from a kind of attention to the text with which I am unfamiliar. Reformed exegesis aims at the thematic and propositional sense by seeking the historical and grammatical meaning of the text, and since individual letters, as such, have no sense, they are not considered as separable semantic indicators.

The prologue to the Ten Commandments as recorded in Exodus 20, woodenly translated, is "I YHWH your God, who brought you out of the land of Egypt, the house of bondage." There is no linking verb in the text of the opening clause, and one needs to be supplied. The verb can go either after the opening "I" or after "YHWH," and where it is placed affects the meaning. "I am YHWH, your God" identifies who the speaker is. "I, YHWH, am your God" identifies to the listeners what the name of their God is. Most translations favor the former, not out of any grammatical obligation, but because that translation seems to make more sense. Earlier in the narrative the person and name of YHWH had already been introduced to the reader (Exod. 3) and to the people in the narrative (Exod. 4:29-31), so it was already understood that YHWH was their God. In Exodus 15:1ff. we read that Moses and the Israelites sang, "YHWH is my strength and my song; he has become my salvation. He is my God, and I will praise him, my father's God, and I will exalt him." Israel knew that YHWH was its God long before Sinai, so Exodus 20:1 is probably not YHWH introducing himself; it should be understood as YHWH identifying himself as the speaker of the commands that follow.

The importance of the prologue is that it sets the proper context for the law of God. Attention is paid not so much to the identity of the God who is uttering the commands as to what YHWH already had done for his people. YHWH does not simply announce a list of laws that must be obeyed if his people are going to avoid captivity. They have already been set free from slavery in Egypt. God had acted on their behalf and released them from the house of bondage, and he had done so independently of any consideration of their conduct. They neither deserved nor earned their liberation. It was a gift of God. So the Decalogue was not a set of requirements that must be met by Israel in order to be redeemed; redemption was God's work and had already occurred before the law was clearly promulgated. Thus the Decalogue taken in context should not be read as moral conditions that must be met to receive redemption. The context provided by the prologue sets up the Decalogue as a rule to teach the people how to live in grateful obedience to God for what he had done already for them. The prologue provides confirmation that, while the Decalogue remains an expression of God's prescribed will, it is not something that must be met as a precondition for redemption.

In the Reformed understanding, the law has three functions. The civic function is to guide public officials in the making of just laws. Another function is to reveal to the sinner her hopeless spiritual condition and to drive her to God's grace in Jesus Christ. (The Heidelberg Catechism replies to the question "How do you come to know your misery?" by simply stating that "the law of God tells me," Q.A. 3.) The third use of the law, and according to John Calvin the principal one, is to provide a rule or guide to teach those redeemed in Jesus Christ how to live in grateful obedience to God for the redemption he has already accomplished for them, in a similar way that it was to be a rule for Israel.

The prologue provides a context that reinforces the third function of the law, but raises a question related to the other two functions of the law. Both of them require that the law is binding on all people and not just on those who have been redeemed. If the Decalogue is a guide for the redeemed, is it only intended for Jews (those redeemed from Egypt's captivity) and later for Christians (those redeemed from spiritual captivity through Jesus Christ), and not for all humanity? The question of the scope of the Decalogue is a question that Professor Diamond considers. Professor Diamond notes that the use of the name Elohim in Exodus 20:1 harks back to creation and so implies the universality of the commandments; and the use of YHWH in verse 2 draws attention to God's covenant with Israel. Thus Diamond recognizes a sense in which the scope is both universal and particular. In the limited space he has available, he does not give compelling evidence for this conclusion, although there are some theological considerations that can give added credence to it. Whether the Decalogue is only for the Jewish (and Christian) community depends on whether the Decalogue is understood as covenantal stipulations *simpliciter,* or whether it is seen as covenantal stipulations grounded in the creation itself. If the Decalogue is grounded in the creation, as Reformed theologians typically think, then it is for all people. On this view the enunciation of the Decalogue to Israel was a blessing to them, a laying out clearly how YHWH's people can live within his divine design intended for all persons. How can those outside the covenant be held accountable for a law given to God's people at Sinai? John Calvin says that an inward law *(dictat lex illa interior)* that is "written, even engraved, upon the hearts of all, in a sense asserts the very same things that are to be learned from the two tables" (Calvin, *Institutes* 2.8.1). Thus all persons have the possibility of knowing God's law. So on the Reformed view of the law, the giving of the Decalogue was like receiving a clear, spoken, owner's manual for human life. The recipients of the law were thus graced by God with a clearer knowledge of how all people should act, and the redeemed understand more clearly how to live in grateful obedience for the redemptive acts of God on their behalf.

The first commandment, "You shall have no other gods before me (lit. before my face)," is clearly linked to the prologue by the fact that the antecedent of the pronoun "me," YHWH, is found in the prologue. Most Christians (Roman Catholics and Lutherans, inter alia) follow the Jewish pattern by including Exodus 20:4-6 as part of the first commandment. Thus the meaning of "you shall not make for yourselves an idol" is taken as a kind of gloss on "you shall have no other gods before me." Protestants in the Reformed tradition take the command not to have idols as a separate commandment (the second) that has to do with the proper worship of YHWH: what is proscribed is using idols of YHWH. One place this Reformed reading has biblical support is Deuteronomy 4:15-18, where the proscription against idols is linked to Israel's not seeing YHWH when the law was spoken. Whether to include Exodus 20:4-6 as part of the first commandment has more to do more with the interpretation of the second commandment (as this volume counts them) than with the first.

The first commandment is ambiguous: Does the phrase "before me" mean that YHWH wants to be the top god of any others we may have (requiring YHWH's primacy), or that YHWH wants to be god to the exclusion of all others (requiring YHWH's exclusivity)? The exclusive view results in a stronger, more restrictive commandment; the primacy view is less stringent and would permit varieties of syncretism. Grammatically either of these is possible, but the exclusive view is affirmed repeatedly throughout the Scripture and is embraced in the Reformed tradition. It is not simply that God wants to be the highest god in our pantheon, rather he desires our complete allegiance and will brook no competition. As stated a few verses later in Exodus 20, God is jealous. He does not tolerate competitors for our allegiance.

This raises yet another question about the first commandment. What other gods are there to compete with YHWH? The commandment seems to assume that there are other gods, otherwise YHWH could have no competitors and the command would not be needed. Other places in Scripture seem to claim that there are no other gods, for example, Isaiah 45:5a has "I am YHWH, and there is no other; apart from me there is no God (Elohim)." So if there are no other gods, how should we understand the first commandment? Two different interpretations are possible: one is that while no other gods actually exist, human persons are prone to imagine or create or fabricate "beings" that they then worship as divine, and the commandment forbids such doings. Two sorts of cases of this come to mind. The clearest one occurs when one fabricates a god *as a god,* e.g., Baal or Isis (the Egyptian goddess of fertility). The other example is when one devotes himself to something, loves something, way out of all ordinate proportion, so that it becomes like a "god" to him. Such a "god" is the center of a person's life, and his time, energy, resources revolve around that thing. Cocaine for an addict would be an example of this kind of "god." It seems to me that this second example is not the sort of problem the first commandment is aimed at preventing. It does not seem to me fitting that an alcoholic Israelite, upon hearing the first commandment at the base of Sinai, should have recognized his devotion to alcohol as a problem the first commandment addresses. That problem more clearly falls under the tenth commandment. Nevertheless, these two kinds of cases are ways to have imaginary "other gods."

The second interpretation of "other gods" is that while there are none in the sense of beings that are almighty, omnipotent, omniscient, etc., there exist in fact spiritual "powers" with lesser qualities that can and do influence human activities, and the commandment forbids our "having" any such "gods," that is, it forbids any worship or allegiance to such powers. Perhaps the first sorts of fabricated gods (like Baal and Isis) are not imaginary gods but names given to actual demonic beings worshiped as "gods." If that is the case, then perhaps the two kinds of interpretations of "other gods" may occasionally collapse into one.

Even so, however, these two interpretations are not contradictory, and it is possible to take the commandment in both of these ways. When we combine these ways of understanding what "other gods" may mean, then the commandment forbids both creating and worshiping imaginary gods or worshiping spiritual powers other than YHWH. This view is taken in the Heidelberg Catechism where idolatry is defined. "Idolatry is having or inventing something in which one trusts in place of or alongside of the only true God, who has revealed himself in his Word" (Q.A. 95). This answer includes both possibilities: creating a god or having a lesser god. Both of these are proscribed.

A final note about the first commandment (and all the others). The

Reformed understanding is that when a commandment is a proscription ("don't do this"), the opposite conduct is prescribed. Similarly, in the two cases when a commandment is a prescription ("do this"), the opposite conduct is proscribed. Thus each commandment entails both prescription and proscription. As applied to the first commandment, this general rule means that not only are all persons to avoid having gods other than YHWH, they also are obliged to trust and worship YHWH alone.

No Other Gods

Daniel Polish

You shall not make for yourself an idol.

Most of us assume we have a perfect understanding of this second "word" and that there is little that needs to be said about it. But the fact is that this "word" has been the source of perhaps more controversy than any of the other injunctions of the otherwise universally affirmed ten. Because the separate "words" are not enumerated in the text itself, one can readily understand why some readers have assumed that the first verse of our "word," ". . . you shall have no other gods before me" (Exod. 20:3 and Deut. 5:7), is the very first injunction. Read in this way, God not only announces God's self ("I am the Lord your God") but at the same time insists that no other gods be accepted alongside the God with whom the children of Israel have entered into covenant. Historically, this has been the way most Christian interpreters have read the ten "words."

But Jewish tradition has elected to identify this verse with the second "word," making it part of what is generally regarded as an injunction against idolatry. Thus the prohibition of other gods is part and parcel of the prohibition of image worship. This raises significant issues to which we will return shortly.

Many people regard this verse as among the most forceful expressions of the monotheistic ideology we associate with the Bible. But a closer reading reveals a significantly more complex reality. We note that this first verse does not appear to deny the existence (or even the efficacy) of other gods. Though some have chosen to read this verse along the lines of "thou shalt not consort with any other (of those whom others consider to be) gods alongside me," the plain reading of the text does not deny the existence of other deities, only their appropriateness for worship by the children of Israel, who have entered into an exclusive covenant with the God of Israel.

The phrase *al p'nai* in this verse is usually translated as "before me," thus causing us to translate this thought as "You shall have no other gods before me." Read in this way, the phrase would seem to suggest the idea of precedence — you shall not give other gods precedence over me. But this is clearly not the intent of the verse. The phrase *al p'nai* usually connotes "alongside me," or better, "in my presence." It is employed as "in the presence of" in Genesis 11:28 ("and Haran died *al p'nai* / in the presence of his father Terah in the land where he was born"). It is also the sense of this idiom in Numbers 3:4. Translated in this way, the verse reads, "You shall have no other gods in my presence" — or ". . . alongside me." When we read the verse in this way, we are struck by the fact that it does not really fit with the idea of strict monotheism in the sense in which we understand it. Rather, it reflects the religious stance that historians of religion would call henotheism — the singular and unique adherence to one god among many existent divine beings.

We encounter this same spirit of henotheism elsewhere in the Bible as well. It can be heard in the famous Song of the Sea, "Who is like you, O LORD, among the gods?" (Exod. 15:11), and conceivably in Psalm 82:1, which translated literally can be read to state: "God stands in the divine assembly, he judges among the gods." Or Psalm 96:4: "For great is the LORD and highly to be praised; he is to be feared above all gods." If this same henotheistic ideology is indeed to be found in the present verse, the belief system reiterated in Exodus 20:3 and Deuteronomy 5:7 reflects the process of evolution of Israelite theology toward the monotheism that came to characterize it by the conclusion of the biblical period. We who read it after the conclusion of this process take it for granted that it speaks in the same monotheistic idiom that we do and ascribes no validity — or existence — whatever to any other divine beings.

What is clear from any historical perspective is that this first verse tells us how to *understand* God. The God who introduces God's self to us in the second "word" expects that we relate to God exclusively. We are to engage in no way with any other deities. We, who are part of the covenant, are not to believe in them or have any kind of dealings with them.

More complex is the issue of exactly what is prohibited by this second "word." Many read it as absolutely forbidding the creation of any kind of graphic image or representation of anything from the world of nature. This understanding has played itself out in various ways in each of the Abrahamic traditions. It is widely believed that the Muslim tradition is the most stringent in adhering to the prohibition of images. Thus Muslim mosques are absolutely devoid of images or even of pictures of great events in Muslim history or sainted leaders or, indeed, of anything from the world of nature. Rather, the decoration of mosques is confined to geometrical forms, vaguely plantlike filigrees, and elaborate calligraphies of quotations from the Qur'an.

In the Christian tradition the interpretation of the second "word" as opposing the representation of anything in the natural world is responsible for the various eruptions of iconoclasm that have dotted the history of Christianity. The church fathers prohibited images outright (Augustine wrote that "the one God should be worshipped without an image"). The most notable expression of this perspective was the iconoclastic controversy of the eighth-century Byzantine Church. Indeed, the advocates of the iconoclastic position explicitly based their argument on this second "word." Their adversaries, called iconodules, agreed that the meaning of this injunction was opposition to images, but argued that it applied only to the ancient Hebrews and to Jews. Bernard of Clairvaux, as part of his ascetic program, vigorously attacked any use of images — or any kind of elaborate decoration, for that matter — in Christian churches. Part of the initial impetus and thrust of the Protestant Reformation was an opposition to the images that had characterized the Catholic churches of the Middle Ages and the Renaissance.

In the Jewish tradition, the issue raised by the second "word" is even more extreme: the so called aniconism that has purportedly characterized Jewish life — the belief that Jewish civilization has produced no art whatsoever in slavish obedience to this understanding of the second verse of our "word." It has been a commonplace to make such statements as:

> Say what you will about the gifted Jews, they have never, up until times so recent that they scarcely begin to count, been plastic artists. Where is the Jewish Michelangelo, the Jewish Rembrandt, the Jewish Rodin? He has never come into being. Why? . . . Is it possible that a whole people cannot produce a single painter? And not merely a single painter of note, but a single painter at all? They never tried their hand at wood or stone or paint. "Thou shalt have

no graven images" — the Second Commandment — prevented them.[1]

> [The second commandment] effectively prevented Jews, again in most places and most times, from engaging in sculpture and painting. Moreover, according to the historians of Jewish culture and art, as a consequence of this blanket prohibition, whatever talent Jews may have had for sculpture and painting became stifled, or at least diverted into related but not prohibited fields. . . . The major arts practiced by the Christian artists, and developed by them to great heights, had no counterparts among the Jews, and for this unquestionably the Biblical prohibition is responsible.[2]

The belief in the absence of Jewish art has become axiomatic. And yet, widespread as this understanding is, *it is not true.* It is maintained despite the tangible evidence of ancient synagogue mosaics, and carved ornamentation; frescoes that adorned home and synagogue through the ages; painted ceilings of synagogues; illuminated manuscripts (of liturgical material, prayer books, even Bibles, as well as more mundane items such as marriage documents, etc.); lavishly decorated ritual objects for use in home and synagogue — all containing elements from the natural world, including representation of human beings. The assertion is made despite the recognition that there is a long history of Jewish artistic endeavor including painting, engraving, even sculpture representing aspects of the created world — and even portraiture. And though there have been differences among various times and locales, where art has flourished among Jews, the realm of these artistic creations was not limited to the religiously disengaged or liberal. All these expressions of the plastic arts have been enjoyed by the pious — even by the religious elite. As the British scholar of Jewish history Cecil Roth has stated in his book *Jewish Art:* "The data assembled above have made it abundantly clear that the conception of representational art for both domestic and synagogal purposes had become fully familiar in Jewish circles long before the beginning of the age of Emancipation."[3]

---

1. Cynthia Ozick, "Previsions of the Demise of the Dancing Dog," in Ozick, *Art and Ardor: Essays* (New York: Knopf, 1983; distributed by Random House).

2. Raphael Patai, *The Jewish Mind* (Detroit: Wayne State University Press, 1996), p. 356.

3. Cecil Roth, *Jewish Art: An Illustrated History,* rev. ed. (London: Vallentine, Mitchell, 1971), p. 17.

Indeed, it is ironic that the great Christian iconoclast Bernard of Clairvaux would denounce excessive ornamentation of churches as being reminiscent of Jewish practice. And Bernard is correct in one regard. Beauty in ritual objects has played a greater role in Jewish life than is generally recognized. Jewish tradition evolved a concept called *hiddur Mitzvah* / the beautification of fulfilling the commandments. Thus the ritual objects used in the fulfillment of mandated practice were not to be utilitarian or austere. Rather they were to be as beautiful as was possible for their owner to secure. The words of Exodus, "this is my God, and I will exalt him" (Exod. 15:2), are explained as follows in the Talmud: "make a beautiful succah in His honor, a beautiful lulav, a beautiful Shofar . . . (etc.)" (Babylonian Talmud, *Shabbat* 133b). Of course, such attention to aesthetic considerations has biblical precedents in the story of the building of the tabernacle in Exodus and the temple in 2 Kings.

And it makes no difference that the authors of these artistic creations may have borrowed motifs and styles from the cultures in which they lived. It makes no difference if they represented the highest level of technical proficiency or not, or were on the cutting edge of their art. It makes no difference that there was not one distinct "Jewish style" that united all the products of their creativity in all times and places. With regard to the question at hand, all that matters is that in all their handiwork they betrayed no inhibition of making representation of things that were "in the heavens above, or the earth beneath, or the water that is under the earth." So the argument that our second "word" was interpreted in Jewish tradition as prohibiting all forms of the plastic arts disregards the evidence of archaeology, literature, and history, and is simply incorrect.

The possibility that what was prohibited was graven images of any kind does, however, open for us one tantalizing avenue of reflection. During the time that Roman rule was violently detested, the party of the zealots among the Jews of Judea refused to handle the Roman coins that bore the representation of Caesar on the grounds that they bore the representation of a human being. Yet more conventional teachers seemed less distressed by the use of human images on coins and employed it as an allegory to make a very different point. In discussing the statement in Genesis 1 that human beings are created "in the image of God" (1:27), "our rabbis taught, if a human king mints many coins from a single mold, they all look exactly the same. But the Holy One . . . shaped all human beings 'in the image of God,' and yet not one of them resembles any other" (Babylonian Talmud, *San-*

hedrin 38a). The implication of this teaching is that the earth is filled with "images" of God. Indeed, we are to treat each of those "images of the divine" as we would treat God in God's own self.

We are presented with an interesting juxtaposition between the coins minted by Caesar and the "coins minted by" God. Perhaps it is this disjunction that Jesus had in mind when he pronounced, "Render unto Caesar the things that are Caesar's and render unto God the things that are God's" (Matt. 22:21; Mark 12:17; Luke 20:25). Perhaps it was the edict of the Zealots that prompted people to ask Jesus the question that resulted in this answer. No wonder his answer left them speechless. It cuts a Gordian knot. For the answer implies "pay the taxes to Caesar with the coins that have Caesar's image on them. Give God that which has God's image stamped on it — yourself." This interpretation gains in credibility when we recall the rabbinic admonition "Give to God that which is God's, recognizing that you and all you have is God's" (*Pirkei Avot / The Sayings of the Fathers* 3:7).

And yet we are still left with a question: If it is not the act of making graphic images in general that is forbidden, what is this injunction intended to proscribe? There are interpreters of this verse who argue that what God is prohibiting is the graphic depiction of God in God's own self. Those who argue thus base their understanding on the events of the golden calf (the Hebrew literally means "the graven calf") described in Exodus 32. There we read that after fashioning this image the people proclaimed, "This is your God, O Israel, which brought you up out of the land of Egypt" (v. 4). The medieval commentator Yehuda Halevi, explaining this incident, said that "'the people did not intend to give up their allegiance to God.' They desired a *visible symbolic representation* of God." Many scholars conjecture that that same desire was what motivated Jeroboam, king of Israel, who pronounced that very same formula, "Here is your God, O Israel . . . ," upon building and dedicating two golden calves of his own (1 Kings 12:26-28). The act may well have represented not the worship of a new deity, but a tangible representation of the existing deity. This interpretation is not the standard reading of our verse, but is nonetheless extremely suggestive and helps us see the episodes in Exodus 32 and 1 Kings 12 more clearly.

Still, though this is not the dominant interpretation of this "word," one aspect of it continues to hold true in understanding the Jewish attitude toward the creation of images. Open as the Jewish tradition has been to the plastic arts, to this day Jewish (and Muslim too, for that matter) openness to representational art does not extend to depiction of the deity. Jewish art, of whatever kind, conventionally does not include representations of God. We will return to this subject below.

The more conventional understanding is that what is prohibited in this second "word" is the worship of other deities. In this case the sentiments of our verses would parallel the words of Isaiah: "I am the LORD, that is my name; and my glory I will not give to another, neither my praise to graven images" (42:8). This more familiar interpretation of this verse seems to be corroborated in verses from Deuteronomy in which we find the contents of this second "word" stated even more emphatically and with greater elaboration:

> For your sake, therefore, be most careful — since you saw no shape when the LORD your God spoke to you at Horeb out of the fire — not to act wickedly and make for yourselves a sculptured image in any likeness whatever: the form of a man or a woman, the form of any beast on earth, the form of any winged bird that flies in the sky, the form of anything that creeps on the ground, the form of any fish that is in the waters below the earth. And when you look up to the sky and behold the sun and the moon and the stars, the whole heavenly host, you must not be lured into bowing down to them or serving them. These the LORD your God allotted to other peoples everywhere under heaven. But you the LORD took and brought up out of Egypt . . . to be his very own people, as is now the case. . . . Take care, then, not to forget the covenant that the LORD your God concluded with you, and not make for yourselves a sculptured image in any likeness, against which the LORD your God has enjoined you. For the LORD your God is a consuming fire, a jealous God. (Deut. 4:15-20, 23-24)

Similar exhortations found in the book of Leviticus also make the full meaning of our "word" explicit: "Do not turn to idols or make molten gods for yourselves: I the LORD am your God" (Lev. 19:4); "You shall not make idols for yourselves or set up for yourselves carved images or pillars, or place figured [Fox uses 'decorated'] stones in your land to worship them, for I the LORD am your God" (26:1).

These verses make clear that the issue for both these citations and our second "word" is not the creation of images or representations of elements from the world of nature, but rather the *worship* of those images. The first-century historian Josephus writes, "Our Legislator has forbidden us to make images . . . for fear that any may be worshipped as gods" *(Against Apion)*. Josephus recognizes that the issue is not the making of images, but their worship. This distinction has been the dominant understanding of the Jewish tradition. One medieval author wrote: "Our Creator, may He be praised, never forbade the production of statues or pictures. He only forbade them with respect to worship and service. As it is written, 'You shall have no other gods before me; Do not make a graven image or any figure' for the purpose of divinity. . . . But Scripture never forbade the making of images or the act of beautifying some work or building" (Jacob ben Reuben, *Sefer Milchamot ha-Shem* 57). The great halakhic decisor Rabbi Meir of Rothenburg wrote a legal opinion about the propriety of illuminated prayer books. He noted, "there is no trespass here against the Biblical prohibition. . . . There are no grounds to suspect [idolatry] with regard to these drawings since they are merely flat patches of color." For Rabbi Meir the issue was not the creation of images but idolatry — the *worship* of those images.

This understanding of the second "word" puts it in the context of the entire biblical polemic against idol worship. That condemnation can be found in many places. We read it, for instance, in the remarkable, biting satire of Isaiah 44:9-20, which exposes the absurdity of worshiping a graven image: "He maketh a god, even his graven image; he falleth down unto it and worshippeth it and prayeth unto it, and saith, 'deliver me, for thou art my god'" (v. 17). We can find the same kind of caustic analysis of the practice of idol worship in Psalm 115:4-9; Jeremiah 10:3-5; and Isaiah 40:18-20, 41:7, and 46:1-2 and 5-7.

If our second "word" is indeed situated in the strand of biblical thought that inveighs against idol worship, we may understand its prohibition as being not against the making of images at all. Separating image making from idolatry explains the Jewish tradition's permissive attitude toward the former, while remaining adamant about the latter. This distinction is present in the other Abrahamic traditions as well. This distinction is one of the reasons the Christian tradition has developed such a vast history of representational art and has produced such a rich iconographic heritage. Even iconoclastic Christian groups evolved their own iconographic patterns. And this difference explains why in Islam, too, contrary to conventional wisdom, the plastic arts are not altogether absent.

Let it be noted that there have been significant differences in the way the various Abrahamic traditions have dealt with the issue of representational art. In the Christian tradition the iconodules maintained that the theology implied in the incarnation of Jesus Christ made tangible representations of the deity permissible for Christians. This understanding made the Christian tradition not only amenable to all graphic art, but allowed for the permission of the representation of Jesus (believed by many Christians to be not only a prophet or significant historical figure, but the second person in the divine Trinity) and of God in God's own self (or God the Father in the trinitarian formulation). However open to the graphic arts and their application to religious purposes Jews and Muslims might have been, both traditions were adamant in proscribing any graphic representation of God as an expression of belief in God's utter intangibility. Indeed, in Islam, depictions of both the deity and the prophet Muhammad are strictly proscribed: as an expression of piety toward the one and special respect for the other.

Historically, the broad consensus of Jewish understanding has heard the second "word" as prohibiting idol worship. An expression of how conventional this interpretation is can be found in the rabbinic teaching that "The Ten Commandments are so closely interwoven, that the breaking of one leads to the breaking of another. But there is a particularly strong bond of union between the first five commandments which were written on one tablet, and the last five which were written on the other tablet. . . . The second: 'Thou shalt have no other gods before me,' corresponds to the seventh: 'Thou shalt not commit adultery,' for conjugal faithlessness is as grave a sin as idolatry, which is faithlessness to God."[4] In passing, we note that the correlation between idolatry and conjugal infidelity is the premise on which some of the teachings of various of the prophets rest — most acutely the first chapters of Hosea.

Having identified the prohibition of the second "word" as being against the practice of idol worship, we must note that the biblical depiction of this practice is not an accurate representation of the practices of various religious traditions that engage in what we would today call image worship. Among image-worshiping members of the Hindu tradition today, for example, we do not encounter the belief that the tangible, physical image to which Hindus pay homage is the actual god they worship. Rather,

4. Louis Ginzberg, *The Legends of the Jews,* 7 vols. (Philadelphia: Jewish Publication Society of America, 1909-38), 3:104.

they understand these images as aids in evoking the presence of their deity or as the transient residence in which the presence of that god temporarily inheres. It might be what we would call a "symbol" or a focus for the expression of veneration to that which it represents but does not contain. Indeed, there are Hindu groups that make it a practice to create elaborate and beautiful images, "invite" them into their homes for a specified period of time, and then, at the conclusion of the designated period, have a ritualized way to "desacralize" the image and dismantle it. Some groups make the images of unfired clay, venerate them for a fixed period of time, and at the conclusion of the celebration place them in the ocean where they are dissolved and returned to their original elements (as, according to Hindu cosmology, are we). This is hardly the way you would treat an object that you believed actually *was* a deity.

Having identified the subject of the second "word" as idolatry, the deeper question arises of what relevance such an injunction could have for modern readers who do not — and will not be tempted to — worship idols. Unless the second "word" is about the creation of any plastic image — which we have earlier discounted — what possible meaning can this prohibition hold for us? How does this injunction retain its validity for us?

While it is true that most of us do not actually worship images, we are still susceptible to giving our allegiance to things other than God. We can identify something as our own absolute and bend all our energies in service to that. In obeisance to that "false absolute," people will be willing to ignore any other considerations, sacrifice the welfare of others, invest enormous expenditures of energy, time, and resources. For some people this "false absolute" might be their nation, their own group of people — no matter how large or how small. We have all heard of people who "worship Mammon." For some, material objects can become an end in themselves. One contemporary writer describing the values of the "new Ireland" said that "so many worship Versace the way their grandmothers worshipped the Virgin Mary."

In *Fear and Trembling,* the Danish theologian Søren Kierkegaard delineates various things, including the otherwise perfectly noble ideal of morality, that can be substituted as "false absolutes" in place of our absolute devotion to God. Paul Tillich identifies God as the object of our ultimate concern. But we can suggest, in an inversion of Tillich, that people are capable of making anything into the object of their ultimate concern, thus turning the object of that commitment into their "God." The psychoanalyst Erich Fromm has written about this: "Idolatry is not the worship of this or that particular idol . . . [it is] the deification of things, of partial aspects of the world and man's submission to such things. . . . It is not only pictures in stone and wood that are idols. Words can become idols, and machines can become idols, the state, power. . . . Science and the opinion of one's neighbors can become idols."[5] Or, in the words of Emerson, "A person will worship something, have no doubt about that. We may think our tribute is paid in secret in the dark recesses of our hearts, but it will out. That which dominates our imaginations and our thoughts will determine our lives, and our character. Therefore, it behooves us to be careful what we worship, for what we are worshipping we are becoming." In light of this, the lesson of the second "word" for us is that absolute devotion to anything other than God must be construed as its own kind of idolatry and is forbidden.

Most commonly we encounter people who make absolutes of themselves, their own interest, their success. While such people do not actually "bow down and worship" themselves, they regard their own happiness and well-being as more important than anything else in the world. They are prepared to sacrifice anything and anybody to that goal. Nothing can stand in the way of their pursuit of their self-interest — even their own better understanding or their own higher selves.

Such willingness to make something other than God serve as your highest goal rightly deserves to be described as its own kind of idolatry. And as such that would be forbidden by our second "word." Indeed, this understanding of the concept of idolatry can explain why this second "word" is propounded at the very beginning of the ten words, right after God's self-introduction. If we choose to violate any of the other "words" to satisfy our own appetites or interests, if we find ourselves making rationales to permit ourselves what the subsequent "words" prohibit, we are in effect defining ourselves and our wants as absolute. Breaking any of the "words" that follow implies that we have made a god of ourselves. Only if we disabuse ourselves of that particular idolatry can any of the injunctions that follow make sense.

It has been suggested that in our day fame itself — indeed, fame for its own sake — is the great idol worshiped by so many. The exploration of this fascination with fame, even more than the creation of an artistic oeuvre,

5. Erich Fromm, *Psychoanalysis and Religion* (London: Gollancz, 1951), p. 118.

33

seems to have been the project of Andy Warhol — almost less an artist than a social theoretician. After all, it was Warhol who pronounced the coming of a time when everyone would have his or her own fifteen minutes of fame. It may be this absolutization of fame that accounts for the public fascination with those who seem to be "famous for being famous." (In this regard, the great emblem of our idolatry might be the totemic figure of Mickey Mouse. Not a day goes by when we do not see his image. But what is he famous for? Apparently he is famous for his fame itself. This to such a degree that one satirical essayist suggested that archaeologists in the distant future might well be misled into imagining that Americans were a people who worshiped . . . a mouse.)

Since our focus is on the subject of religion, let us attend to some paradoxical implications of this second "word" for religion itself. Having noted that even such virtues as patriotism, group loyalty, and morality can become idolatrous, let us note that we can idolatrously valorize our own religious group as well. In the tale of the Grand Inquisitor contained in his *Brothers Karamazov,* Dostoyevsky portrays a church hierarchy that is prepared to condemn Jesus Christ as a heretic for endangering the well-being of the very church founded in his name. This sense of the primacy of the welfare of the church itself, rather than the message to which it is supposed to testify as absolute, lies at the heart of the current tensions between the Vatican and the Jewish community about the actions of the Catholic Church during the Holocaust. Did the Church act on its highest principles (understood as its obligations to the message of God: the ideals of love and compassion)? Or did it compromise those values for the sake of protecting its own, more temporal, interests? For any religious group, the group itself, be it a particular congregation, an ecclesiastical body, or the very tradition itself, can become valorized to the extent to which it, rather than the God it is supposed to profess, becomes the object of ultimate concern. In our desire to honor our religious group, we can raise it to a position even higher than God in our functional esteem. Thus our very religious identity can become an idolatry.

Which leads to the most profound challenge of the second commandment: even the idea of God we hold can become an idol. If Kierkegaard is prepared to grant his conception of God superiority to every other human consideration, is it possible that Kierkegaard's conception of God has become a kind of idol in its own right? In one particularly moving essay, Martin Buber recalls a dialogue in which his interlocutor challenged him:

"How can you bring yourself to say 'God' time after time? How can you expect that your readers will take the word in the sense in which you wish it to be taken? What you mean by the name of God is something above all human grasp and comprehension, but in speaking about it you have lowered it to human conceptualization. . . . When I hear the highest called 'God' it sometimes seems almost blasphemous." Buber reports that as part of his reply, he noted "that certainly . . . [people] draw caricatures and write 'God' underneath."[6]

Buber's lesson is very much akin to Paul Tillich's profound insight that God as God is in God's own self must not be confused with the more finite, necessarily limited, understanding of God that we also call God. The danger for us is that we might confuse our own understanding or image of God with the reality of God that will always elude our ability to comprehend with our minds or express with our words or symbols. The reality of God in all God's fullness, the God that is responsible for the being of all things, is the God above God (as we imagine/understand/represent God to be). Our image of God can never fully contain the God above God. What we call God is only a symbol for that which cannot be described. To imagine that our symbol exhausts what can be said about God runs the risk of turning our symbol into an idol. Our image of God can, itself, become an idol that we replace for the reality of God.

What Buber and Tillich prescribe to prevent our *idea* of God from becoming an idol in place of the *reality* of God, is the dialectical movement that would have us worshiping, revering, and communing with God as best as we can comprehend God, while at the same time remaining aware that God in the fullness of God will ultimately elude us. There is precedent for this dialectical movement in Jewish tradition. We hear it in the speech King Solomon delivered when he dedicated the temple he built in Jerusalem: "But will God really dwell on earth? Even the heavens to their utmost reaches cannot contain you, how much less this house that I have built!" (1 Kings 8:27). Solomon, to whom tradition ascribes exceeding wisdom, understood the dialectical movement of seeking God in the temple he had built and yet understanding that no finite edifice could contain God. This understanding is at the core of the meaning of the book of Job. When God appears in the whirlwind in chapter 38, the thrust of God's message is that

6. Martin Buber, *Eclipse of God: Studies in the Relation between Religion and Philosophy* (New York: Harper, 1957), pp. 7-8.

"human minds are not able to comprehend me as I am in my fullness." The God of Job warns us against making an idol of our limited understanding of God and God's ways — imagining that we can explain God when such wisdom is beyond our limited capacities.

Included in the liturgy of the Jewish worship service, significantly, at numerous points of every traditional service, and most pointedly at the conclusion of every service, is the prayer called the Kaddish/the doxology, which includes the assertion: "Blessed, praised and glorified, exalted, extolled and honored, magnified and lauded be the Name of the Holy one, blessed be He; though He be high above all the blessings and hymns, praises and consolations, which can be uttered in the world." It is as if the closing words of the service are admonishing us not to imagine that we had captured a literal image of God nor related to God in God's fullness. The service ends on a note of modesty, affirming the limits of our efforts and implicitly cautioning us not to imagine that the image we carry out of the service is a literal representation of God. The God of our imaginings ought not to become an idol for us.

The second "word" ends with a number of assertions that warrant our attention. The self-identification of God as being jealous has often provoked surprise and bewilderment. But the fact is that, close as the emotion of jealousy might be to God's demand that we not have commerce with other (conceivable) deities — or, in modern terms, not subscribe to other ultimate concerns — the literal meaning of the Hebrew is closer to the words "zealous" or "impassioned." It is as if God were cautioning, "I respond intensely to such infractions."

Perhaps more perplexing is the image of God punishing children and subsequent descendants for the wrong actions of a parent or ancestor. But whatever might have been the intent of the verses before us, other parts of the Bible are explicit in rejecting such a perspective.

> The fathers shall not be put to death for the children, neither shall the children be put to death for the fathers; every man shall be put to death for his own sin. (Deut. 24:16)

> The soul that sinneth, it shall die; the son shall not bear the iniquity of the father with him, neither shall the father bear the iniquity with him; the righteousness of the righteous shall be upon him, and the wickedness of the wicked shall be upon him. (Ezek. 18:20)

> In those days they shall say no more: "The fathers have eaten sour
> grapes, and the children's teeth are set on edge." But every one shall
> die for his own iniquity; every man that eateth the sour grapes, his
> teeth shall be set on edge. (Jer. 31:29-30)

Thus, any intergenerational retribution that might have been suggested by
our "word" never did take root in biblical, and subsequent Jewish,
thought.

Many apologists have hastened to point out that even while the con
cluding section of our "word" does suggest a multigenerational retribution
of three or four generations, it envisions a far greater horizon — a thousand generations — of promise and reward. God's "anger" might express
itself over a period of time. But God's loving concern lasts infinitely longer.
And we do find expression of this very idea in the Bible itself. As Isaiah
writes:

> For a small moment have I abandoned thee;
> But with great compassion will I take thee back.
> In a little wrath I hid my face from thee for a moment
> But with everlasting kindness will I have compassion upon thee.
>
> (Isa. 54:7-8)

Commentators also note that this "word" ends on a note that identifies
the basis of the human response to God as love. And more, the concluding
words underscore a connection between love of God and attentiveness to
God's commandments.

This "word" concludes by talking in terms of the emotional component of our relationship to God. The sounding of this note might seem in-
congruous to Christian readers who have been accustomed to thinking of
love as a New Testament quality, while characterizing the "Old Testament"
as a document of law. It is paradoxical that many Christians assume that in
the famous exchange in Matthew 22:36-40 Jesus is enunciating a new
teaching.

> And one of them asked him a question to test him. "Teacher, which
> is the great commandment in the Law?" and he said to him, "'You
> shall love the Lord your God with all your heart, and with all your
> soul, and with all your mind.' This is the great and first command-
> ment. And a second is like unto it, 'You shall love your neighbor as

yourself.' On these two commandments depend all the law and the prophets."

In fact, what Jesus is doing in this exchange is citing verses from the Hebrew Bible (Deut. 6:5 and Lev. 19:18) that he thinks epitomize the entire work — as numerous rabbis of that time cited epitomic verses or "general principles" to summarize the entire Torah. Indeed, the Deuteronomy verse has come to be included as part of every Jewish worship service as a reminder to worshipers of what the entire exercise represents.

It is also noteworthy that the Jewish tradition links the concept of God's love for us with the concept of mitzvah/commandment and responsibility. The verses from Deuteronomy 6 that speak of loving God go on to talk about the commandments and our responsibility to incorporate them into our lives, make them part of our everyday experience, impart them to the generations who come after us. And the liturgy of the Jewish tradition perpetuates that association. When the liturgy speaks directly of God's love for us, it consistently joins that idea with the concept of God's revealing of the Torah. The traditional liturgy for every morning service states:

> With abounding love have You loved us. . . . O put it in our hearts to understand and discern, to mark, learn and teach, to heed, to do and to fulfill in love all the words taught in Your Torah. Enlighten our eyes in Your Torah, and let our hearts cleave to Your commandments. . . . Blessed are You, O Lord, who has chosen Your people Israel in love.

The corresponding evening prayer asserts:

> With everlasting love have You loved Your people, the house of Israel. Torah and commandments, statutes and ordinance have You taught us. . . . We will rejoice in the words of Your Torah and Your commandments forever. . . . Blessed are You, O Lord, who loves Your people Israel.

The conjunction of Torah and love is inescapable.

For Jews, love of God is no alien idea. Nor is the notion of God's love for us. In Jewish tradition that divine love is identified with Torah and commandment that are understood not as a burden but as tokens of our mutual commitment to one another. Indeed, one rabbinic commentary describes the Torah in terms of a marriage contract between God and the people of Israel:

> Rabbi Abba bar Kahana [commenting on the verse "this I call to mind, therefore I have hope," Lam. 3:21] said: this may be likened to a king who married a lady and wrote her a generous ketubah/marriage contract: "so many state apartments I am preparing for you, so many jewels I am preparing for you, so much silver and gold I give you."
>
> The king left her and went to a distant land for many years. Her neighbors used to vex her, saying, "Your husband has deserted you. Come and be married to another man." She wept and sighed, but whenever she went into her room and read her *ketubah* she would be consoled. After many years the king returned and said to her, "I am astounded that you waited for me all these years." She replied, "My lord, king if it had not been for the generous *ketubah* you wrote me, then surely my neighbors would have won me over." (*Lamentations Rabbah*)

Which brings us full circle to "I am the Lord your God. . . ." For, at bottom, this second "word" is about that same sense of love and commitment. Its ultimate subject is the people's responsibility for fidelity to the loving God with whom they are bound in covenant.

Response

Leanne Van Dyk

The Bible story books my parents often read to me as a child included watercolor pictures of the prophet Moses coming down from Mount Sinai with the two stone tablets of the law in his arms. The commandments were numbered, with Roman numerals, usually, thus making clear which commandments were which. If only it were so clear. The commandments, of course, are not numbered in the biblical text, and so the demarcation of the commandments has long been disputed in the Christian and the Jewish traditions. For example, the Lutheran tradition, among others, includes what this volume identifies as the first commandment and the second commandment as one. The Jewish tradition ends the first commandment after the divine self-identification and makes the second commandment include both the prohibition of other gods and the prohibition of idolatry. Again, the Lutheran tradition divides the tenth commandment into two, distinguishing the coveting of someone's wife from the coveting of someone's property. There are deep theological and historical reasons at stake in all these differences. For the purposes of this response to Rabbi Polish's chapter on the second commandment, it is sufficient to focus primarily on the second commandment identified as the prohibition against idolatry.

What, precisely, is the temptation that this commandment warns against, the actions this commandment prohibits? The translation of the Hebrew word *pesel* is often rendered "idol" or "image," a visible representation of Yahweh. The commandment warns against construing anything that is created for the God that is creator. The second commandment's comprehensive wording, "You shall not make for yourself an idol, whether in the form of anything that is in heaven above, or that is on the earth beneath, or that is in the water under the earth," makes it clear that an inventory of all created reality does not reveal an alternative or rival for God's sovereign being. God's mystery and reality are discontinuous with everything else. God is God. Created reality is not God. Therefore, to assign ultimate worth to anything that God created replaces God's rightful place as creator and is idolatrous.

The most obvious application of this commandment, as Rabbi Polish rightly points out, is the prohibition of material idols. The Abrahamic faiths all prohibit the fashioning and worshiping of the forms of deities. Thus the obvious ban of the commandment is against idol worship. But idolatry is a temptation that takes shape in far more subtle cultural disguises. For contemporary believers in both Jewish and Christian communities, perhaps the violation of the second commandment is an attempt to "locate and thereby domesticate Yahweh in a visible, controlled object."[1] Any object that takes on the character of ultimate value not only becomes an idol, thus replacing God, but also makes the implicit claims to spatially locate and limit God.

Psalm 20:7 echoes the second commandment in its declaration, "Some take pride in chariots, and some in horses, but our pride is in the name of the LORD our God." The creatures (horses) and the objects (chariots), both symbols of military might, are not where ultimate hope and destiny lie; rather, in God is where they lie. Any other option is a violation of the commandment and a fall into idolatry. It is not difficult to apply more contemporary categories to this example to see our own culture's headlong plunge into the adoration of symbols of violence, domination, and power.

The subtle temptations of the second commandment are identified by Rabbi Polish as the giving of our allegiance to anything other than God. Any "false absolute" can become the focus of idolatry, the making of an image. Polish says, "In obeisance to that 'false absolute,' people will be willing to ignore any other considerations, sacrifice the welfare of others, invest enormous expenditures of energy, time, and resources." The familiar idols of nation, money, might, power, prestige, status, and material possessions immediately come to mind. For adolescents, the idols may be brand-name clothing or shoes, brands that constantly shift, thus continually replacing the idols with their successors, or body piercings or a coveted place in the social order.

In the cultural matrix in which North Americans live and move and

---

1. Walter Brueggemann, *The New Interpreter's Bible*, vol. 1 (Nashville: Abingdon, 1994).

have their being, idolatry can beckon not only in material possessions but also in images. Often possessions and images exist in intimate connection. The idolatry of images is especially striking in connection to the second commandment, because a familiar translation of *pesel* is "image" — "You shall not make for yourself an *image*. . . ." This culture is saturated with images — commercial images, media images, photographic images, Internet images, logos and icons and symbols that portray a whole complex of values — and the sheer ubiquity of images, especially in an electronic age, makes idolatry an even more nuanced concern. Just four years after television was introduced, 10 million American homes had television sets. Just twenty years after the early years of the Internet, this form of communication, commerce, and information has exploded to millions of sites and has become a staple of modern life. Clearly, the appetite for images among North Americans seems to know no bounds.

Cultural critic Barry Sanders comments, "As soon as the child enters into electronic training — one that begins with television viewing — without knowing it, he or she has opted for a very specific cognitive track, with a complete set of values, goals, and beliefs."[2] These values and beliefs are surprisingly clear and plainly stated. Sanders says, "No commercial carries a warning that the product it advertises may be beyond one's reach. Instead, TV offers images of happy, usually young people enjoying their brand-name abundance. In fact, those people have found happiness because of their new gadgets and goodies."[3] The belief system being promoted by ubiquitous electronic images is that these products or these experiences will offer joy, completion, and wholeness, or, in a word, salvation.

In contemporary North American society, two generations have encountered the value-shaping effects of television and one generation of the Internet. Faith traditions committed to resist the temptations of idolatry face fresh challenges in countering these pervasive influences and finding their identity and values in the one true God, the creator of heavens and earth.

The critique of images and how uncritical consumption of images can shape values, beliefs, and actions is not limited to massive consumption of

2. Barry Sanders, *A Is for Ox: Violence, Electronic Media, and the Silencing of the Written Word* (New York: Pantheon Books, 1994), p. 141.

3. Barry Sanders, *The Private Death of Public Discourse* (Boston: Beacon Press, 1998), p. 147.

electronic images, however. Even a classic modern art form, the photograph, comes in for a stinging rebuke by Susan Sontag in her essay *On Photography*. She links our culture's fascination with the photograph to a form of idolatry. She argues her case by noting that the photograph *is* another kind of image. "In the preface to the second edition (1843) of *The Essence of Christianity*, Feuerbach observes about 'our era' that it 'prefers the image to the thing, the copy to the original, the representation to the reality, appearance to being' — while being aware of doing just that."[4] She claims further that one of the primary activities of our society is the production and consumption of images, and that these images have enormous power over our imaginations, our beliefs, and our actions.

Sontag believes that the peoples of nonindustrialized countries display some deep intuitions in their aversion to being photographed. They perceive "it to be some kind of trespass, an act of disrespect, a sublimated looting of the personality or the culture," whereas people in countries familiar with "reality TV" somehow feel more real when they are photographed and seek out this affirmation.[5]

Sontag, who died recently, was no doubt aware that her essay went against the grain of massive public acceptance of the intrusion of photography into every aspect of our lives. A North American culture so accustomed to baby pictures, school pictures, graduation pictures, wedding pictures, family pictures, and vacation pictures, all digitized, edited, and loaded onto personalized Web sites, can hardly stop for a moment to think about the implications. Yet photography is a form of imagery that has enormous power to distort, distance, frame, flatten, interpret, normalize, obscure, and simplify.[6] It is not neutral. It is not value-free. It too has the potential to become an idol. The insights of Barry Sanders and Susan Sontag do not suggest that a photograph, a Web site, a television program, a highway billboard themselves become idols — although there is nothing to rule this out — but that the values, beliefs, attitudes, and actions that these symbolic systems encourage can become idols, drawing people away from true worship of God.

In further witness to the powerful effect of ceaseless electronic images on the formation of values and vision, Edmund Morris's editorial in the

---

4. Susan Sontag, *On Photography* (New York: Farrar, Straus, and Giroux, 1973), p. 153.
5. Sontag, *On Photography*, p. 161.
6. I owe this insight to Marilyn Chandler McEntyre.

New York Times of October 17, 2005, reflects with dismay on his University of Chicago students' disinterest in learning about the written original drafts of great works of literature and musical composition. He remembers one of his lectures in particular, in which the students "weren't listening so much as watching. To them, I was just the latest in a lifetime's succession of images, another talking head." Morris wonders how much is lost in a culture of Internet-ready images, what kind of superficiality it breeds and jaded disinterest it fosters in the very students he hopes to ignite with curiosity and hunger for learning.

According to these cultural observers, none of whom, it must be admitted, had any comment on the second commandment, images demythologize the world. Another way of saying the same thing is that uncritical consumption of images removes God from the world. This is a violation of the second commandment — to remove God from the world in the blind and addictive service of images, the power of which we are often naively unaware. One of the most urgent tasks of theologians, pastors, and rabbis is to remythologize the world, to envision a world that pulses with the energy, love, and beauty of God.

Rabbi Daniel Polish reminds us of "the most profound challenge" of the second commandment — that even a concept of God can become an idol. When we confuse our constructed concepts and doctrines of God for God's own holy self, then we have fallen into a violation of the second commandment. Speaking from my own arena of experiences, I think it must be admitted that an honest survey of the contemporary Christian ecclesial and theological scene brings confession to this failure. Too often the worship "wars," the God-talk divide, the sexuality debate, the biblical interpretation differences, the ecumenical struggles, and the small steps of interfaith dialogue bring theologians and church leaders to a commitment to the construct, the formulation, the symbol. Precision and clarity are in fact high values in theological conversation and ecumenical and interfaith dialogues. But the deep caution of the apophatic Christian tradition and, as Polish notes, the dialectical Jewish tradition must give due modesty to these efforts at precision and clarification. God is beyond all our words, concepts, images, symbols, and imaginings. For Christian believers, only one Word is adequate to convey God, and that Word was spoken in the incarnation of Jesus Christ. Idolatry and excessive attachment to imagery are possible even with respect to the incarnate Jesus Christ, however, for Christians have not been immune to a wide range of reductionisms in their understandings of Jesus.

Daniel Polish ends his chapter with a rabbinical story about a king who wrote a generous and loving marriage contract and then left for many years. His fiancée was distressed at his long absence but stayed faithful to her promise to him, despite her neighbors' jeers. When the king returned, he asked her why she had remained true to him. She replied that it was the generous marriage contract, which so clearly stated his intentions to her. Polish makes the same connections to the tables of the law. These are God's clear, loving intentions for us, founded on his self-identification, "I am the Lord your God. . . ." Everything that follows flows from these words that bind God to us and bind us to God. The prohibition against idolatry and excessive attachment to imagery is only an implication of God's identity, God's gracious inclination toward us and our faithful response.

The Blessing of God's Name

R. Kendall Soulen

You shall not make wrongful use of the name of the LORD your God, for the LORD will not acquit anyone who misuses his name.

Speaking about God

Most of the time, Christians and Jews talk to God and about God unselfconsciously, and this is as it should be. Without a measure of childlike confidence, one would scarcely dare to pray, praise, confess, teach, or comfort in God's name. If every time a person spoke in faith she stopped to second-guess herself, faith itself would soon whither. Yet from time to time Christians and Jews do become self-conscious as they speak to and about God. They become afraid that what they say is tinged with frailty, vacuity, or falseness. Then they may falter and fall silent. And this too is as it should be. For as experience shows, it is easy when speaking of God to cross the line that separates childlike confidence from foolish and culpable presumption.

According to both Christian and Jewish traditions, the mingling of the ordinary and the momentous that colors all religious language is especially concentrated in *the name of God*. Indeed, it is God's name that imbues the language of faith with both qualities. Because God has a name and makes it known, we can speak to God and about God in a way that is not presumptuous but is ordinary in the best sense of the word, as becoming to our lips as conversation with a beloved spouse or child or friend. Rightly understood, the very self-evidence with which Christians and Jews have called upon God down through the ages points to the undergirding mystery of biblically informed speech, the gift of God's name. For by this gift

47

God has made it possible for his people to approach him personally, gain his attention, address him, and communicate with him.

But the gift of God's name also imparts profound gravity to religious speech. It raises the stakes on "God talk" by an infinite degree. It makes it impossible for our religious language to be merely a free-floating flight of exploration and fancy, or a dispassionate analysis of doctrinal grammar or logic, or a colorful and heartfelt supplement to our rhetorical resources. What we say and how we say it go to the heart of our relationship to God. And so the use and misuse of this language is always, ultimately, a matter of life and death.

Both the use and the abuse of God's name are the concern of the third commandment. The commandment warns against misusing the name even as it presupposes its indispensability for the daily life of faith. To reflect on the third commandment, therefore, is to meditate on how the awesomeness of God's name is to be made visible in its every ordinary use.

The Third Commandment in Context

We get important clues about the meaning of the third commandment by considering its context within the Decalogue as a whole. The first table of the Decalogue is all about preserving the integrity of the covenantal relationship that the Lord has established between himself and God's people, Israel, or, as the church reads the Decalogue, the enlarged people of God made real through Jesus Christ. In the first two commandments the Lord prohibits Israel from violating the covenant in *extra mural* fashion, by forsaking the Lord for other gods or idols. The next two commandments, in contrast, are concerned with what we might call the *intra mural* integrity of the covenant. Here the looming danger is not relationship to false gods, but false relationship to YHWH, Israel's God. The fourth commandment guards against this danger by directing Israel to remember what God has done, singling out the Sabbath for its own sake and also to represent all God's other generous benefits. But the third commandment, the topic of this essay, guards the *intra mural* integrity of the covenant at an even more intimate and sensitive point. Its concern is the proper acknowledgment of *who God is*, a concern that the Scriptures naturally express by invoking God's name.

Literally rendered, the third commandment states, "You must not lift up the name of the LORD your God frivolously/falsely."[1] The misuse that God appears to have directly in view is swearing an oath in God's name with the intent to deceive or in trivial circumstances. By nature such oaths make God a party to foolishness at best or villainy at worst. What is worse, perhaps, they contradict and obscure the fact that God's testimony is supremely reliable and weighty. (If it were not, of course, then the act of invoking God as a witness would be vacuous, a fact that suggests that making a false oath is the epitome of all self-contradictory speech-acts, the irrational act par excellence.)

Significantly, however, God does not choose to use the words that elsewhere in Scripture refer most directly to swearing falsely (Lev. 19:12). Instead, God uses the broader and more polyvalent term that is commonly translated "in vain." This suggests that God's concern in the third commandment is more than defective oaths. More broadly, we might say, the commandment warns Israel away from any word or deed that belies or belittles the integrity with which God speaks and acts in God's own name. False oaths certainly do that, but so do other forms of speech, such as, for example, false prophecy (cf. Jer. 14:13-16; 23:16; Ezek. 22:28). Or, in positive terms, we might formulate God's instruction this way: "Use my name in a way that corresponds to how I use it."

But how does God use God's name? Or, more to the point, we may wonder, how on earth can human beings use God's name in a way that corresponds to God's use? In fact, the Bible is rather clear on both points. According to a large if disparate choir of biblical witnesses, God uses God's name to two chief ends: to make it known and, in so doing, to bless God's people. Human beings, in turn, reflect God's use of the name when they demonstrate by word and deed that they "know that the Lord is God" and "bless God's holy name" in return.

Seen in this light, the third commandment offers a vista into the heart of the whole sweep of God's history with creation. To better appreciate this vista, we will explore three marks that characterize how God uses God's name to make it known and to bless, and some implications for how God's people are to use God's name.

---

1. Herbert B. Huffmon, "The Fundamental Code Illustrated: The Third Commandment," in *The Ten Commandments: The Reciprocity of Faithfulness*, ed. William P. Brown (Louisville: Westminster John Knox, 2004), p. 207.

God's Name Declares God's Uniqueness

A first way in which God uses God's name is to declare God's uniqueness. From the encounter at the burning bush, to God's majestic self-declarations in Isaiah, Jeremiah, and Ezekiel, to the vision of a new heaven and a new earth vouchsafed to John, no other note associated with God's name sounds throughout the Scriptures more brilliantly and urgently than that of the sheer incomparable uniqueness of God. "I *am* the LORD: that *is* my name: and my glory will I not give to another, neither my praise to graven images" (Isa. 42:8).

As the mark of God's uniqueness, God's name shows that God is both *identifiable* and *uncircumscribable*.[2] When in the third commandment God refers to "my name," he is not referring to an abstraction or an ineffable idea. God is referring to YHWH, the name God uses to identify himself at the opening of the Decalogue: "I am YHWH your God." This, of course, is the same name God made known to Moses at the burning bush (Exod. 3:15), and "made great" by delivering Israel from Egypt. The most remarkable thing about the name YHWH is that it is a personal proper name more or less like any other, except that it belongs to God. God uses the name to identify himself, and by making it known, God permits others to use it in the same way, to "call on his name."

Yet God's name also betokens God's uncircumscribability. As *God's* personal proper name, YHWH is in fact *not* like any other name. Unlike the names of the animals under Adam's dominion and most human names, God's name does not originate in human invention or whimsy. Uniquely among all personal proper names, it radiates the abysmal eternity of God. At the burning bush God supplies the name YHWH with his own interpretive gloss, "I am who I am" (Exod. 3:14), a perpetual warning against every attempt to define or delimit God's being.

Taking our cues from the preceding, we might formulate a first way of obeying the third commandment in the following way. *Speak of who God is in a way that honors God's mystery, and honor God's mystery in a way that extols who God is.* The opening of Psalm 113 illustrates this balance beautifully.

---

2. Here I am indebted to Christopher Morse's excellent discussion of God's being and name of God in *Not Every Spirit: A Dogmatics of Christian Disbelief* (Valley Forge, Pa.: Trinity, 1994), chap. 7.

Praise the Lord!
Praise, O servants of the Lord,
    praise the name of the Lord!
Blessed be the name of the Lord
    from this time forth and for evermore!
From the rising of the sun to its setting
    the name of the Lord is to be praised!
The Lord is high above all nations,
    and his glory above the heavens!
Who is like the Lord our God,
    who is seated on high,
who looks far down
    on the heavens and the earth?

(Ps. 113:1-6)

The psalmist celebrates who God is by invoking the Tetragrammaton with percussive insistence, while at the same time using vivid images to underscore the "infinite qualitative distinction" between this God and everything else (God must look "far down" just to see the heavens, creation's farthest edge!). Today we do not always find the psalmist's balance easy to strike. Some believe that God's mystery can be protected only by denying that God can be reliably identified at all! (The tiresome repetition of the saying "You can't put God in a box" often tends toward such a denial.) Others, it seems, are so eager to invoke God by name that they fail to heed the warning it contains, "I am who *I* am." According to the third commandment, however, God's incomparable identity and God's uncircumscribable mystery must not be played off against each other. Apart from God's concrete whoness, God's mystery would be empty, blank and featureless, and thus no real mystery at all. But apart from God's uncircumscribability, God's identity would be a datum to be described and manipulated, a sterile fact, and thus not the identity of God.

The ancient Jewish practice of honoring the Tetragrammaton by not pronouncing it, still customary among Jews today, is wonderfully suited to teach the heart to recognize both the identity and mystery of God.[3] Christians have sometimes caricatured the practice as a craven and sub-

---

3. On the Tetragrammaton in the New Testament and intertestamental period, see the fine book by Sean McDonough, *YHWH at Patmos: Rev. 1:4 in Its Hellenistic and Early Jewish Setting* (Tübingen: Mohr Siebeck, 1999).

Christian superstition (Calvin). In fact, the practice is even more integral to the New Testament than to the Old. Everywhere in the New Testament we notice a heightened scrupulosity with respect to the third commandment, as in the pervasive use of pious circumlocutions in place of God's name, or in Jesus' own command to refrain from all oaths, not just false or frivolous ones (cf. Matt. 5:33-37). Even when noticed, the theological passion that informs this restraint is often misunderstood. Its root is not a general cultural sense of God's increased *remoteness* or *quarrelsomeness,* as is sometimes suggested. Its root, rather, is a passionate, end-time longing that God at long last overshadow our human talk about God *with God's talk about God.* Whenever Christians pray "Hallowed be thy name!" they are, in effect, saying, "God, use your name as you have promised! Sanctify it, so that all the earth may know that you are God!" And by referring to YHWH's name *indirectly,* they formulate this petition in a way that underscores its content, pointing away from themselves and toward the incomparable identity and uncircumscribable mystery of God.

God's Name Declares God's Reliable Presence

A second way God uses God's name is to declare God's reliable presence to God's people. That, at any rate, is the joyous message of the burning bush. God's shattering "I am who I am!" has hardly ceased tolling when God continues his reply to Moses: "Tell the Israelites, 'I AM sent me to you'" (Exod. 3:14). With that, God repeats God's pun/name in a new and comforting register: God makes it a promise to *be with* Moses and the Israelites in their need and distress.

We find the same glorious movement from *God is who God is!* to *God is who God is for us!* in the continuation of Psalm 113. At last mention, we recall, YHWH was looking "far down upon the heavens and the earth." The psalm continues:

> He raises the poor from the dust,
> and lifts the needy from the ash heap,
> to make them sit with princes,
> with the princes of his people.

(Ps. 113:7-8)

With plunging suddenness the God who is high above all things is also at the side of the poor and needy, raising them up from dust and ashes. We get an almost dizzying sense of God in motion, stooping, *reaching down, bending low* not merely to the earth, but to the lowest of earth. Here, too, as at the burning bush, God declares God's uniqueness by coming to the side of endangered human beings.

Over the span of the biblical story, the link between God's name and God's faithful presence grows ever stronger, from the burning bush, to the temple in Jerusalem where God makes God's name to dwell (cf. Deut. 12:11; 1 Kings 8:23-29), to (for Christians) the wonder of the child in Bethlehem, called "Emmanuel" (Matt. 1:23). But here we must be careful to understand the message of God's name aright. If God's name proves time and again to be the place of God's reliable presence toward us, then this is because *God's name conforms to God's most holy character, and not to our desires and expectations.* This comes through loud and clear in the story that recounts how YHWH declared his name to Moses a second time, after the incident of the golden calf. God "descended in a cloud" and "stood with" Moses and "proclaimed the name" (Exod. 34:5):

> The LORD, the LORD, a God merciful and gracious, slow to anger, and abounding in steadfast love and faithfulness, keeping steadfast love for the thousandth generation, forgiving iniquity and transgression and sin, yet by no means clearing the guilty, but visiting the iniquity of the parents upon the children and the children's children, to the third and the fourth generation. (34:6-7)

God's name brings God's reliable presence, yes. But God's being there is trustworthy because God is both merciful and righteous toward us, both gracious and exacting, both slow to anger and at times angry. True, God promises that the former qualities outweigh the latter, even vastly so. Nevertheless, God uses God's name to declare that God is both the one and the other. Even in the jubilation of Psalm 113 we hear the overtones of God's judging righteousness, as we picture "the princes of his people" shocked out of their self-sufficiency by God's new seating arrangements for the poor.

In light of the preceding, we can draw one or two further lessons for what it means for God's people to use God's name rightly. First, all talk that touches on divine things, however light of heart or learned it may be, takes place *coram Deo,* in the presence of God. Christians and Jews are prohibited from supposing that they can ever talk about God behind God's back, as it were, whether idly in the manner of a gossip or jokester, or full of serious intent, like a doctor discussing her patient. Secondly, Christians and Jews must cultivate a scrupulous honesty with regard to the character of God's reliable presence toward us. We must avoid confusing God's *I am with you* with the trouble-free maintenance of our life projects. (Moses' plans, after all, didn't survive his encounter with the burning bush.) Above all, we must avoid cleaving asunder what God has joined in God's name, namely, God's mercy and God's justice. The human spirit strains against this rule, for nothing, it seems, comes more easily to us than a desire to distribute God's justice toward others and God's mercy toward ourselves. Conversely, our American religious life today sometimes suggests God's job is to be a supportive presence that helps everyone to do whatever it is he or she chooses. In truth, to speak rightly in God's name is to strive to make clear to ourselves and others that God-with-us is neither an indulgent and sentimental grandparent nor a malicious and vindictive tyrant, but YHWH, the living God of steadfast love and righteousness.

God's Name Declares God's Transforming Blessing and Claim

A third way God uses God's name is to pronounce God's blessing. At the close of the Ten Commandments, God promises, "In every place where I cause my name to be remembered, I will come to you and bless you" (Exod. 20:24). Here we have the "logic" of God's name in a nutshell: from God's uniqueness ("wherever I cause my name to be remembered") to God's presence ("I will come to you") to God's blessing ("I will bless you"). Aaron's well-known blessing, pronounced daily over the people, expresses the connection between God's name and God's blessing even more forcefully:

> The LORD spoke to Moses, saying: Speak to Aaron and his sons, saying,
> Thus you shall bless the Israelites: You shall say to them,
>> The LORD bless you and keep you;
>> the LORD make his face to shine upon you, and be gracious to you;
>> the LORD lift up his countenance upon you, and give you peace.
> So they shall put my name on the Israelites, and I will bless them.
>> (Num. 6:22-27)

When God wishes to bless the Israelites, he causes his name to be "put" on them, again and again, like an extravagant quantity of fragrant oil poured over their heads.

The blessing that God confers through God's name gives a great benefit to those who receive it, indeed, the greatest benefit of all: life in fellowship with God. Yet we would badly misunderstand the nature of this benefit if we overlooked the fact that it *claims and transforms* those who receive it, so that they are suited for the service of God's name before the eyes of the world. In the Bible, a common sign of coming under God's sway is that a person's own name is changed. As people are swept up into fellowship with God, their personal proper names melt and take new shape before the transforming presence of God's uniqueness. Abram becomes Abraham, Sarai becomes Sarah, Jacob receives the name Israel, and so on, until ultimately God has what God desires: "a people called by the name of the LORD" (Deut. 28:10). No wonder the psalmist ultimately ascribes to God's name not only the *redemptive* power that rescues Israel from destruction time and again, but the *creative* power that undergirds the universe.

> If it had not been the LORD who was on our side
> — let Israel now say —
> if it had not been the LORD who was on our side, . . .
> then over us would have gone
> the raging waters.
> Blessed be the LORD. . . .
> Our help is in the name of the LORD,
> who made heaven and earth.
>
> (Ps. 124)

By the transforming power of God's name, God creates a people whose life is a parable of creation's own deepest secret.

There are two distinct but interlocking axes along which God shapes Israel into a community able to "know that the LORD is God" and "bless God's name." A first axis is its practices of worship and cultic purity. We have already noted the divine promise that sustains these practices: "In every place where I cause my name to be remembered I will come to you and bless you" (Exod. 20:24). This promise has its echo when the people bless God's name in return, in ways both communal and individual, both prescribed and spontaneous.

Then the Levites . . . said, "Stand up and bless the LORD your God from everlasting to everlasting. Blessed be your glorious name, which is exalted above all blessing and praise." (Neh. 9:5)

Then the women said to Naomi, "Blessed be the LORD, who has not left you this day without next-of-kin; and may his name be renowned in Israel!" (Ruth 4:14)

Bless the LORD, O my soul,
  and all that is within me,
  bless his holy name.

(Ps. 103:1)

Especially in the Psalms, Israel offers praise with the intent of moving the rest of creation to join in blessing God's name.

Make a joyful noise to the LORD, all the earth. . . .
  Give thanks to him, bless his name.

(Ps. 100:1a, 4b)

My mouth will speak the praise of the LORD,
  and all flesh will bless his holy name forever and ever.

(Ps. 145:21)

Yet, as these verses hint, God's blessing also creates a second axis of mutuality that exists *within* God's people and *between* God's people and the nations (cf. Gen. 12:1-5). Already in worship and praise, the people are knit together in a new way, as a community whose focus and ultimate loyalty is God. But if the community is to reflect the glory of God's name, its worship must be accompanied by ongoing practices of daily living, which draw the common and ordinary tasks of life into the orbit of God's uniqueness and give them something of its imprint. A last glance at the closing verse of Psalm 113 provides a simple but moving illustration.

He gives the barren woman a home,
  making her the joyous mother of children.
Praise the LORD!

(Ps. 113:9)

After having first praised God's name on a cosmic scale and then celebrated God's dramatic upending of unjust economic and political arrangements, Psalm 113 ends with a scene of surprising domesticity: a happy mother presiding over a noisy household. Yet the picture has bite, for the woman's endless rounds of chores and satisfactions are the measure of how *fine-grained* and *all-consuming* the transforming power of God's blessing is. The people Israel is this household writ large. The law of Moses is its schedule of domestic chores and satisfactions. In the large family as in the small, God's blessing penetrates and transforms every nook and cranny of the household's common life, and makes its daily rhythms a witness to God's name.

God blesses with God's name in order to create a people whose lives will be altogether and in every part a sanctification of God's name. We should not be surprised, therefore, when God equates, as though in passing, the keeping of *all* God's commands with the observance of the third commandment. "Thus you shall keep my commandments and observe them: I am the LORD. You shall not profane my holy name, that I may be sanctified among the people of Israel: I am the LORD" (Lev. 22:31-32).

We can now draw a further lesson about observing the third commandment. To honor God's name, to "know that the LORD is God," is to desire that the transforming claim of God's blessing pour its drenching oil over every inch of our lives, from our deepest desires to our merest cycles of daily existence, and make of them something new and pleasing to God: a hymn of praise to God's name.

The Profanation and Vindication of God's Name

Up to this point we have chiefly considered the right use of God's name, and its abuse only in passing. Yet to leave the matter there would be untrue to the third commandment, with respect both to its literal wording and to its canonical setting. The third commandment explicitly states the sanction attached to its violation (curiously, it is the only commandment to do so): "for the LORD will not acquit anyone who misuses his name." Moreover, the Decalogue appears halfway between two markedly different occasions when God declares God's name to Moses. The first comes just before God will "make a name" for himself by liberating Israel (Exod. 3), while the second comes just after Israel has poured contempt on God's name by worshiping the golden calf (Exod. 34). This setting invites us to consider how God deals with God's people when they profane God's name, and what this implies for how we are to use God's name.

The sin of the golden calf represents Israel's wholesale failure in its primary vocation: to be a people whose existence and conduct resound to the glory of YHWH's name. The severity of Israel's failure is dramatically underscored by YHWH's initial reaction to the crisis. "I have seen this people, how stiff-necked they are. Now let me alone, so that my wrath may burn hot against them and I may consume them; and of you I will make a great nation" (Exod. 32:9-10). This passage is exceptionally interesting because it explicitly considers the possibility that YHWH might be so angered by Israel's sin as to wipe it out and create a new people in its place. And in fact, there is a sad tradition in Christian theology of appealing to this and similar passages to support the teaching that God has in fact rejected the Jews on account of their sins and made the Gentile church to be God's people in their place. Yet the thrust of the passage itself points in a direction exactly contrary to all such supersessionistic misuses. At the crucial moment, Moses intercedes:

> O LORD, why does your wrath burn hot against your people, whom you brought out of the land of Egypt with great power and with a mighty hand? Why should the Egyptians say, "It was with evil intent that he brought them out to kill them in the mountains, and to consume them from the face of the earth"? Turn from your fierce wrath; change your mind and do not bring disaster on your people. Remember Abraham, Isaac, and Israel, your servants, how you swore to them by your own self, saying to them, "I will multiply your descendants like the stars of heaven, and all this land that I have promised I will give to your descendants, and they shall inherit it forever." (32:11-13)

Moses' intercession is successful, for "the LORD changed his mind about the disaster that he planned to bring on his people" (32:14). Seen in context, the passage raises the possibility of God's abandoning Israel because of its sins only to reject that possibility. For our purposes, it is especially noteworthy that Moses succeeds in changing God's mind by appealing to the oath that God swore "by your own self." If God destroys Israel, Moses warns, the Gentiles will talk. God's reputation will suffer. By reminding God of the promises he has made, Moses shows that what God has in mind is inconsistent with God's own character and purpose. It is at odds with YHWH's name. God punishes Israel for their genuine and grievous sin, but preserves them as his people for his name's sake.

Throughout Israel's long history, the themes of this story recur time and again: intercession on behalf of a disobedient people, and God's pardon, forgiveness, and reforming discipline for the sake of God's name. From Ezekiel in the time of the exile we hear: "Therefore say to the house of Israel, Thus says the Lord GOD: It is not for your sake, O house of Israel, that I am about to act, but for the sake of my holy name, which you have profaned among the nations to which you came. I will sanctify my great name . . . and the nations shall know that I am the LORD, says the Lord GOD, when through you I display my holiness before their eyes" (Ezek. 36:22-23). And from Isaiah:

> For my name's sake I defer my anger,
>   for the sake of my praise I restrain it for you,
>   so that I may not cut you off.
> See, I have refined you, but not like silver;
>   I have tested you in the furnace of adversity.
> For my own sake, for my own sake, I do it,
>   for why should my name be profaned?
>   My glory I will not give to another.
> Listen to me, O Jacob,
>   and Israel, whom I called:
> I am He; I am the first,
>   and I am the last.
>
> (Isa. 48:9-12)

According to these and other passages, the holiness of God's name towers above the abject failure of God's people to live in a way that reflects God's holiness in return. Still, God does not abandon God's people, but sanctifies God's name before the nations in a yet more awesome and glorious way: by forgiving and restoring the fallen. These considerations suggest two further lessons concerning the use of God's name, lessons that are among the most important of all. First, with respect to ourselves, it is not possible to speak truthfully to God and about God without regularly confessing our sin, and without continually renewing our commitment to greater obedience. Second, with respect to the others, it is infinitely easier to speak worthily of God by interceding for the fallen than by reading them out of the people of God.

The Name Above Every Name and the Name of Jesus

All the themes that we have considered in this essay come together in a striking way in the New Testament witness to Jesus Christ. Perhaps the best way of gaining an overview of both the continuity and the novelty of this witness is to read the following passage from Paul's letter to the Philippians in the light of Psalm 113:

> 5 Let the same mind be in you that was in Christ Jesus,
> 6 who, though he was in the form of God,
> did not regard equality with God
> as something to be exploited,
> 7 but emptied himself,
> taking the form of a slave,
> being born in human likeness.
> And being found in human form,
> 8 he humbled himself and became obedient to the point of death —
> even death on a cross.
> 9 Therefore God also highly exalted him
> and gave him the name
> that is above every name,
> 10 so that at the name of Jesus
> every knee should bend,
> in heaven and on earth and under the earth,
> 11 and every tongue should confess
> that Jesus Christ is Lord,
> to the glory of God the Father.
>
> (Phil. 2:5-11)

Psalm 113 told of the condescension of YHWH and the rescue of human beings. Paul's hymn tells a similar though somewhat more intricate story. It begins not with YHWH's condescension but with Christ Jesus, who, though himself in want of nothing, became a human being on the "ash heap" (113:7) for the sake of others. God honored Jesus' condescension by delivering him from death and restoring him to his former condition. Moreover, in God's own act of supreme condescension, God gave to Jesus God's own name ("the name that is above every name" [v. 9], an oblique reference to the Tetragrammaton). The hymn then ends in the way that Psalm 113 began, with all creation joined in praise of God's name, thus dissolving once and for all the distinction between the covenant's *intra mural* and *extra mural* integrity that we noted at the start of this essay. But now at the conclusion of the hymn, God's name (designated this time by "Lord" [v. 11], another oblique reference to the Tetragrammaton) bears the mark of mutuality that formerly characterized God's relation to creation. True to God's condescension, creation praises God's name with the words "*Jesus Christ* is Lord," while true to Christ's condescension, Christ receives creation's praise "to the glory of *God the Father*."

In reflecting on this hymn, one scarcely knows what to marvel at more. Is it the fidelity with which it preserves earlier associations between God's name and God's uniqueness, reliable presence, transforming power, and forgiving judgment? Or is it the over-the-top way in which these associations are reshaped by the gospel? In either case, we can formulate one last rule concerning the Christian observance of the third commandment. Speak in Jesus' name so as to give glory to the God of Israel, and glorify the God of Israel by speaking humbly but confidently of Jesus.

Response

Rochelle L. Millen

Whenever studying or teaching the texts of what has come to be known as the Ten Commandments,[1] I frame them through the lens of the words written by Abraham Ibn Ezra, the medieval Spanish biblical commentator.[2] Ibn Ezra goes beyond the usual understanding of the structure of the Ten Commandments. The customary division, as indicated by R. Kendall Soulen, is one in which the first five commandments are "all about preserving the integrity of the covenantal relationship that the Lord has established between himself and God's people, Israel." Jewish commentators designate these first five as emphasizing the relationship between God and human beings, while the second five explicate fundamental relationships among human beings. One might say the first five utterances are theological while the last five are ethical. The fifth, honoring one's parents, straddles both categories and serves as a transition. Ibn Ezra, however, complicates this seemingly straightforward division.

In his introduction to the Ten Commandments, Ibn Ezra suggests a threefold division of Jewish precepts or mitzvoth.[3] According to his classi-

---

1. In Judaism they are known as *aseret hadibrot* or the Ten Utterances. The word *dibra* (*dibrot* in the plural) is a Mishnaic term referring to divine speech for *devarim*, meaning "words" in Deut. 5:20 (SPS) (5:22 NRSV): ". . . these words *(devarim)* which the LORD spoke . . . to your whole congregation. . . ," as well as Deut. 4:13 (NRSV). See Moshe Greenberg, "The Decalogue Tradition Critically Examined," in Moshe Greenberg, *Studies in the Bible and Jewish Thought* (Philadelphia: Jewish Publication Society, 1995), pp. 279-80.

2. Ibn Ezra, who lived from 1089 to 1164, was not only a biblical commentator but also a poet, grammarian, philosopher, astronomer, and physician. See "Ibn Ezra, Abraham," in *Encyclopedia Judaica* (Jerusalem: Keter Publishing, 1972), 8:1163.

3. Ibn Ezra in *Mikraot Gedolot Rav Peninim: Shemot* (in Hebrew) (Jerusalem: Levin-

fication, all precepts can be divided not only into positive and negative (what to do and what not to do), but also into precepts of the heart and mind, of speech, and of action or doing. Ibn Ezra views the precepts of the heart as the most important and brings proof texts to support his claim. He sees the first five as manifesting a progression from heart and mind (the first two) to speech (the third) to family relations and actions (the fourth and fifth). In the second set of five, however, the progression is reversed. That is, commandments six, seven, and eight prohibit deeds (murder, adultery, and theft), the ninth proceeds to word (false witness), and the concluding precept concerns heart and mind (coveting).[4] This structure reflects the ideal religious person, one whose thoughts and feelings find expression in both speech and action; heart and mind alone are insufficient. Similarly, good deeds and social justice are inadequate if they are not a manifestation of appropriate speech and intended by the feelings of one's heart and mind. Ideally, the inner self — our rationality and affect — and outer self — how we act in the concrete world of daily life — should be intertwined and derive from the same spiritual source.

Seen in this framework, the third utterance, or commandment, "Do not take the name of God your Lord in vain. God will not allow the one who takes His name in vain to go unpunished,"[5] represents the midway point between that which one believes, feels, and knows and how one's beliefs, feelings, and knowledge spill over into actions toward others. Thus God's name is a gift to us, a means to articulate and actualize faith in the very words we utter during both the prosaic and more grand moments of everyday human existence.

The notion Soulen brings to our attention, that "God uses God's name to declare God's uniqueness," is foundational in Judaism. According to rabbinic sources, the purpose of the various names of God in Hebrew

Epstein Publishing, 1973), pp. 359-64. A partial English translation may be found in Nehama Leibowitz, *Studies in Shemot, Part I* (Jerusalem: Jewish Agency, 1976), pp. 342-43.

4. Whether or not coveting is purely a precept of the heart is disputed. *Mekilta* and Maimonides argue that "coveting" is an actual deed. Ibn Ezra and Radak argue against this view. See the discussion in Nehama Leibowitz, *Studies in Shemot [Exodus]*, Vol. 1, trans. Aryeh Kaplan (Jerusalem: World Zionist Organization, 1976), pp. 344-46.

5. Translation of Aryeh Kaplan, *The Living Torah* (New York: Maznaim Publishing, 1981), p. 353. The recently retranslated JPS version reads: "You shall not swear falsely by the name of the Lord your God; for the Lord will not clear one who swears falsely by His name." *The Tanakh,* 2nd ed. (Philadelphia: Jewish Publication Society, 1999).

Scriptures is didactic: to teach us, through God's very designations, God's attributes, attributes we are required to emulate. Indeed, how do we come to "know" God? We come to "know" God through God's actions in the world, about which we are given partial understanding through the very appellations given to God in the texts that describe those actions. Thus, aspects of God's uniqueness are conveyed in God's very names, and the text specifically wishes to designate God as *Yhwh Elohekha*, "Lord, your God," in this third utterance.

A central meaning of YHWH (sometimes vocalized in English as "Yahweh" or "Jehovah"), as Soulen informs us, is "to declare God's reliable presence to God's people." God's "being-with-us," God's "being-present-to-us" is derived from the four letters that constitute the name "Lord," or YHWH. How is this so? While the verb "to be" appears in Hebrew in past, future, and imperative constructions, it does not have a present tense, which is understood. Were one to say in Hebrew, "I am a teacher," the Hebrew words would correlate with "I teacher," and "am" would be presupposed. However, were the verb "to be" to appear in the present tense, its grammatical form would be the name of God translated into English as "Lord." That is, YHWH literally means "be-ing" or "beingness"; or, regarding God, the God who is faithfully present to us. This is further explicated in Exodus 3:14, when God declares God's self as "I Will Be Who I Will Be."[6] In rabbinic theology this attribute of God is expressed through God's mercy. The name YHWH is a manifestation of God's qualities of mercy and compassion.

In contrast, the name Elohim, which in the third utterance appears subsequent to YHWH and with a possessive pronoun, i.e., "your God," indicates God's attribute of justice,[7] according to rabbinic literature. Thus in this command God speaks to the people through both the attribute of compassion and the quality of justice, similar to the use of both names in

6. Soulen translates this phrase in Exod. 3:14 in the present tense, "I am who I am." Indeed, this is the translation that appears in the JPS *Tanakh*. But others translate the phrase in the future tense, which is certainly its literal meaning. See Kaplan, *The Living Torah*, p. 271, and his notes there.

7. The biblical text offers other appellations of God, such as Shaddai and Makom (the latter in the book of Esther). Here the focus is on the names used in the third utterance. For a detailed discussion of the various Hebrew names of God as analyzed in kabbalistic, talmudic, and midrashic sources, as well as in the works of biblical commentators, see S. A. Adler, *Aspaklaria: Compendium of Jewish Thought* (in Hebrew) (Jerusalem, 1999), pp. 211-49.

the second story of creation, Genesis chapter 2.[8] One interpretation of the inclusion of both names of God in the third commandment is that misuse of God's name of mercy will call forth God's aspect of *din*, or justice. But other commentators disagree. They turn to the similar verse cited by Soulen, Leviticus 19:12: "You shall not swear falsely by my name," and using the rabbinic hermeneutic that declares that nothing in the biblical text is purposelessly repeated, state: "What need is there for this text [Lev. 19:12] when it has already been stated, 'Thou shall not take the name of the Lord thy God in vain'? You might have thought that one is not culpable except when His specific name [the Tetragrammaton] is involved. Whence that the prohibition applies to all the names of God? The text adds, 'By My name' — whatever name I have."[9] This refers specifically to the use in Leviticus 19:12 of the word "my name," since it is clear that this verse refers to a *false* oath, which differs from "taking God's name in vain."

And what is this difference? The classic commentator Rashi asks precisely this question. He defines "in vain" as "for nothing" and inquires, "What is a vain oath? If a person swore to change that which is known, that a pillar of stone is of gold." Nahmanides interprets similarly, stating: "This text has been interpreted by the Sages to mean that it is forbidden to swear by the hallowed Name in vain, as for example, he who swears that something is or is not so, where the matter is self-evident — that a pillar is made of marble, and he is standing by and all can see that it is so."[10] Unnecessary oaths are a serious offense, and only in the third commandment (as well as regarding idolatry) is punishment made explicit. The gravity of unnecessary oaths derives in part from their behavioristic impact. A person who indulges himself or herself by bolstering claims through swearing in God's name loses the sense of human limitations, exaggerates his or her power, and soon moves from vain oaths to false ones. "In vain" can lead to per-

---

8. See Joseph B. Soloveitchik, "The Lonely Man of Faith," *Tradition: A Journal of Orthodox Thought* 7, no. 2 (Summer 1965): 5-67. Soloveitchik discusses the use of "Elohim" to designate the God of perfect justice, who creates the natural universe, which manifests the preciseness and perfection of science in Genesis chapter 1. This is distinct from the use of both names in the creation of the historical-moral universe in chapter 2. A world inhabited by humanity requires God's compassion.

9. *Sifra*, quoted in Nehama Leibowitz, *Studies in Shemot, Part I*. The *Sifra* is also quoted by Rashi on that verse.

10. Ramban (Nahmanides), *Commentary on the Torah: Exodus*, translated and annotated by Charles Chavel (New York: Shilo, 1973), pp. 302-3.

jury, a betrayal not only of the many laws of justice, but also of Isaiah's proclamation, "You are my witnesses, says the LORD" (Isa. 43:10). According to others, "in vain" can also refer to using God's name in incantations, sorcery, and magic, each a kind of illusion.[11]

The formidable power of God's names — their truth, moral weight, uniqueness, and referencing of God as Creator — can only be invoked in ways that affirm human acknowledgment and gratitude, recognizing our own holiness in that of God. From this principle derives an interesting *halakhah,* or Jewish law. One way of "taking God's name in vain" is by reciting an unnecessary blessing, or benediction. The discussion in Babylonian Talmud *Berakhot* 33a may seem strange; indeed, in what way(s) is it appropriate to limit praise given to God? Benedictions in Judaism often have a formal structure in which gratitude is expressed to God for allowing humans to benefit from certain aspects of the world God has created. An example is the blessing said before eating bread: "Blessed are You, Lord, King of the universe, who brings forth bread from the earth." The converse of this articulation of praise and appreciation is the use of God's hallowed names for purposes that are frivolous, even if the trivialization occurs in some form of blessing. This concept of *berkhah levatalah,* pronouncing a vain or unnecessary benediction, is only marginally related to the issue of spontaneity and regularity as part of religious ritual but is central to understanding the third utterance.

One final point before concluding this brief response. It is interesting to me that Soulen associates Exodus 32:9-10 with the "sad tradition" of "supersessionistic misuses" of biblical texts in Christian theology. That Christian exegesis reads the journey of the ancient Israelites to maturation[12] as a history of rebellion that foreshadows God's alleged abandonment of the Jewish people in favor of the Gentile church is surprising. It is a reading back into biblical history, an attempt to see diverse events in Hebrew Scripture only through the lens of Christian texts and not on their own, as intrinsic parts of a purposeful narrative. Indeed, it is

---

11. See Martin Buber, *Moses: The Revelation and the Covenant* (San Francisco: Harper Torchbooks, 1958), p. 132, and U. Cassuto, *A Commentary on the Book of Exodus,* trans. Israel Abrahams (Jerusalem: Magnes Press, 1974), pp. 243-44.

12. Classical Jewish commentators read the forty-year journey in the desert as a result of God's realization that the people need to slough off the imprint of years of slavery and gradually develop the autonomy and inner freedom to commit themselves to God at Mount Sinai.

to deny the validity of the Pentateuch as the history of the Jewish people and claim it as the early history of Christianity. One might point to Acts 7:40-53 as hinting at such an interpretation.[13] But deriving supersessionism from Acts 7:40-53 is quite a leap. Certainly Soulen is correct to lament the misuse of such texts. Theological distortions of Hebrew Scripture have been condemned by post-Holocaust Christian theologians, from Clark Williamson to John Roth to Stephen Haynes to Mary Boys.[14] In addition, as Soulen indicates, the biblical text itself contradicts the notion of theological abandonment, preserving the Israelites as God's people for the sake of God's name.[15]

The graciousness of God permits us to use God's names in ways that cultivate our holiness and thereby our continued cognizance of God's holiness. Although God is known through several appellations, YHWH remains foundational. The utterances of our lips are expressions of heart and mind, and ultimately, as Ibn Ezra reminds us, of actions, which can promote or deter justice and goodness, the triumph of godliness. Not only are graven images prohibited in the second commandment, but also, in the third commandment, is the desecration of God's unique names. Even God's enemies take God's name in vain (Ps. 139:20); surely God's faithful cannot do so.

13. My thanks to Professor Barbara Kaiser for discussing this passage with me.

14. See, for instance, Clark M. Williamson, *A Guest in the House of Israel: Post-Holocaust Church Theology* (Louisville: Westminster John Knox, 1993); Stephen R. Haynes, *Reluctant Witnesses: Jews and the Christian Imagination* (Louisville: Westminster John Knox, 1995); Mary C. Boys, *Has God Only One Blessing: Judaism as a Source for Christian Self-Understanding* (Mahwah, N.J.: Stimulus/Paulist Press, 2000).

15. Rashi understands the word *bakh* in Exod. 32:13 as referring not to anything finite upon which God might swear, such as the heavens or the earth, but rather to God's very name, which endures forever.

The Sabbath Day

David Novak

Remember the sabbath day, and keep it holy.

I

Shortly before his death in 1949, the lay French Catholic theologian Aime Palliere, a man who had very close ties to Jews and Judaism throughout his life, wrote an article entitled "Why Wouldn't You Observe the Sabbath?" The article was addressed to religiously lax Jews who, it seems, were less observant of the Sabbath than was Palliere, who himself also kept a number of other commandments of the Torah that Jewish tradition designates as being obligatory only for Jews. Indeed, Palliere may have been aware that the Talmud teaches that someone obligated by the Torah to keep a commandment (in this case a Jew) has a greater obligation to keep that commandment than someone (in this case a Christian like Palliere) who only keeps it voluntarily (*Kiddushin* 31a). So, it seems, Palliere was saying to the Jews: "If I keep the Sabbath, you should keep it all the more so!"

In a volume where Jewish and Christian theologians reflect on each of the Ten Commandments, Palliere's question has great significance, especially regarding the Sabbath, inasmuch as the observance of the Sabbath has been a great divide between Judaism and Christianity. With the exception of certain Sabbatarian Christian groups (like the mostly American Seventh-Day Adventists), for almost all their history the vast majority of Christians have not observed the Sabbath on the seventh day of the week (Saturday), but they have either made Sunday an altogether different celebration (of the resurrection of Jesus) or they have pretended — as far as

Jews are concerned — that Sunday can have the sanctity Saturday has had for Jews, including the sanctity it had for Jews like Jesus and his disciples. (Some Reform Jews in the past wanted to transfer the Sabbath to Sunday so as to better accommodate themselves to a still predominantly Christian culture, but their efforts met with little long-range success even in their own community.) In other words, should Christians observe the Sabbath on the day Jews have always observed the Sabbath, and in a way similar to the way Jews have always observed the Sabbath? Thomas Aquinas, for example, was of the opinion that Christians should not observe any of the laws specifically designated for the Jews as truly divine commandments after the coming of Christ (*Summa Theologiae* II/1, q. 103, a. 3-4). He no doubt included the observance of the Sabbath (q. 100, a. 3, ad 2). Nevertheless, many Christians would not necessarily follow Aquinas on this and other points as well.

This question of Christian observance of the Sabbath is important because an early talmudic text, which could well be speaking of the Christians as Jewish schismatics, asserts that the reason the Ten Commandments are no longer part of the synagogue liturgy (but read only when they appear in the weekly scriptural lectionary) is because the "schismatics [*minim*] say that they [the Ten Commandments] alone were given by God at Sinai" (Jerusalem Talmud, *Berakhot* 1:8/3c). For Jews, of course, all the Mosaic commandments are perpetually obligatory (Num. 15:23 and *Kiddushin* 29a; *Makkot* 23b-24a). But if Christians regard *all* the Ten Commandments to be perpetually obligatory, then why do so few of them keep the Sabbath? (John Calvin, in many ways the most biblical of the Reformed theologians, clearly struggled with this question in *Institutes* 2.8.29-34.) Surely, most Christians ignore the Jewish Sabbath, but not because the Talmud states that it is forbidden for Gentiles to observe the Sabbath (*Sanhedrin* 58b). Rather, most Christians ignore the Jewish Sabbath because they believe that Jesus has dispensed them from observing the Sabbath once and for all (Matt. 12:8). The Jews, on the other hand, do not seem to want Gentiles observing the Sabbath because the Sabbath constitutes a special intimacy between God and his elect people (Exod. 31:17 and *Mekilta* thereon), something into which no one outside the covenanted community is entitled to intrude. (Most Christians believe that God's intimacy with the church is constituted by something else, namely, the sacraments celebrating the life, ministry, death, and resurrection of Jesus.) In other words, both Judaism and (almost all) Christianity, for very different reasons, to be sure, have concluded that the Sabbath is for Jews and not for Christians. Nevertheless, by looking at the two versions of the Ten Commandments, in Exodus and Deuteronomy respectively, especially the two versions of the Sabbath commandment, I would like to reopen the question, at least theoretically, as part of the joint Jewish and Christian reflections on the Ten Commandments being conducted in this volume. We now need to look at the two versions of the Sabbath commandments in the two versions of the Decalogue in the Mosaic Torah.

II

The first version of the Sabbath commandment in the Decalogue reads: "Remember [*zakhor*] the Sabbath day to make it holy [*le-qadsho*]" (Exod. 20:8). The reason given is "because [*ki*] in six days the LORD made the heavens and the earth, the sea and all therein, and he rested on the seventh day; therefore [*al ken*] the LORD blessed the Sabbath day and hallowed it" (20:11). Here the Jewish tradition locates both a positive and a negative injunction. Positively, hallowing the Sabbath means there are certain sacred practices reserved for the Sabbath, such as the sanctification prayer (*qiddush*) uttered over wine that is then drunk by all the participants in the sacred Sabbath dinner who have responded "amen" to that prayer. Negatively, there is the prohibition: "you shall do no labor [*mel'akhah*]" (20:10).

But what is "labor"? Here an objective standard is needed. If *labor* is what is physically exhausting, then the prohibition of labor would be as particular and subjective as everyone's unique bodily condition. Yet it is clear that just as the positive commandment to hallow the Sabbath denotes *communal* (hence unanimous) action, so should the negative commandment to cease from labor denote *communal* (hence unanimous) inaction (*Berakhot* 20b). (Actually, though, in rabbinic law, a Jew is not to exhaust himself or herself even in acts that are themselves permitted on the Sabbath or do anything that even appears to be compromising the holiness of the Sabbath day [Isa. 58:13 and *Shabbat* 113a-b].) So, the rabbis assumed that there are thirty-nine labors prohibited by scriptural law. They derived this number and what it counts for by noting that before Moses gathered the people to give them the specific commandments to build the dwelling place (*mishkan*) or sanctuary (*miqdash*) in the wilderness, he reiterated the positive and negative commandments about keeping the Sabbath (Exod.

71

35:1-3). The rabbis speculated about thirty-nine different acts required for the building of the sanctuary that they assumed had also been revealed to Moses (but transmitted orally rather than in writing like Scripture). These are the labors that are perpetually prohibited on the Sabbath because of the juxtaposition of these two commandments in Scripture (*Shabbat* 97b). In other words, what was mandated to be done for the building of the sanctuary on the six days of the workweek, these very acts are prohibited from being done on the Sabbath. (The sanctity of the sanctuary and the sanctity of the Sabbath are connected in a number of other ways as well [*Yevamot* 6a-b].) But since the building of the sanctuary is commanded only to the Jews (even though Gentiles were allowed to bring sacrifices to the sanctuary and, later, to the Jerusalem temple), so it would seem that the prohibition of labor on the Sabbath too is commanded only of Jews.

The connection of the Sabbath and the sanctuary is not as artificial as one might initially think. A number of ancient and modern biblical scholars have plausibly pointed out that the sanctuary is meant to be the model or the microcosm of the created universe itself as macrocosm. (This was also true of other sanctuaries and temples in antiquity.) If that is the case, then the reason given in Exodus for keeping the Sabbath — the commemoration of God's completion of creation — makes more sense in terms of which acts are prohibited on the Sabbath. These acts are the acts necessarily involved in Israel's imitation of God's creation of the macrocosm (which no human could have actually experienced) in both creating and completing the creation of the microcosmic sanctuary, first in the wilderness and then in Jerusalem (which became for many the *axis mundi*, the "center of the universe"). It also makes sense as regards the restriction of the Sabbath to Israel since only Israel knows through God's revelation to her just what was involved in the process of creation. No human was actually present at the initial event of creation, hence no human could possibly figure out for himself or herself just what happened in that prehistorical period of time.

Despite all this, the greatest of the medieval Jewish theologians, Moses Maimonides (1135-1204), who in his legal works reiterates the rabbinic restriction of the observance of the Sabbath to Jews, nonetheless, in his more philosophical reflection on the Sabbath, notes that it is given "in order that the principle of creation of the world be established and universally known in the world through the fact that all people refrain from working on one and the same day" (*Guide of the Perplexed* 2.31, trans. S. Pines, p. 359). Although Maimonides is not making a practical ruling here that *all people should* observe the Sabbath, he seems to be suggesting that if they discover the Sabbath on their own, that might not be a bad thing after all. (I shall return to this point later.) This implied suggestion is consistent with Maimonides' philosophical approach, for he assumes that human beings with reason unaided (but surely helped) by historical revelation can themselves apprehend God's ongoing creation of the universe. Just as all humans can discover for themselves the existence of God, whose very apprehension inspires worship, so they can discover for themselves God's purposive (hence limiting) creation of the universe and be inspired to imitate God's cessation from creation on the Sabbath as an act of worship. Whether humans could actually discover that the Sabbath is the seventh day without historical revelation traditionally transmitted is questionable though. But Maimonides seems to be more interested here in the idea of the Sabbath than its actual dating.

III

In the version of the Ten Commandments in Deuteronomy, a different version of the Sabbath commandment is given. "Keep [*shamor*] the Sabbath day to make it holy [*le-qadsho*]" (Deut. 5:12). Here the reason is different from the creation reason given in Exodus. Rather, the Sabbath is to be kept "in order [*le-ma'an*] that your male slave and your female slave rest like you, so that you remember that you were a slave in the land of Egypt and the LORD brought you out from there . . . therefore [*al ken*] the LORD your God commands you to observe [*la'asot*] the Sabbath day" (5:14-15).

The key difference between the reason given in Exodus and the one given here is that this reason is based on actual experience. The Jews know what a slave has to do because they themselves were slaves in Egypt. As such, not only are they not to act like slaves on the Sabbath, even if that "slavery" is slavery to their own projects and ambitions, but they are also not to treat Gentiles living under their rule, whether they be "slaves" or "sojourners" (the *ger* mentioned in 5:14), like slaves or even servants on the Sabbath. (And, in fact, they were not to treat their slaves at any time with the brutality they themselves experienced in Egypt [see Exod. 1:13-16; 2:11; 21:26-27].) "A sojourner you shall not persecute, for you know about the life of the sojourner [*nefesh ha-ger*] because [*ki*] you were sojourners in the land of

Egypt" (Exod. 23:9). So, whether as sojourners in Egypt, which is what Israel originally was (Gen. 47:4-6), or as the slaves they became because of Pharaoh's paranoia (Exod. 1:8-14), Israel knows firsthand what it is like to be treated as less than the image of God, which is the nature of every human being (*Avot* 3:18). Especially on the Sabbath, which celebrates the creation of the world of which the human creature is paramount (Gen. 1:26-28; 2:7; 3:22; Ps. 8:5-7), any human being living under the control of Jews should have Sabbath rest as his or her right, along with the Jews with whom he or she is living. One might well see this as an example of the commandment to the Jews to "love your neighbor as yourself" (Lev. 19:18; Gen. 5:1; Jerusalem Talmud, *Nedarim* 9:3/14c), or in this case, "the sojourner who dwells with you, you shall love him as yourself because you were sojourners in the land of Egypt; I am the LORD your God" (Lev. 19:34).

In rabbinic law, both sojourners (known as "resident aliens") and slaves are not to be made to work by Jews on the Sabbath because they are bound by at least some of the same Torah law as the Jews themselves (*Avodah Zarah* 64b; *Hagigah* 4a). But since sojourners were living under Jewish rule more voluntarily than were slaves, Jews could not prevent them from working on the Sabbath for themselves as they could their slaves. Nevertheless, Jews are not allowed to directly request any Gentile to work for them on the Sabbath, even though a Gentile might do work for a Jew on the Sabbath on his or her own initiative (*Shabbat* 19a; 121a-122b; 150a). All this indicates that the more political-historical meaning of the Sabbath put forth in Deuteronomy became the basis of more concrete Jewish practice than did the more ontological meaning put forth in Exodus. Nevertheless, the teaching of Deuteronomy's Decalogue extended less universally than did the teaching of Exodus's Decalogue.

Even in the version in Deuteronomy, the influence of the Sabbath and its structured rest extends beyond the confines of the Jewish people per se. Taking the Sabbath to be a "delight" (Isa. 58:13), which means it is beneficial to anyone to whom it is extended, and extending its rest to Gentiles over whom a Jew has some economic or political control, can be seen as part of what the Talmud sees as extending Jewish beneficence to Gentiles at hand for the sake of peace *(shalom)*, which is a Jewish value par excellence (*Gittin* 61a). Indeed, one of the names of the God to be imitated is *Shalom* (Judg. 6:24 and *Leviticus Rabbah* 9.9; also, *Shabbat* 133b; Maimonides, *Guide of the Perplexed* 3.54). And if the Jews are obligated to extend peace even to their enemies (Deut. 20:10-11; Jerusalem Talmud,

Shevi'it 6:1/36c), how much more so are they obligated to extend peace to those already living among them in peace? And, on a personal level, I was gladdened to hear from a Gentile a long time ago, how much he appreciated what he saw to be the basic humanity of his Jewish boss who did not require him to work on the Jewish Sabbath as well as on Sunday. Perhaps this Gentile would have even praised the "God of the Jews" had he known that his boss's motives were religious and not just humane (see Jerusalem Talmud, *Bava Metzi'a* 2:1/8c).

IV

What we see here is a difference between two types of Jewish universalism in regard to the Sabbath. In neither view is the Sabbath something exclusively for the Jews, even if the Jews have unique responsibilities for it. The problem with the more universalistic view of the Sabbath (and other commandments as well) as a celebration of creation, though, is that it implies a kind of religious imperialism. It implies that the experience of all people of the creativity of God not only *is* but *ought to be* the same as that of the Jews. It implies that the Sabbath is a matter of natural law, and that Judaism has a greater grasp of natural law than any other tradition in the world. However, that presupposes that all people do experience or should experience creation as limited in space and in time as do the Jews. But hasn't that *Jewish* experience of the world already been prepared for the Jews by the creation narrative of Scripture? As such, how can one see something like the Sabbath, which is such an integral part of that historical narrative, as a matter to be discerned by unaided reason about ordinary human experience of the natural world?

According to Scripture, creation is limited in space; it is thus finite, even if we cannot perceive its finite limits. Hence, in this ontological view, God transcends the finite spatial order. It cannot contain God (1 Kings 8:27; Isa. 66:1-2); and because of that, God can say, "I will be wherever I will be" (Exod. 3:14). That means God can be anywhere or nowhere in the universe, but not "everywhere," since that would mean the pantheistic notion that God is coextensive with the universe. But this pantheistic God is not truly transcendent as only the Creator God can be. God's general transcendence of the universe enables God to be present at any particular place in the universe God so chooses to be (Isa. 55:6). Nevertheless, God can also "hide his face" from us (Ps. 27:9), which is God's ability to be absent from us in a way that we can never be absent from him (see Ps. 139:1-12).

And, according to Scripture, creation is limited in time. The world has an originating event and a terminating event (Gen. 1:1-5; Isa. 54:10; 66:22). The originating event is "the day God created" (Ezek. 28:13-15). The terminating event is "the end of days" (Ezek. 38:16). Hence, in this ontological view, God transcends the temporal order at both ends. God locates the world spatially and temporally; the world, though, is not where God can be located through ordinary human experience and human reason about it (Gen. 28:11-19; *Genesis Rabbah* 68:9). The Sabbath is God's way of locating us in time. As for our location in space, a Jewish community takes it to be a divine mandate to mark off various spatial boundaries *(tehum)* within which a Jew may move about and interact with his or her neighbors (Exod. 16:29; *Eruvin* 51a; *Shabbat* 34a). This is seen to be following the way God marks off various spatial limits in the universe (Gen. 1:4-5; Jerusalem Talmud, *Berakhot* 8:7/12c). To this ontological message Israel bears witness. "You are my witnesses, says the LORD, my servant whom I have chosen, that you are to know and be faithful [*ve-ta'aminu*] to me, and understand that I am he, before whom no god has been created, and after me none will be" (Isa. 43:10).

Clearly, the Jewish observance of the Sabbath is the greatest act of testimony of God's transcendence of historical time, which alone enables God to enter into historical time whenever he so chooses. Conversely, a God who is coextensive with historical time would be in no position to hallow any specific part of it any more than a person could judge his own lifetime while still bound within it. "Hallowing" means both separating and elevating, which is something that can only be done by the Maker of the whole, but not by any of the parts that are made. In the same way, only the Creator of the universe could elect one people within his universe for a special (hallowed or sacred) covenantal relationship. Both the Sabbath and Israel have primordial status conferred upon them (*Pesahim* 54a and 87b). Indeed, the Sabbath is considered Israel's bride (*Genesis Rabbah* 11:8 on Gen. 2:3). But none of this is part of our ordinary experience of the natural world. The natural world seems to be eternal, as Aristotle thought, and eternal and infinite as Spinoza thought. In the natural world we all experience, there does not seem to be any chosen day any more than there seems to be a chosen people. So, when the Friday night synagogue liturgy that ushers in the Sabbath after sundown speaks of the Sabbath as a "remembrance [*zekher*] of the work of creation [*ma'aseh br'esheet*]," it is not referring to a metaphysical inference from what we would call the "scientific" experience of the world. Rather, this "remembrance" is what we remember from the scriptural account of creation, the account that ends with the words: "Heaven and earth with all their orders [*tsva'am*] were contained. God completed his labor which he had made on the seventh day and on the seventh day he refrained [*shavat*] from all the labor he had done. Then God blessed the seventh day and hallowed it because [*ki*] he had refrained from all his labor which he had created and made" (Gen. 2:1-3). Indeed, according to the Talmud, although the Sabbath occurs *in* this world and is measured by this-worldly phenomena like the light of the sun and the stars, it is not an experience *of* "this world" at all but, rather, an experience of one-sixtieth of the world-to-come (*Berakhot* 57b). (A "sixtieth" in rabbinic law designates a minute amount that is, nonetheless, not simply nothing.) As such, the Sabbath is an experience of the supernatural, which is not to be confused with what is irrational. Like all of what has been revealed, it most definitely has a logic, a logic that the rabbis and their theological successors until the present day have continually plumbed and developed.

We now have three possible ways of explaining the essential reason of the Sabbath. One, there is the metaphysical way, which was attractive to the medieval theologians. The need for the Sabbath is explained by the experience of finite created nature. The problem with this view, though, is that it is built upon a scientific worldview that is impossible to cogently assert, let alone demonstrate in the world since the sixteenth century (after Galileo). Two, there is the explanation of the Sabbath as a remembrance of the exodus from Egypt, the release from the type of slavery where one's time is controlled by an illegitimate human master rather than by the one legitimate, rightful, divine King. This view is consistent with the large place in Judaism for the remembrance of what a contemporary Jewish philosopher called "root experiences." And three, there is the biblical ontological view that celebrates the event of creation and its completion on the seventh day, which are celebrations of what Scripture reveals happened at a time that no human could have possibly experienced himself or herself. Here the mediating testimony of scriptural revelation is indispensably foundational.

Neither the second (historical) view nor the third (theological) view, unlike the first (metaphysical) view, can be eliminated by modern science. Neither of them is talking about a world that is the subject of the ordinary experience of physical nature. And the second and third views do not contradict each other; instead, they complement each other. Thus the second (historical) view presupposes the third (theological) view. It will be recalled that the Exodus account of the Ten Commandments' teaching of the Sabbath bases the institution of the Sabbath on the remembrance of creation and its completion, while the Deuteronomy account bases it on the remembrance of the exodus from Egypt and its egalitarian implications. Indeed, Scripture itself sees Deuteronomy as building upon what was taught earlier in the Pentateuch (Deut. 1:5; see 2 Kings 23:25). The priority of Exodus to Deuteronomy is not only chronological, it is logical as well. Only the Creator God would have the power and wisdom to be able to redeem Israel from slavery to the mightiest empire the world had theretofore seen. There is no "natural," that is, usual, interpretation for what happened at the event of the exodus (Deut. 4:18-20; see Moses Nahmanides, *Commentary on the Torah:* Genesis 1:1). The exodus is the closest any human being could possibly come to experiencing the creation of the world by God (Judah Halevi, *Kuzari* 1.25). And now, like the creation of the world, one can experience the exodus only by experiencing the scriptural account of the exodus. Without the account of Exodus, creation would have no connection even to any possible human experience. And without the account of creation, the exodus could easily look like nothing more than a historical fluke, a marvelous prison escape, but one that could possibly be repeated by other human actors at some other time and some other place. The exodus, though, is not an event within any ordinary historical process.

Here is where the question of Christian appropriation of the Jewish Sabbath admits of some sort of answer, however incomplete and vague it might indeed be. And the answer might well have more theoretical than practical implications.

Both Jews and Christians share an experience of the text of Scripture qua Hebrew Bible/Old Testament to be the revealed word of God (however transmitted by human scribes and interpreters). In fact, Maimonides, who was normally rather hostile to Christian teaching and practice, nevertheless ruled that Jews may study the text of Scripture with Christians precisely because this theological precondition can be assumed (as is not the case with Muslims, whose metaphysics he often preferred to that of Christians). This theological situation, by the way, is unique between any two historical traditions in the world today (and perhaps yesterday as well). Accordingly, this certainly means that Christians can "remember the Sabbath day as being holy" in terms of their appreciation of the scriptural doctrine of creation. Whether or not such Christian appreciation of the Jewish-scriptural Sabbath leads to their actually "keeping the Sabbath," both in terms of positive action and negative inaction, need not be on the agenda of the Christian study of Scripture, especially when conducted in dialogue with Jews. Such dialogue should not be expected to lead to foreseeable practical results.

Finally, the fact that some Christians have already practically appropriated the Jewish-scriptural Sabbath has had an effect on Jewish theology. So, although the Talmud proscribes any Gentile observance of the Sabbath, as we have seen, some important masters of Jewish practical theology (halakhah) were of the opinion that this talmudic proscription applies only to Gentiles who voluntarily and haphazardly observe the Sabbath. However, if such a Gentile — who is unlikely to be anyone but a scripturally serious Christian — takes upon himself or herself regular Sabbath observance as a religious obligation (mitzvah), Jews are minimally not to discourage such supererogatory piety on the part of such Gentiles (*Biur Halakhah* on *Shulhan Arukh:* Orah Hayyim, 304.3). In fact, Jews might actually encourage it. And surely, such Christian observance of the Sabbath, however rare, is based upon their Christian appropriation of the scriptural narration of creation and, perhaps, the scriptural narration of the exodus as well. As such, at least the Jewish Sabbath has not been superseded by such Christians after all, even if it yields more theoretical than practical commonality at present.

For one of the greatest theological meditations on the Sabbath, one that has inspired a number of Jews to retrieve the experience and practice of the Sabbath in their own lives, I urge readers to study the book by my late revered teacher Abraham Joshua Heschel, *The Sabbath: Its Meaning for Modern Man* (New York: Harper and Row, 1966).

Response

Marguerite Shuster

A few months ago, while accompanying a friend to an appointment in West Los Angeles, I spotted a banner in front of a local Hebrew academy that read "Hang in there. . . . Shabbat is coming!" That banner, with its promise of Sabbath relief and joy, generated a longing in me as a Christian — a religiously serious Christian, but not one noted for real strictness of Sabbath, or Lord's Day, observance. I thus read David Novak's article with anticipation, finding it illumining in many ways, and often moving.

That the Sabbath has been such a key factor in the maintenance of Jewish identity ("More than Israel has kept the Sabbath, the Sabbath has kept Israel" — Aḥad Haʿam, 1898) means that it should be particularly incumbent upon Christians not to presume somehow to "hijack" the day, as if they could blithely leave behind the formal aspects of its observance by their Jewish brothers and sisters, imbue it with their own practices, and label what they do "Sabbath keeping." At the same time, Christians who honor the full authority of the scriptures of the Hebrew Bible must not fail to ask how the fourth commandment ought to bear on their own conduct. To lay my own cards on the table from the beginning, I myself embrace the basically Augustinian view that the Decalogue shows the shape that Jesus' summary of the law (Matt. 22:37-40; Mark 12:30-31) must have in this world; it thus does not lose its authority for Christians who also affirm that their salvation is by grace alone. But that view, though giving an orientation to the Decalogue as a whole, is most especially short on specific guidance with respect to the fourth commandment, given the challenges to aspects of its observance found in the Gospels and Epistles.

Continuity and Change

When Novak wrestles with whether Gentiles ought to be encouraged to keep the Sabbath, he clearly seems to be asking whether they should take up the fully elaborated Jewish practice of observance. It seems to me that that question, while surely a legitimate one, is at least a somewhat different question from whether Christians ought to be encouraged to be far more scrupulous about keeping the fourth commandment. What may be too quickly hidden from view is that not just Christian practices of weekly observance, but also Jewish ones, are at least a step removed from the commandment itself — that they themselves involve an aspect of change, and not just a direct continuity. That the thirty-nine acts required for building the sanctuary figure the sorts of work forbidden on the Sabbath, since the building of the sanctuary represents on a smaller scale God's own work of creation, is a meaningful and evocative way of thinking; but it is surely at some remove from Exodus 20:8-11 and Deuteronomy 5:12-15, as well as Genesis 2:2-3. And it is surely at least in significant part because Jesus understood the rabbinic elaboration of the Sabbath commandment to go beyond the actual demand of the Law that he mounted the challenges reported in the Gospels. (Of course, such challenges find a sort of precedent in the Hebrew prophets, who were quick enough to criticize the sort of observance that missed the intent of the Law, e.g., Isaiah 1:12-13.)

While it may be easy to overemphasize the continuity on the Jewish side, it is also easy to overemphasize change on the Christian side. Novak speaks of the Christian Sunday as "an altogether different celebration" or, alternatively, of what may feel to Jews like a pretense "that Sunday can have the sanctity Saturday has had for Jews." It is quite true that for the early church fathers and for the Protestant Reformers, a great gap was to be fixed between the Sabbath and the Lord's Day (though even so, that the observance of the Lord's Day remained a weekly one is a not inconsiderable continuity, given that no convincing precedent for a weekly observance is to be found outside of God's revelation to Israel).[1] By contrast, the Puritans, whose views so heavily influenced much of mainline Protestantism in America, clearly intended to honor the fourth commandment in assuming an almost complete continuity between the Jewish Sabbath and the Chris-

---

1. Gerhard F. Hasel, "Sabbath," in *Anchor Bible Dictionary,* ed. David Noel Freedman, 6 vols. (New York: Doubleday, 1992), 5:849-56.

tian Sunday, save only for the change of day from the last day of the week to the first, acknowledging the resurrection of Jesus. (See especially the Westminster Confession 21.7-8.)[2] The first day soon brought its own set of well-elaborated prohibitions. (I recall from my own growing-up years the forbidding in our household of attending movies on Sunday, for they were the epitome of worldliness.) The "blue laws" enacted to protect the observance of the day were named from the color of the cover of the book in which they were bound, but in their effect on many, they might just as well have been named for the mood they evoked — a clear violation on the Christian side of God's intent for his day (Isa. 58:13).

However, even if we were frankly to acknowledge continuity and change in observance of the fourth commandment on both the Jewish and the Christian side, and sometimes a common sinful missing of the mark in allowing the letter of the law to overrun its spirit, there is no point in denying not only the prominence of Sabbath conflicts in the Gospels, but also the forcefulness of Pauline injunctions against the necessity of observing days and seasons (Rom. 14:3-6; Gal. 4:9-11; Col. 2:16-17; though it must be acknowledged that some have questioned whether "days" or "sabbaths" refers to the weekly Sabbath). Lacking these, one might well doubt that Christians would in fact worship on a different day than Jews, despite the day on which the resurrection took place. After all, Jews, too, and not just Jesus, could make the point that the Sabbath was made for humankind and not humankind for the Sabbath (Mark 2:27).[3] But there were obvious worries on the part of Paul and his followers that a focus on observance of the Law would obscure the fact (as Christians see it) of the radical newness present in Jesus, that something — anything — besides faith in Jesus Christ might be seen as key to salvation. Indeed, it seems plausible that it was the very centrality of Sabbath observance to Jewish self-understanding, and not just that Sabbath keeping has a ceremonial character lacking in, say, avoidance of swearing or murder or adultery, that made it a particular issue for early Christians and may have led them to underplay its positive meaning throughout the biblical texts they themselves affirmed as sacred writ.

2. For a summary of the historical material, see Paul K. Jewett, *The Lord's Day* (Grand Rapids: Eerdmans, 1971).

3. See the Midrash Mekilta *Shabbata* 1 to Exod. 31:13-14 (later than Jesus, ca. A.D. 180). Note, however, the interpretive qualifications suggested by Robert A. Guelich, *Mark 1–8:26*, Word Biblical Commentary, vol. 34A (Dallas: Word, 1989), p. 124.

Response to "The Sabbath Day"

Common Affirmations

Granting the reality of what I as a Christian would take to be proper differences in observance, including a difference in the day that emphasizes new creation in Christ above completion of the old creation, I believe not only that Jews and Christians share a great deal in their understanding of the fourth commandment, but also that Christians (and secular Jews) would do well if their actual practice more closely resembled the carefulness of traditional Jewish celebration, for beliefs cut off from practices threaten to become vacuous. We would do well if our lives as a whole were better governed by the orientation toward humility, justice, hope, and refreshment that the fourth commandment offers us. Giving these values concrete shape in a world where that shape is likely to be scorned and resisted takes concerted purpose and attention, purpose and attention that help us rightly to see our whole lives as lived before God.

Humility

To rest from our labors because the world has already been created, and because our final trust rests in God and not in ourselves, goes flatly against the violent manipulativeness and rabid promotion of self-reliance that permeate our whole culture, not to mention the relentless acquisitiveness that seems to head the list of our values. One sometimes wonders if we are afraid to stop because if we did, we might be forced to notice not just the diminishing returns in our own lives, but also the effects of our assaults on the created order that it cannot forever sustain. (One thinks here of the meaning not just of the weekly Sabbath, but of the seventh-year rest for the land.) We worry about the costs of stopping that we can count; we ignore the costs of not stopping, for we do not know how to count them. We are afraid to trust in a world that seems arbitrary and erratic at best; we ignore the fact that all we do assumes trust in the existence and regularities of a creation not under our control. If there is no sovereign God who holds and sustains us and the world, we are in far worse trouble than we generally care to think about. A vital lesson in humility comes from acting on the recognition that everything depends on Someone other and more faithful than we. If God is sovereign, we are not.

Justice

Rest is not just for us but also for others. Whatever slavery we have known and have been delivered from, or wish to be delivered from, we must spare our brothers and sisters (and must spare whatever may stand in for the animals that few of us still use in our daily labors — one might, for instance, think of laying off of the consumption of power that makes for ever-diminishing habitat for animals).[4] What if, one day in seven, we were not only to rest ourselves and refuse to ask others to work for us, but also to reflect for a time on ways we might make our own living less burdensome to others during the rest of the week?

Hope

Both Jews and Christians acknowledge an eschatological aspect to their observance of the fourth commandment. Not only Christians, but also Jews, see it as a sign of the world to come, of resurrection, of eternity.[5] Jews have believed that if two Sabbaths were perfectly observed, the Messiah would come; Christians, who believe the Messiah has come, still affirm that a Sabbath rest remains for the people of God (Heb. 4:9). That this is not all there is, that God has something better for us, relativizes our present efforts. We rest from what is not ultimate, in the service of what is.

Refreshment

I put last what generally comes first in the current Christian cottage industry of writings on "Sabbath," in which the emphasis is on the need for respite from our frenetic lives. The emphasis has legitimacy, in the sense that rest one day in seven can be understood as a creation ordinance with universal scope, modeled on God's own creative activity and rest. It *is* better for our health and, yes, productivity, that we have regular periods of re-

4. "Nothing is as hard to suppress as the will to be a slave to one's own pettiness" (Abraham Heschel, *The Sabbath*, p. 89, in *"The Earth Is the Lord's" and "The Sabbath"* [New York: Harper and Row, 1966]).

5. Heschel, *The Sabbath*, p. 73.

freshment. God made us that way. God cares about this aspect of our well-being. Yet making merely instrumental what God named as holy is an offense against the deeper purpose of the day. It further tends to the merely individualistic, in which "I" rest in whatever way I decide upon, without necessarily being joined to others in common acknowledgment of community and purpose before God. Rest so conceived may serve our bodies and psyches at some level without touching either our interpersonal or our spiritual loneliness, so that the fruits of the best gift are offered in the end not to the Lord but to one or another idol of our own making. True rest comes when we know ourselves as members of a community held in God's hand.

*   *   *

We are a people nervous about holiness, for we have it confused with being sanctimonious and obnoxious (and we are probably altogether unclear on what it really means for a *day* to be holy, even in the sense of its being "set apart"). We are nervous about worship as an expression having intrinsic worth, often wanting our communities of faith to prove their mettle in some more conventional marketplace of usefulness. We are ready to mouth truths about the Lord's claim upon our whole lives, yet reluctant to give the Lord exclusive claim upon a single day of the week. And the thought that such a day is intended to be a source of delight (Isa. 58:13-14) is almost beyond our conceiving. We have much to learn. Careful attention to the fourth commandment would rightly reshape the whole of our lives, teaching us to live the rest of the week in the light of the one day that is different from all the others, the one day that tells us that the other days are, in the end, not for naught.

Honoring Parents

Byron L. Sherwin

Honor your father and your mother.

The biblical narrative is replete with stories of dysfunctional families. Human family life begins with a fratricide (Gen. 4:8-12). Though he is the father of the "Abrahamic faiths," Abraham is not a father to emulate. Though he courageously argues with God about the fate of the wicked inhabitants of Sodom (Gen. 18), Abraham does not contend with his wife Sarah when she orders him to expel his son Ishmael from his home (Gen. 21). Nor does Abraham protest against God's command to kill his son Isaac (Gen. 22). Throughout their lives, Isaac and Ishmael must have suffered from post-traumatic stress syndrome because of what their father did to them.

Isaac and Rebekah play favorites between their sons, and tear their family apart. Jacob, the father of the tribes of Israel, deceives his own father Isaac and alienates his brother Esau (Gen. 25–27). Jacob's obsessive favoritism toward his son Joseph provokes violent jealousy among his other children. Jacob, who wrestles with God and man (Gen. 32), responds passively to the seduction of his concubine by his son (Gen. 36:2) as well as to the rape of his daughter Dinah (Gen. 34). This patriarch of the people of Israel is the father of a highly dysfunctional family where acts of jealousy, intrigue, deception, and crime abound, and where filial honor and devotion seem out of place (Gen. 29–36).

Later on, Moses emerges as the great liberator, lawgiver, leader, and prophet of the people of Israel. Yet he is not extolled as a great father to his own sons. David, the ancestor of the Messiah, has irrevocable differences with his son Absalom who plots not only dishonor but also treason against his father, and with his son Amnon who rapes his own sister (2 Sam. 13). In sum, many of the leading figures of Hebrew Scripture whom we admire, extol, and seek to emulate, were great in many ways, but not as parents. Though parents of a people, they left much to be desired as parents of their own children. Many of them, whom we honor, were not honored by their own children, nor did they adequately honor their own parents.

Though few tasks in life are more challenging or more important than being a good parent, and though first-time parents are compelled to undergo "on-the-job training," Scripture offers little guidance regarding the art of parenting. More often than not, Hebrew Scripture offers us parental models to be eschewed rather than admired.

Despite the paucity of desirable parental models to emulate in Hebrew Scripture, Jewish commentaries on Hebrew Scripture seem to have been aware of the need to address the issue of parent-child relations. They were inevitably struck by the asymmetry in biblical law and ethics between the attention given to filial obligations and the lack of attention given to parental responsibilities. More often than not, scriptural injunctions about how parents ought to treat children focus on harsh punitive actions to be taken against children who challenge parental authority (see, e.g., Exod. 21:15; Lev. 20:9; Deut. 21:18-21), rather than offering guidance for effective and nurturing parenting. Perhaps, precisely because of this asymmetry, Jewish commentators throughout the ages interpreted the fifth of the ten commandments in ways that address not only the duties of children to their parents, but also those of parents vis-à-vis their children. Though the commentators probed, examined, interpreted, and amplified scriptural injunctions regarding filial duty, they did not hesitate to link filial duty — especially as set down in the fifth commandment — with parental responsibility. For the commentators, offering guidance for beneficial parent-child relations and for salutary family life was a significant feature of their exegesis of the text of the fifth commandment: "Honor your father and mother, so that your days may be long in the land that the LORD your God is giving you" (Exod. 20:12; Deut. 5:16).[1]

1. This essay draws upon some of my previously published work on parent-child relations in Jewish tradition: Byron L. Sherwin, *In Partnership with God: Contemporary Jewish Law and Ethics* (Syracuse: Syracuse University Press, 1990), pp. 130-49; Byron L. Sherwin and Seymour J. Cohen, *How to Be a Jew: The Ethical Teachings of Judaism* (Northvale, N.J.: Jason Aronson, 1992), pp. 163-91; Byron L. Sherwin, *Jewish Ethics for the Twenty-First Century* (Syracuse: Syracuse University Press, 2000), pp. 88-109.

The commentators considered self-serving and manipulative behavior to be an obstacle to parent-child relations that should, in their view, be based upon mutual love, trust, and respect. For this reason, some of the commentators found the text's promise of longevity of the child as a reward for obeying this commandment, and by implication a curtailed life for disobeying it,[2] to be self-serving and mercenary. As the fourteenth-century rabbi Bahya ben Asher put it, "A person must not serve his or her parents for the sake of an eventual inheritance, for some honor that can be gained from such service, or from any selfish consideration."[3] Similarly, the eleventh-century rabbi Bahya ibn Pakuda admonishes parents who are motivated by self-aggrandizement or other benefits in their support and nurturing of the child.[4] Precisely because the commentators found Scripture's promise of a concrete reward for filial duty to be problematic and inadequate, they proposed alternative rationales for observing the fifth commandment.

According to the sixteenth-century rabbi Don Isaac Abravanel, there is really no need to offer either a rationale or a reward for observing this commandment. That it is a divinely revealed commandment should suffice. In his words,

God wanted to explain to you that it is improper to base worthwhile virtues and qualities upon the human intellect. Rather, they should be observed because it was commanded by God to follow them, so that one might cleave to God and achieve fulfillment and goodness. Their observance cannot be justified from any other perspective, such as rational legal ethics . . . even though human reason establishes that a person will revere his parents from youth, your motivation in revering your parents and in observing the commandments should be because I [God] commanded you regarding it. For this reason the text states: "I am the Lord your God" (Exod. 20:2), i.e., that your motivation derives from God's commandment rather than from another motivation.[5]

2. *Mekhilta de'Rabbi Yishmael*, ed. Hayyim Horovitz and Israel Rabin (Jerusalem: Wahrmann, 1960), "Yitro," chap. 5, p. 232.

3. Bahya ben Asher, *Kad ha-Kemah* (Lwow, 1892), "Kibbud Av," p. 107a.

4. Bayha ibn Pakuda, *The Book of Direction of the Duties of the Heart*, trans. Menahem Mansoor (London: Routledge and Kegan Paul, 1973), p. 177.

5. Don Isaac Abravanel, *Commentary on the Torah* (in Hebrew) (Jerusalem: Benei Abravanel, 1964), 2:109-11, on Lev. 19:3.

Abravanel was responding to the view of earlier commentators that filial duty is both natural and rational.[6] The twelfth-century commentator Abraham Ibn Ezra, for example, claimed that it is rational and natural for a child to reciprocate parental acts of generosity and care with honor and gratitude.[7] However, various other commentators noted that if filial duty were indeed natural and rational, it would be superfluous for God to command it. It would be like having a commandment to perform natural bodily functions, like breathing. Rather, some commentators assert, ethical imperatives are required to subdue rather than to require following one's natural impulses. For example, greed, avarice, pride, and jealousy are natural impulses that need to be restrained. In this view, precisely because it is not always either rational or natural to honor parents, a commandment to do so is necessary. In instances in which a parent is extremely ill, senile, abusive, or morally corrupt, a person may not naturally be drawn to honor his or her parents. It may well be rational — as Ibn Ezra and others suggest — to reciprocate parental generosity with filial duty. But neither are all parents generous, nor are all children either grateful or rational.[8]

In the case of a morally corrupt parent, the question is raised as to whether the commandment to honor parents is absolute and unconditional. It would seem, at first blush, that the commandments, especially each of the Ten Commandments, are "categorical imperatives." But are they? This question is already addressed in early rabbinic literature: "'You should each revere his father and mother and keep My Sabbaths: I am the Lord your God' (Lev. 19:3). . . . One might think that a person is obliged to obey one's parents, even if they ask one to transgress a commandment of the Torah. Therefore, Scripture says 'and keep My Sabbaths,' i.e., all of you [parents and children] are obliged to honor Me [i.e., God]."[9] In other words, the obligation to observe the other commandments, such as the Sabbath, studying the Torah, and not worshiping "other gods," trumps the obligation to honor parents where there is a conflict of obligation. When

6. See, e.g., Yosef Bekhor Shor, *Commentary on the Torah* (in Hebrew) (Jerusalem: Tehiya, 1956), 1:92, on Exod. 20:12; *Sefer ha-Hinukh*, ed. and trans. Charles Wengrov (Jerusalem: Feldman, 1978), no. 33, pp. 180-83. See also Gerald Blidstein, *Honor Thy Father and Mother* (New York: Ktav, 1975), pp. 8-19.

7. Abraham Ibn Ezra on Exod. 20:12, in *Mikra'ot Gedolot* (New York: Tanach, 1959).

8. See, e.g., Moses Hafetz, *Malekhet Mahshevet* (Warsaw: Cahana, 1914), p. 148b, on Deut. 5:16.

9. *Sifra* (New York: Ohm, 1947), sec. "Kedoshim," p. 97a; see also *Yevamot* 5b.

both the parent and the child share an obligation, e.g., to observe the Sabbath, that obligation supersedes the obligation of filial duty.

Whether a child is obliged to honor a morally deficient parent is a matter of dispute among the medievals. Maimonides is among those who consider the fifth commandment to be unconditional and hence unrelated to the behavior of the parent. In Maimonides' words, "Even if one's parent is an evil person, a habitual transgressor, it is [nonetheless] the duty of the child to honor and to revere that parent."[10] For others, however, the focal point of the parent-child relationship is how well the parent helps shape the intellectual, moral, and spiritual development of the child. From this perspective, only the parent who nurtures this development is worthy of honor and reverence. The parent who neglects or who frustrates it becomes unworthy of filial honor. For example, as the fourteenth-century rabbi Israel ibn Al-Nakawa puts it, echoing earlier views, "If the parent is a sinner, and his intention is to mislead the child and to prevent his child from doing the will of the Creator — for example, if the parent teaches the child to murder, rob or steal, or something similar, or even to transgress a single religious precept — then the child is obliged to reject the commands of his parent, to rebel against the parent's dicta and to refuse [to obey] the parent's words."[11] Indeed, the twelfth-century rabbi Eliezer of Metz goes so far as to say, "If one's parent is wicked, even to the point of failing to observe even a single commandment in the Torah, one is free from honoring or revering such a parent."[12]

Besides instances in which filial duty may be suspended, there are occasions when it may be restricted. For example, Jewish case law (i.e., *responsa*) addresses a conflict between filial obligation and obligations to one's spouse. In a case from thirteenth-century Spain, a young bride asks the court for relief from being abused by her mother-in-law. She and her husband lived in the same house as her in-laws. Her mother-in-law constantly belittled her, creating ongoing tension between her and her in-laws, and consequently between her and her husband. She finally demands that she and her husband move elsewhere, telling the rabbinic court, "I refuse

10. Moses Maimonides, *Mishneh Torah — Book of Judges*, "Laws of Rebels" (in Hebrew) (New York: Friedman, 1963), 6:7; Joseph Karo, *Shulhan Arukh — Yoreh De'ah* (Vilna: Romm, 1911), 240:18; 241:4.

11. Israel ibn Al-Nakawa, *Menorat ha-Ma'or*, ed. H. G. Enelow (New York: Bloch, 1931), 4:18.

12. Eliezer of Metz, *Sefer Yere'im* (Livorno: Rokeah, 1837), sec. 56, p. 49b.

to live with people who cause me pain and suffering." On the basis of the biblical claim that a husband and wife become "one flesh" (Gen. 2:24), one person, a new family, the court ruled that in such cases filial duty may be limited.[13] As a midrash puts it, "until a person marries, his love centers on his parents. But when he marries, his love is bestowed upon his wife. . . . Does a man then leave his parents regarding the obligation to honor them? Rather, his soul cleaves to the soul of his wife."[14]

Talmudic and medieval sages were also keenly aware of the profound psychological strain that may be placed upon a child attempting to fulfill his or her filial responsibilities. Caring for one's parents, for example, may stretch the limits of a child's fiscal resources and psychological endurance, especially if the parent becomes senile, chronically ill, or financially destitute. Though a child is not freed in such cases from filial responsibility, a child may be encouraged to arrange professional care for the parent.[15] In addition, the behavior of an overbearing parent might psychologically inhibit the child from rendering honor and reverence, and might encourage the child to reject the obligations of filial duty altogether. Consequently, the parent is enjoined from becoming unreasonably demanding.

Medieval sources caution parents not to be too overbearing and too exacting with children in matters pertaining to their honor, lest the child see no option but to rebel against the parent, or in extreme cases is driven to self-destructive behavior.[16] Indeed, Jewish law provides a mechanism to permit (and even to encourage) parents to "waive honor" due them in circumstances in which honoring them could lead to the moral degeneration of the child, the stifling of the personal development of the child (e.g., by an immoral parent), the imposition of undue psychological stress on the child (e.g., by an inflexible, abusive, and/or overbearing parent), or situations of irreconcilable tension between filial duty and the child's duties to

---

13. See Solomon ibn Adret, *Responsa* (in Hebrew) (Pietrikow: Belkhatavsky, 1883), part 4, no. 168, p. 25b; see also Blidstein, *Honor*, pp. 83-98, 100-109.

14. *Pirkei de-Rabbi Eliezer* (Warsaw, 1852), p. 73a; see also Moses Nahmanides, *Commentary on the Torah* (in Hebrew) (in *Mikra'ot Gedolot*) on Gen. 2:24.

15. Maimonides, "Laws of Rebels," 6:10; see also Karo, *Shulhan Arukh — Yoreh De'ah*, 240:10.

16. See, e.g., *Sefer Hasidim*, ed. Reuven Margaliot (Jerusalem: Mosad ha-Rav Kook, 1960), pars. 152, 565, pp. 153, 372. On the apprehension that an overbearing parent might even drive a child to suicide, see Joseph Yuspa Hahn, *Yosif Ometz* (Frankfurt: Herman, 1928), p. 279.

his or her spouse and/or children.[17] In such instances, filial duty is clearly not considered to be an absolute, unconditional imperative.

In most occasions in which filial duty is either set aside or limited, it is usually because another duty is considered to be of greater value or significance than filial duty. To better understand when and why this is so, it is necessary to see how the talmudic and medieval rabbis delineated the obligations of a child toward a parent as well as those of a parent to a child.

Rabbinic exegetes were reluctant to delineate required actions or attitudes of a child toward a parent. The fifth commandment requires the child to "honor" his or her parents, though elsewhere in the Pentateuch (e.g., Lev. 19:3) the child is required to "fear" or "revere" his or her parents. Yet the rabbis realized that leaving the meaning of "honor" and "reverence" vague would provide little guidance on how to observe these scriptural imperatives. Though the commentators considered the duties of a child vis-à-vis a parent to be limitless, they nonetheless specified certain required attitudes and actions, with the understanding that their fulfillment only partially satisfied an obligation of infinite demands.[18]

The Bible requires a child to honor and revere his or her parents, but does little to explain what specifically is required. Consequently, the Talmud proceeds to describe what constitutes honor and reverence: "What is 'reverence' and what is 'honor'? 'Reverence' means that a child must neither stand in his [parent's] place, nor sit in his place, nor contradict his words, nor tip the scales against him [in a scholarly dispute]. 'Honor' means that he [i.e., the child] must give him [i.e., the parent] food and drink, clothe and cover him, lead him in and out."[19] Underlying these and other specific duties imposed upon the child is the expectation not only of their performance, but their performance with a certain attitude. Attitude

17. See *Kiddushin* 32a; *Sefer Hasidim*, pars. 152, 565, pp. 153, 372; Maimonides, "Laws of Rebels," 6:8. On *mehila* or the waiving of honor due parents, see, e.g., Blidstein, *Honor*, pp. 126-27, 155-56.

18. According to the second-century rabbi Shimon bar Yohai, the obligation to honor parents is the most difficult of all commandments of the Torah to fulfill; see *Midrash Tanhuma*, ed. Solomon Buber (Vilna, 1885), "Ekev," no. 3, p. 9a. See *P. Mishnah Pe'ah* 1:1, and *Kiddushin* 31b where the obligations of children to parents are described as "beyond measure." In his commentary to the Mishnah, Maimonides notes that "the obligations a child owes his parents are too numerous to list"; see Moses Maimonides, *Commentary to the Mishnah* (in Hebrew), ed. Joseph Kapah (Jerusalem: Mosad ha-Rav Kook, 1963), on *Kiddushin* 1:7, p. 197.

19. *Kiddushin* 31b.

as well as action are required. The aim of the deed is to articulate the attitude. When the attitude is absent, the deed is incomplete. For example, the Talmud records a case of a person who was deemed reprehensible, not because he failed to fulfill certain obligations toward his father, but because of the attitude that accompanied his actions: "A man once fed his father on pheasants [i.e., the most expensive food]. When his father asked him how he could afford them, he responded, 'What business is it of yours old man, grind [i.e., chew] and eat. . . .' A man once fed his father fatted hens. Once the father asked, 'Son, where did you get such hens?' The son replied, 'Old man, eat and be quiet; just as dogs eat and are quiet.'"[20]

In this view, the reward of longevity for honoring parents refers, not as the biblical text seems to infer, to the longevity of the child, but rather to the longevity of the parent. By helping to ensure that the "creature needs" and personal dignity of the parent are addressed, the parent's life may be protected, enhanced, and extended. Unlike other biblical commandments, where specific deeds are required and certain attitudes and intentions are hoped for but not required, filial duty demands both particular actions and attitudes.

Long before the current "sandwich generation" of "baby boomers," the medieval commentators were especially sensitive to the potential financial and psychological conflicts that honoring parents while simultaneously dealing with the needs of one's own family might entail. For example, if honoring parents includes seeing to their basic needs, who is obliged to finance fulfilling them? If the parent has the means, the parent pays, according to Jewish law. However, what if neither the parent nor the child is wealthy, and the child is struggling financially to support his or her own family? According to the dominant view in Jewish law, the child, in such a circumstance, is not obliged to pay more than he or she can afford in order to support the parent. The child's duty to his or her spouse and children overrides the obligation to the parent.[21]

As was noted above, few biblical verses deal with the obligations of a parent toward a child. The talmudic rabbis, however, offered some guidelines, later amplified by the medievals, regarding the obligations of parents

20 *P. Kiddushin* 1:7 and Rashi's commentary on *Kiddushin* 31a-b (in standard editions of the Talmud).

21. See, e.g., *Shulhan Arukh — Yoreh De'ah*, 240, and the gloss of Moses Isserles' on 240:5; cf. *Kiddushin* 32a, *P. Kiddushin* 1:17; Ahai Gaon, *She'iltot*, ed. S. K. Mirsky (Jerusalem: Mosad ha-Rav Kook, 1964), 3:164-65, no. 56.

toward children. According to the Talmud, "A father is obliged to circumcise his son, to redeem him [if he is a firstborn; see Num. 18:15], to teach him Torah, to have him wed, and to teach him a craft. Some say, to teach him to swim too."[22] A variant reading of this text adds, "to teach him practical citizenship *(yishuv medinah)*."[23] This text emphasizes the following obligations: (1) pedagogy — conveying the intellectual and ethical teachings of the religious tradition, i.e., of the Torah (see, e.g., Deut. 6:4-9; 11:13-21),[24] (2) making the child a committed member of a covenantal community, (3) providing the means for the child to become economically independent of the parent, (4) teaching the child "survival skills," e.g., how to swim, (5) mentoring the child in sociopolitical behavior, i.e., how to become a moral and productive member of a family and of a society. In sum, the obligations of the parent vis-à-vis a child are primarily pedagogic. The parent's success in parenting is determined by how effective a role model and a pedagogue he or she is, and by how well the parent helps the child to become socially, morally, intellectually, and financially independent of the parent.

As ibn Al-Nakawa put it, the focal point of parent-child relations is not the child's honoring the parent but the parent's role in the development of the child. Consequently, for ibn Al-Nakawa and others, only the parent who guides and nurtures this development is worthy of honor, reverence, gratitude, and love.[25] For various commentators, love of the parent for the child is natural and needs not be commanded. Love of the child for the parent may be earned or freely given but not commanded. The child's love tends to be focused on his or her children, and only secondarily on his or her parents. As a talmudic adage puts it, "A parent's love is for his or her child; a child's love is for his or her children."[26]

22. *Kiddushin* 29a; see also Blidstein, *Honor,* pp. 122-36. Note that financial support of children by parents is not listed in this talmudic text; on the issue of parental obligations to financially support their children, see, e.g., *Ketubbot* 49-50; Karo, *Shulhan Arukh — Even ha-Ezer,* pars. 71, 73.

23. *Mekhilta de-Rabbi Yishmael,* "Bo," chap. 18, p. 73.

24. The requirement to teach one's children the Torah was codified in the medieval legal codes; see, e.g., Karo, *Shulhan Arukh — Yoreh De'ah,* 245:1. Teaching the child moral values is discussed in many sources throughout the ages, see, e.g., Prov. 1:8; Tob. 4:12; *Yevamot* 62b, and as already noted in medieval Jewish ethical *(musar)* literature such as ibn Al-Nakawa's *Menorat ha-Ma'or,* 4:18.

25. Ibn Al-Nakawa, *Menorat ha-Ma'or,* 4:18.

26. *Sotah* 49a.

From this perspective, honoring parents is not an end in itself. Rather, honoring parents is a means to a variety of ends. Such ends coalesce with the goals of proper parenting, such as the spiritual and moral development of the child, the continuity of religious tradition, and the social stability of society. Honoring parents and proper parenting lead to the recognition that a person is not a self-made "sovereign self"; they lead to the awareness of who and of what transcends us.

The commentators point out that honoring and revering parents is a conduit to honor and reverence for the ultimate parent — God.[27] Among the pedagogic roles incumbent upon parents is teaching the child to honor and to revere the parent of all parents, the parent of the first human parents — God. In this regard the medieval commentators indicate that the Ten Commandments were divided into two tablets, with five commandments in each. The first tablet contained the first five commandments and the second contained the second five. The first tablet deals with the obligations toward God while the second deals with obligations toward other human beings. That the fifth commandment is part of the first tablet indicates that the commandment to honor parents is ultimately and primarily a commandment to honor the divine parent, and only secondarily a commandment to honor one's human parents.[28] The Talmud describes each person as an amalgam of body and soul, where God provides the soul and the human parents provide the raw materials for the body.[29] Hence, each child has three parents, three partners in his or her creation: God, mother, and father — each due honor and reverence.

Filial duty derives from an awareness of that which transcends us, from the awareness that each of us is a creature of the Creator, a child of human forebears, a link in a chain of religious tradition, a member of a community. According to medieval Jewish philosophers, such as Maimonides and Gersonides, filial duty has sociopolitical as well as religious implications. It strengthens the family, the fundamental sociopolitical unit upon which society is based. The family serves as the primary conduit for the continuity of the intellectual, spiritual, and moral values of a society. When families become dysfunctional, society becomes destabilized.[30] Fil-

27. See, e.g., *Sefer ha-Hinukh*, no. 33, p. 183.
28. See, e.g., Moses Nahmanides on Exod. 20:12-13, in his *Commentary on the Torah* (in Hebrew).
29. *Niddah* 31a. See also *Zohar* (Vilna: Romm, 1883), 1:49; 3:83a.

ial duty is, therefore, a means to ends that transcend the self and the individual family. For Abravanel, observance of the fifth commandment profoundly affects the continuity of Judaism as a living religious, intellectual, and moral tradition.[31]

Not only God but also various types of human beings are included by the commentators in the category of "parent." For example, the respect shown by Moses to his father-in-law Jethro was interpreted to mean that filial honor and respect extend to in-laws.[32] As a late medieval text puts it, "The reason why a person must honor his in-laws is because a husband and wife are considered as one person, and the parents of one are considered the parents of the other."[33] Nonetheless, as was already noted, various commentators and legal decisors restrict the honor due both to parents and to in-laws when it causes irreconcilable marital tensions between husband and wife.

In Jewish law there is no concept of legal adoption. The adoptive parent is considered to be the "legal guardian" of the child. The name (e.g., *x* son/daughter of *y*) and identity of the adopted child remain that of its biological rather than of its adoptive parents. Nonetheless, the honor due biological parents was extended to stepparents, to adoptive parents, and even to an older sibling.[34] The commentators are ambiguous on whether filial duty extends equally to grandparents. Some maintain that filial duty does indeed extend to grandparents, while others are keenly aware of the temptation of children to honor their doting grandparents more than their parents.[35]

In recent decades the question of who is a "father" or "mother" has become increasingly complex because of sociological changes in the struc-

---

30. Moses Maimonides, *Guide of the Perplexed,* trans. Shlomo Pines (Chicago: University of Chicago Press, 1963), book 3, chap. 41, p. 562; Levi ben Gerson [Gersonides], *Commentary on the Torah* (in Hebrew) (Venice: Bomberg, 1547), pp. 50b-51a, on Exod. 20:12. See also Plato, *Laws* 790.

31. Abravanel, *Commentary on the Torah,* 2:190-91, on Exod. 20:12; see also Joseph Albo, *Sefer ha-Ikkarim,* ed. and trans. Isaac Husik (Philadelphia: Jewish Publication Society, 1930), 3:251-52.

32. *Mekhilta de-Rabbi Yishael,* "Yitro," chap. 1, p. 190; see also Karo, *Shulhan Arukh Yoreh De'ah,* 240:24.

33. Eliezer Azikiri, *Sefer Hareidim* (Jerusalem, 1987), chap. 12, p. 76.

34. See, e.g., *Ketubbot* 103.

35. See, e.g., *Yevamot* 62b; cf. *Bava Batra* 143b; *Sotah* 49a. See also Moses Isserles' gloss on Karo, *Shulhan Arukh — Yoreh De'ah,* 240:5; Azikiri, chap. 12, pp. 75-76. According to the *Zohar,* 2:233a, "a person loves his grandchildren more than his children."

ture of families, and because of developments in reproductive biotechnology.[36] For example, is a child raised by a gay couple where one person may be the child's biological parent obliged to honor the parent's partner and/ or the child's biological father or mother (e.g., the sperm or ovum donor)? For a child with more than one "mother" — e.g., a "genetic mother" (e.g., an egg donor), a "birthing mother," and a "social mother" (i.e., an adoptive mother) — who is eligible for "honor"? Is the child obliged to honor only one or more than one? Though the majority of Jewish legal decisors define the "mother" as the birthing mother, some maintain that a child can have more than one mother, each of whom is due parental honor. With the continued development of reproductive biotechnology, e.g., reproductive cloning, the issue of who is a father or mother will become increasingly complex.[37]

As has been noted, the parent is primarily viewed by Jewish tradition as a pedagogue. Parents are obliged to teach their children the Torah and to cultivate moral virtue. Parents who are unable to do so are obliged to hire teachers to do so. Because the teacher serves as a surrogate parent — thereby fulfilling the most crucial function of parenting, i.e., pedagogy — the honor due parents was expanded to include teachers. However, since parents as well as children are obliged by Jewish law to study the Torah, Jewish legal decisors ruled that even though the obligation to honor teachers derives from the obligation to honor parents, when there is a clash between honoring the teacher and honoring the parent, honoring the teacher and studying the Torah take precedent.[38]

In sum, how well a child fulfills the fifth of the ten commandments as the rabbis interpreted it may ultimately depend upon how well the parent has succeeded in the challenging task of parenting the child. In this regard, the following is told of the nineteenth-century rabbi of Zhitomer: "The rabbi of Zhitomer was once walking along with his son when they came upon a drunken man and his drunken son, both stumbling in the gutter. 'I

---

36. On parental identity, especially as it relates to developments in reproductive biotechnology, see, e.g., Emmanuel Feldman and Joel Wolowelsky, eds., *Jewish Law and the New Reproductive Technologies* (Hoboken, N.J.: Ktav, 1997); Michael Broyde, "The Establishment of Maternity and Paternity in Jewish and American Law," *National Jewish Law Review* 24 (1997): 27-65.

37. See, e.g., Sherwin, *Jewish Ethics*, pp. 111-17.

38. See, e.g., Karo, *Shulhan Arukh — Yoreh De'ah*, 240:13; 242:1; 245:4, and in the Talmud, *Megillah* 16b.

envy that man,' the rabbi said to his son. 'He has accomplished his goal of conveying his values and his lifestyle to his son. I can only hope that the drunkard is not more successful with his son than I am with you.'"[39]

39. Quoted in *Beit Pinhas* (Bilgoray: Weinberg, 1926), pp. 9b-10a n. 14.

Response

Anathea E. Portier-Young

The success of the popular reality television shows *Supernanny* and *Nanny 911*[1] testifies to the difficulties of parenting in a fast-paced culture of consumerism, permissiveness, and instant gratification. Indeed, the challenges of child rearing in any age have made it tempting to view the commandment to honor mother and father as a trump card that parents may play in a match of wills against their children.[2] In the Christian tradition, the use of the Decalogue as a cornerstone for the catechesis of young children contributes to a popular misconception that the fifth commandment mandates that young children obey their parents on pain of divine displeasure and even an early death (cf. Exod. 21:15, 17).[3]

---

1. The "11 Commandments of Nanny 911" can be downloaded from http://www.fox .com/nanny911/.

2. Ivor Bailey, in a sermon entitled "The Ten Commandments: 5. Honour Your Father and Mother," *Expository Times* 102 (1991): 206-7, cites a lament from ancient Egypt: "We are seeing the decay of good family life; parental control is a thing of the past and children no longer obey their parents." In his sermon "The Duties of Children to Their Parents," Cotton Mather addresses the perennial problems of back talk, clowning, impudence, and disobedience, any of which may bring on "The heavy Curse of God." For full text see http://www .spurgeon.org/~phil/mather/dut-chi.htm. A glimpse of contemporary application of the fifth commandment to young children may be found in posted responses to Johann Christoph Arnold's online article, "Honor Father and Mother." The article and responses are available at http://www.christopharnold.com/articles/jca/Honor-Father-Mother.htm.

3. Brian Haggerty, *Out of the House of Slavery: On the Meaning of the Ten Commandments* (New York: Paulist, 1978), notes (p. 75), "Centuries of tradition and practice have significantly altered the interpretation of the command to honor father and mother. What was once a forceful statement of the obligations society owes to the elderly has become a child's commandment, one that enjoins young children to obey their parents." It is worth noting

Response to "Honoring Parents"

By contrast (and it is a salutary contrast), Sherwin follows the Jewish tradition in taking for granted that the primary audience for this commandment, as for all the others, is the adult.[4] In his essay he underscores the crucial link between honoring parents and honoring God, the "ultimate parent." Honoring father and mother leads above all to continuity of religious and moral tradition.[5] Parents are thus fundamentally understood as teachers of their children, and are charged with the task of forming their children into adults who live in obedience to God's laws. It is out of this matrix that the grown child will truly be able to honor mother and father.[6]

---

here that placing unrealistic expectations on children is a major contributing factor in child abuse (see National Research Council, Panel on Research on Child Abuse and Neglect, *Understanding Child Abuse and Neglect* [Washington, D.C.: National Academy Press, 1993], p. 115). Thus, while it is tempting to find in this commandment an antidote for permissive parenting, the dangers of this application are all too real. Expectations for children's behavior must take into account stages of development and the lengthy and complex process of moral formation. For a sensitive discussion of the problem this commandment poses for the *victims* of child abuse, see Marshall S. Scott, "Honor Thy Father and Mother: Scriptural Resources for Victims of Incest and Parental Abuse," *Journal of Pastoral Care* 42, no. 2 (1988): 139-48. Scott also follows Brevard Childs and Martin Noth in arguing that the commandment is directed not to young children, but rather to adult children, specifically heads of households (p. 141). Anthony Phillips (*Ancient Israel's Criminal Law: A New Approach to the Decalogue* [New York: Schocken, 1970], pp. 81-82) points out further that Israelite law made serious offenses against one's parents a crime to be handled in a court of law, thus protecting children by prohibiting parents from taking matters into their own hands. Brueggemann ("The Commandments and Liberated, Liberating Bond," *Journal for Preachers* 10, no. 2 [1987]: 15-24, 21) emphasizes that the commandments serve as "guides for God's liberating activity" as exemplified in the exodus. When they do not work toward this end, as in the case of child abuse, they must be reexamined.

4. Cf. Haggerty, *Out of the House*, p. 74: "As all the stipulations of the covenant, the command to honor father and mother was addressed to adult Israelites."

5. According to Phillips (*Ancient Israel's Criminal Law*, p. 81), the original purpose of the injunction to honor one's parents was to ensure continuity of faith from generation to generation. The benefits to parents, namely, that their children would care for them in their old age, that they would not be expelled from the family home, and that they would receive proper burial, were secondary to this originating intent. Yet Phillips (pp. 80-81) also notes that the biblical tradition developed in such a way as to emphasize the rights of and care for the elderly, on which see further below.

6. Cf. the words of the Trent Catechism (*The Catechism of the Council of Trent for Parish Priests,* trans. John McHugh and Charles Callan, 11th printing [New York: Joseph F. Wagner, 1949], p. 419): "[H]aving properly trained up their children to the service of God and to holiness of life, they may, in turn, experience at their hands abundant fruit of filial affection, respect and obedience."

I intend my response to complement Sherwin's treatment of the fifth commandment by drawing on resources from within the Christian tradition.[7] I begin with a discussion of three related themes: gift, gratitude, and community. I then explore concrete applications of the commandment to honor mother and father with specific attention to prayer, care for the elderly, community support for caregivers of the elderly, and the growing problem of elder abuse. While Sherwin has noted a lack of model parents in the biblical tradition, there are a few examples of model children, chief among them Ruth and Tobias. Here I pay special attention to the book of Ruth, a text we share with our Jewish sisters and brothers, as one narrative illustration of exceptional filial devotion.[8]

Gift, Gratitude, and Community

The fifth commandment is accompanied by the double promise of a long and good life in the land (Exod. 20:12; Deut. 5:16), a promise taken up and expanded in Ephesians 6:1-3. Yet elsewhere in the tradition it is not the hope of reward that is lifted up as motivation for obedience to the command, but rather gratitude for gifts already received.[9] Jesus ben Sira urges his readers to remember the singular gift of birth: "With all your heart

7. In this essay I refer to the commandment to honor mother and father as the fifth commandment except when citing sources that treat it as the fourth.

8. The example of Tobias is likewise remarkable. The tale emphasizes the vital function of community as well. See n. 48, below. Roughly contemporaneous with the book of Tobit, Sirach also provides significant insight into the fifth commandment. For Roman Catholics, Sir. 3:1-8, 12-16 is the lectionary text for the Feast of the Holy Family.

9. See Michel Sales, "The Honor of Becoming Children: What It Means to Honor One's Father and Mother," *Communio* 22, no. 1 (Spring 1995): 5-27, esp. 7-12; and Christophe Potworowski, "The Attitude of the Child in the Theology of Hans Urs von Balthasar," *Communio* 22, no. 1 (1995): 44-55, esp. 53-54. Hans Urs von Balthasar (*Unless You Become Like This Child*, trans. E. Leiva-Merikakis [San Francisco: Ignatius, 1991], p. 49, cited in Potworowski, p. 53) speaks of the gratitude of a child as a lifelong disposition: "To be a child means to owe one's existence to another, and even in our adult life we never quite reach the point where we no longer have to give thanks for being the person we are. This means that we never quite outgrow our condition of being children, nor do we therefore ever outgrow the obligation to give thanks for ourselves or to continue to ask for our being." The themes of gift and gratitude are also prominent in the Jewish tradition. For a discussion, see Gerald Blidstein, *Honor Thy Father and Mother: Filial Responsibility in Jewish Law and Ethics* (New York: Ktav, 1975), pp. 8-19.

honor your father, and do not forget the birth pangs of your mother. Remember that it was of your parents you were born; how can you repay what they have given to you?" (Sir. 7:27-28). For Aquinas, this gift of life is followed by the gifts of nourishment, support, and instruction.[10] We honor our parents more than any other authority because they alone have given us birth. We support them in their old age because they have supported us. We obey them, to the extent that we are able, because they have instructed us. The *Catechism of the Catholic Church* similarly understands gratitude as foundational for honor: "Respect for parents *(filial piety)* derives from *gratitude* toward those who, by the gift of life, their love and their work, have brought their children into the world and enabled them to grow in stature, wisdom, and grace."[11]

John Paul II, in his 1994 "Letter to Families," laid particular emphasis on the gift of life, noting that as "benefactors" of their children parents participate in the supreme goodness of God.[12] This gift of life and benefaction engenders the reciprocal gift of honor, which is an acknowledgment of the other, namely, the parent, as an individual person.[13] This acknowledgment of the other is a fundamental component of the Decalogue as a whole and an antidote to the individualism of contemporary culture.[14]

10. "The Catechetical Instructions of St. Thomas," available online at http://www.ewtn.com/library/SOURCES/TA-CAT-2.TXT.

11. *Catechism of the Catholic Church* (New York: Doubleday, 1995), 2215.

12. "Letter to Families," 15.3, available online at http://www.vatican.va/holy_father/john_paul_ii/letters/documents/hf_jp-ii_let_02021994_families_en.html.

13. "Letter to Families," 15.12. This honoring is "a sincere gift of person to person" (15.4).

14. "Letter to Families," 14.5; Mona Fishbane, "'Honor Thy Father and Thy Mother': Intergenerational Spirituality and Jewish Tradition," in *Spiritual Resources in Family Therapy*, ed. Froma Walsh (New York: Guilford, 1999), pp. 136-56, 145. Joseph Chorpenning uses the phrase "antidote to individualism" in "The Holy Family as Icon and Model of the Civilization of Love: John Paul II's *Letter to Families*," *Communio* 22, no. 1 (1995): 77-98, 79. Drawing on the work of Emmanuel Levinas, Patrick Miller ("The Good Neighborhood: Identity and Community through the Commandments," in *Character and Scripture: Moral Formation, Community, and Biblical Interpretation*, ed. William P. Brown [Grand Rapids: Eerdmans, 2002], pp. 55-72, 67) asserts that "[t]he moral community effected by the Commandments is one in which human self-understanding is found in an encounter with the Other." As has often been noted, the fifth commandment forms a bridge between those commandments that have to do primarily with God and those that have to do primarily with neighbor. The Decalogue leads us, then, from the encounter with God, through the encounter with family, to the encounter with neighbor. Cf. Miller, p. 68. For Holbert (*The Ten Commandments: A Preaching Commentary* [Nashville: Abingdon, 2002], p. 72), the first five com-

According to Reinhard Hütter, we "encounter God's commandments" in "a dense web of relationships, and in light of particular challenges."[15] The "community of remembrance and interpretation"[16] within which we "embody our obedience to God and our service to humanity"[17] is first of all the family, itself a "community of faith" and "realization of ecclesial communion."[18] The "communion between generations" established by the fifth commandment reaches beyond the boundaries of the individual family and into the broader community.[19] In this way the fifth commandment highlights our responsibilities not only toward our parents, but also toward our children, neighbor, and God. We honor our parents by according them a place of dignity within this broader community.[20]

The particular challenges of honoring parents in their old age are manifold. For some, the remembrance of past wrongs creates a barrier to the practice of charity. For others, the transportation revolution has severed or weakened the "communion between generations," such that extended families rarely share a dwelling, and are often separated by great

---

mandments express the fundamental orientation of community; without them, the community will pass away. As such, the honoring of mother and father illuminates our relationships with God and neighbor, and binds the two together. Cf. *Catechism of the Catholic Church,* 2212: "The fourth commandment *illuminates other relationships in society*" (emphasis in original). We recognize each human being as a child like ourselves, and above all as a child "of the One who wants to be called 'our Father.'"

15. Reinhard Hütter, "The Twofold Center of Lutheran Ethics: Christian Freedom and God's Commandments," in *The Promise of Lutheran Ethics,* ed. Karen Bloomquist and John Stumme (Minneapolis: Fortress, 1998), pp. 31-54, 45.

16. Hütter, "The Twofold Center," p. 45.

17. Hütter, "The Twofold Center," p. 44.

18. John Paul II, Apostolic Exhortation *Familaris Consortio* (The Christian Family in the Modern World), November 22, 1981, 21.3, http://www.vatican.va/holy_father/john _paul_ii/apost_exhortations/documents/hf_jp-ii_exh_19811122_familiaris_consortio _en.html; cf. *Lumen Gentium* 11.

19. John Paul II, "Letter to Families," 15.2. According to Carroll Simcox (*Living the Ten Commandments: A Guide to Christian Obedience* [New York: Morehouse-Gorham, 1953], p. 75), "Honouring our father and mother begins at home, but it reaches backward and forward and spreads out. It creates and quickens that bond which embraces a longer period of time than this: a piety toward the dead, however obscure, and a solicitude for the unborn, however remote."

20. *Familiaris Consortio* 17 highlights four tasks for the Christian family: "1) forming a community of persons; 2) serving life; 3) participating in the development of society; 4) sharing in the life and mission of the Church."

distances. Medical advances enable individuals to live longer despite complex medical problems, which nonetheless may require high levels of care and monitoring. As a result, adult children may feel strained by the demands of caregiving or may withdraw from the relationship entirely. This withdrawal is facilitated by an individualistic ethos, which suggests that aging individuals ought to provide the means for their own care, such that their needs will not impinge upon the lives of others, even their children. Further, in a culture that is increasingly driven by the rhythms of production and consumption, individual worth is measured according to potential for either. Members of society who do not promise to contribute to this economy are a liability rather than an asset.[21] Finally, in a culture that privileges what is "new" over what is "old," the wisdom of elders is perceived as outmoded and memory as such is undervalued. In an industrialized society the aged are too often demoted from a place of honor to one of dishonor and seclusion. Their dignity may be compromised by a perception of helplessness, by impersonal forms of caregiving, and even by abuse.

These challenges do not diminish the force of the fifth commandment. They are the real context out of which God's prophetic word calls us to lives of obedience and service. In Mark's Gospel, Jesus affirms the mandate of the fifth commandment, emphasizing the concrete form honor must take (Mark 7:6-13).[22] In the section that follows, I discuss ways in which the fifth commandment may be actualized in the lives of individuals, families, and larger faith communities.

Prayer

Often neglected in treatments of the fifth commandment, one of the simplest and most powerful ways of honoring mother and father is through prayer.[23] Prayer will play a special role in cases where children and parents

---

21. Cf. the prophetic critique of Jay Marshall, *The Ten Commandments and Christian Community* (Scottdale, Pa.: Herald, 1996), pp. 63-65. Brueggemann ("Commandments," p. 18) sees that in the fifth commandment "[t]he entitlement of communal dignity is extended to old people who have lost their usefulness to society."

22. Hütter ("The Twofold Center," p. 44) writes that "God's commandments allow us to embody our obedience to God and our service to humanity in concrete historical practices and activities."

23. In a treatment of the "Manner of Honoring Parents" (pp. 412-13), the Trent Cate-

struggle to forgive one another for past injuries. Yet even when this is not the case, the commandment to honor mother and father cannot be accomplished apart from prayer.[24] In the Lord's Prayer above all, Christians become mindful of our status as children, following Christ's example of humble reverence. Through such prayer we are conformed more and more to Christ, and so grow in our ability to give freely of ourselves to those who have already given us the supreme gift of life.

Care for the Elderly

If prayer is necessary for the honoring of parents, it is not sufficient. A concrete praxis of care is also a necessary component of honoring parents, especially as they age or grow ill.[25] As Sherwin notes, this can include opening one's home, providing physical care and material support, and observing deference and humility in speech and manner. Moreover, children can affirm their parents' personal dignity through healing touch, by attending to likes and dislikes, by providing opportunities for personal enrichment, by honoring parents' decisions about their care, by listening to stories and complaints, and by including parents in family activities.[26] Children can also work to ensure that aging or ailing parents are not isolated within the home but rather are surrounded by a community of faith

---

chism lists spontaneous love first and intercessory prayer second. Other acts of honoring, including obedience, seeking and following parents' advice, and providing for their bodily needs, follow on that of prayer. John Paul II ("Letter to Families," 4.2) similarly emphasizes the importance of prayer by, for, and with family.

24. *Catechism of the Catholic Church*, 2745, asserts: "Prayer and *Christian life* are *inseparable*, for they concern the same love and the same renunciation, proceeding from love; the same filial and loving conformity with the Father's plan of love; the same transforming union in the Holy Spirit who conforms us more and more to Christ Jesus. . . ."

25. According to Haggerty (*Out of the House*, p. 74), the fifth commandment "called upon [adult Israelites] to provide physical care and material support for their elderly parents who were no longer fully able to provide for themselves. It prohibited members of the covenant community from turning their backs on the elderly and leaving them to their own devices."

26. Such a list is by no means exhaustive. The "United Nations Principles for Older Persons" (1999) (http://www.un.org/esa/socdev/iyop/iyoppop.htm) lists five principles around which the basic rights of older persons are organized: independence, participation, care, self-fulfillment, and dignity.

that will "strengthen their weakness, assist them by their counsel," and, as death nears, "animate them to the hope of immortality."[27] In extreme illness and at the end of life, children play a key role in ensuring that parents can participate in religious rites and devotions that convey grace and strength to them in their time of need. In this context children can ensure access to the sacraments, for example, and to pastoral care. After the death of a parent, children continue to honor their parents by attending their funerals, ensuring proper burial,[28] executing their wills and final wishes, and, for those who practice prayer for the dead, continuing to offer intercessory prayer on the parents' behalf.[29]

Support for Caregivers

The fifth commandment binds us to honor not only our own parents, but all elders (cf. Lev. 19:32), and to support those who care for them (cf. Mark 3:35; Matt. 12:50). In the United States, 16 percent of the adult population provides unpaid care to a recipient age fifty or older, providing an average of twenty-one hours per week of care.[30] These caregivers help aging family and friends with such tasks as managing finances, grocery shopping, housework, and transportation, and such aspects of personal care as dressing, bathing, and eating. Caregiving at this level can cause significant stress. In a recent study, 40 percent of women and 26 percent of men caregivers reported "very high levels of emotional stress." Many caregivers compromise job security and sacrifice job benefits to provide care.[31] Over time caregivers become vulnerable not only to emotional stress, but also to poor health and economic hardship.[32]

27. *Catechism of the Council of Trent*, 414.

28. It should be recalled that Esau and Jacob buried their father together (Gen. 35:29).

29. *Catechism of the Council of Trent*, 414.

30. "Caregiving in the U.S.: Executive Summary" (study conducted by the National Alliance for Caregiving [NAC] in collaboration with AARP, 2005), p. 1. A majority (61 percent) of these caregivers are women, and a majority are children of the care recipient (pp. vi-vii) (http://assets.aarp.org/rgcenter/il/us_caregiving_1.pdf).

31. "Caregiving in the U.S.," p. 4. Fifty-seven percent of caregivers surveyed "say they are going to work late, leaving early or taking time off during the day to provide care." Some (particularly women) have to take leaves of absence, lose job benefits, or quit their jobs (p. 22).

32. "Caregiving in the U.S.," p. 32.

In the face of such strain, it is noteworthy that the number one "cop-ing strategy" reported by caregivers (73 percent) is prayer, while a signifi-cant number also seek spiritual counseling.[33] Just as so many caregivers have recognized the importance of their faith for sustaining them in their service to the aging and infirm, so communities of faith must recognize their duty to support and honor the work of these caregivers in our midst.[34] Caregivers need help finding time for themselves; keeping their care recipients safe; balancing work and family; managing stress; finding easy activities to do together with their care recipients; learning how to talk with doctors; making end-of-life decisions; and choosing assisted living fa-cilities, nursing homes, or home care agencies.[35] The fifth commandment must continue to challenge communities of faith to discern how they can support and honor the work of caregivers and help to meet these manifold needs.[36]

Elder Abuse

There is a darker side to the fifth commandment. The positive formulation to honor mother and father hints at prohibitions stated elsewhere against cursing and striking one's parents.[37] Though we would wish to imagine that such abuse occurs only rarely, we do not have that luxury. Reports of elder abuse are rising throughout the world. In the United States alone nearly two million individuals sixty years of age or older suffer abuse each

33. "Caregiving in the U.S.," p. 20.

34. The NAC/AARP study concludes with a call to action (p. 32): "[W]e need to help current at-risk caregivers so that they can continue to provide care to family and friends without sacrificing their health, financial security and quality of life in the process." This can be done in many ways, including encouraging families to plan for the future and advocating for policies and programs (and in the case of faith communities, administering programs) that will provide much-needed services such as training, transportation, meals-on-wheels, adult day care, and respite services (pp. 32, 24).

35. "Caregiving in the U.S.," p. 26.

36. I support Hütter ("The Twofold Center," p. 52) in his judgment that the fifth com-mandment conveys a "radical social and economic critique," including a demand for "just economic structures."

37. These prohibitions are expressed elsewhere in the Pentateuch: cursing: Exod. 21:17; Lev. 20:9; Deut. 27:16; striking: Exod. 21:15. Cf. Patrick D. Miller, Jr., "The Place of the Decalogue in the Old Testament and Its Law," *Interpretation* 43, no. 3 (1989): 229-42, 236.

year.[38] In 37 percent of cases reported in the United States, the abusers were adult children.[39] In countries such as India and Japan, where respect for elders has long been a core cultural value, "westernization and industrialization have been identified as social factors exacerbating abuse."[40] Such abuse can take several forms, including physical, emotional, and psychological abuse, financial exploitation, and neglect.[41] Abuse frequently occurs in situations of family stress and socioeconomic hardship; as aging parents and caregivers become isolated from their community, the risk of abuse increases.[42]

The fifth commandment speaks a prophetic word in the face of this reality. We honor our parents not only by our direct actions toward them, but also by working to effect just socioeconomic structures and networks of support for the elderly and their families. Faith communities must play a role in raising awareness and prevention of elder abuse, as well as in providing counseling, support, and assistance for victims.[43]

Biblical Models for Honoring Mother and Father

Jesus himself is often, and rightly, cited as a model of filial devotion, obedience, and humility. Both in his attitude toward his human parents and in his divine sonship he images for us a perfect mode of honoring parents.[44]

---

38. "National Elder Abuse Incidence Study (1998)," cited in Sally Balche Hurme, "Perspectives on Elder Abuse," AARP, 2002. http://assets.aarp.org/www.aarp.org_/articles/international/revisedabusepaper1.pdf, p. 4. A summary of the study's findings is available at http://www.aoa.gov/eldfam/elder_rights/elder_abuse/elder_abuse.asp.

39. "Abuse against Older Persons" (report of the UN Secretary-General, Preparations for the Second World Assembly on Ageing, 2002), §§28-29. Available at http://www.un.org/esa/socdev/ageing/waa.oldrep1.htm.

40. Hurme, "Perspectives on Elder Abuse," p. 3.

41. "Abuse against Older Persons."

42. "Abuse against Older Persons," p. 20.

43. In an analogous type of initiative, the Catholic Church has responded to the clergy sex-abuse scandal in part by taking the lead as educators in the field of child abuse recognition and prevention. In the Diocese of Raleigh, North Carolina, for example, diocesan educators have trained over three thousand people, including the staff of the state-run Prevent Child Abuse program. For more information on the Child and Youth Protection program, see http://www.dioceseofraleigh.org/what/youth/

44. E.g., Sales, "Honor of Becoming Children," pp. 20-23.

Jesus' (and David's) ancestor Ruth provides a companion model of filial devotion. Her free gift of self affords dignity and new life to a grieving mother.

Ruth's mother-in-law Naomi is a foreigner among the Moabites. Following the death of her husband, and later her two sons, Naomi wishes to return to her homeland. Despite Naomi's objections, Ruth goes with her to Judah, where she herself is a foreigner, risks isolation, and makes herself vulnerable for the sake of her mother-in-law's well-being.

Naomi's first words to Ruth invoke God's *chesed,* the divine loyalty and generosity shown to God's covenant partners, and acknowledge that Ruth herself has done *chesed* toward Naomi (1:8).[45] Ruth's future husband Boaz remarks on her singular devotion to Naomi: "Of course it has been told to me — everything that you have done for your mother-in-law after the death of your husband, that you left-behind your father and your mother and the land where you were born and went to a people you didn't know at all a day or two ago!" (2:11).[46] Boaz knows she has risked her own security on behalf of Naomi, and responds by providing her with enough food for them both (2:14).[47] Later, when she receives permission to glean in Boaz's fields, she provides for Naomi from the grain she has gathered (2:18). As Ruth continues the work of harvesting, she makes her home in Judah with her mother-in-law (2:23).

Naomi now calls Ruth "daughter" (3:1), reciprocating the honor Ruth has paid her by instructing Ruth in how to gain security for them both. Her language hints at the transformation that Ruth's devotion has engendered in her. Ruth responds with total submission: "Everything that you say, I will do" (3:5). At the story's end, Ruth has borne a son to Boaz. The women who are present at the birth proclaim new life and support for Naomi, who has received love from her bride-daughter (4:15), and now a son (4:17). Through Ruth's devotion Naomi is transformed from a bitterly bereaved mother and widow (1:13) to a joyful mother and grandmother, honored in her old age, surrounded by family and a community of faith, and newly aware of God's gift to her of life and support.[48]

---

45. On this theme in Ruth, see the sensitive treatment by Ellen Davis, *Who Are You My Daughter? Reading Ruth through Image and Text* (Louisville: Westminster John Knox, 2003), esp. p. 17. For Davis (p. 17), "this distinctive quality of loyal kindness is the criterion on which human character is judged throughout the book."

46. Translation is that of Davis, *Who Are You?* p. 48.

47. See Davis, *Who Are You?* pp. 49, 55.

48. In similar fashion, the devotion of Tobias brings new life to his ailing and depressed

Conclusion

Gift, gratitude, and community constitute the fundamental matrix out of which we actualize the command to honor mother and father. We realize this call in concrete practices, including prayer, care for the elderly, support for caregivers, and attention to the problem of elder abuse. The biblical character Ruth provides a model of exemplary filial piety that all of us may imitate: through her gift of courage and devotion, she restores dignity to her bereaved mother-in-law, and together they celebrate new life.

father, and deep joy to his mother. See Anathea Portier-Young, "Alleviation of Suffering in the Book of Tobit: Comedy, Community, and Happy Endings," *Catholic Biblical Quarterly* 63, no. 1 (January 2001): 35-54. The example of Tobias is lifted up in the concluding paragraph on the fourth commandment in the *Catechism of the Council of Trent*, 419.

What Have You Done?

John K. Roth

You shall not murder.

Some versions of the Decalogue's sixth commandment substitute "kill" for "murder." In either case those key words require definition if the commandment is to make sense, but how much difference does it make if the sixth commandment contains one rather than the other? The answer is, *a great deal.* That response and the question that prompts it make an apt place to start what I call wrestling with the sixth commandment, an engagement with the imperative that is the most necessary, although not sufficient, condition for human civilization.[1]

The wrestling in this essay has multiple parts, which can be identified in part by four additional questions: (1) How has the sixth commandment functioned and fared in history? (2) What does this commandment reveal about humankind? (3) What does it suggest about God? (4) What place does it have in humanity's future? As we shall see, the struggles involved with those issues are, quite literally, matters of life and death.

Definitions

As a prelude to addressing the four questions above, two further steps need to be taken. The first involves definitions that inform this essay's wrestling.

1. Among the sources that have been most helpful in my thinking about the Decalogue, I want to mention especially William P. Brown, ed., *The Ten Commandments: The Reciprocity of Faithfulness* (Louisville: Westminster John Knox, 2004).

According to the most reliable biblical scholarship, "murder," not "kill," is the best English term to use in translating the Hebrew text. That decision is significant, for the meanings of "murder" and "kill," although closely related, are not identical.

All murder is killing, but not all killing is murder. To kill means to inflict or cause death, which also happens in murder, but distinctions exist because killing acts can be accidental and unintentional. Killing acts of that kind are not murder, which typically requires an intention, often including premeditation and careful planning, to inflict or cause death. In addition, murderous intentions are usually inflamed by anger, malice, envy, greed, fear, hate, revenge, or some other violence-inciting emotion. Not all killing actions fit that description, but typically murderous ones do.

Historically, the sixth commandment, along with others in the Decalogue, has been understood to be addressed to human beings — to Jews, to Christians, and indeed to all persons and communities — whose distinctiveness includes a capacity for murder that is not found in any other part of the natural world. Various interpretations of its meaning can be found, but they all share and depend upon the understanding that the imperative applies to human beings who are commanded not to do certain things that are within their power. Obvious though this point may be, awareness of it helps to underscore other crucial differences between "kill" and "murder."

The sixth commandment is unequivocal and absolute. Allowing no exceptions, it does not say, "Murder is wrong in situation x, but it may be permissible in situation y." Murder, the commandment entails, is wrong — period. Killing, however, is not so easily interpreted that way, unless one stipulates that "killing" means "murder." In fact, unless killing is qualified in that way, or in some other way that restricts the meaning of that term to forms of killing that are intentional but unjustifiable or inexcusable, a commandment that said "You shall not kill" would be so ambiguous, even nonsensical, that it would be impossible for human beings to obey it no matter how good they might be or how hard they might try.

To see why that situation holds, notice that human life depends on killing. That statement, of course, is as problematic as it is evident, as much in need of qualification as it is bold. Therefore, to avoid misunderstanding, I need to clarify what I do and do not mean by it. I do not mean, for example, that human life depends on war; it does not, although sometimes war is unavoidable and even necessary to defend human life. Nor do I mean that human civilization depends on capital punishment; it does not, although there may be times and places where justifiable reasons for executions can be found. What I do mean is that human life and civilization cannot exist, let alone thrive, unless people eat, quench their thirst, obtain shelter, raise and educate their young, and, in short, take the actions that are necessary to sustain human life. Unfortunately, those actions cannot be taken without killing. As the philosopher Philip Hallie cogently put the point, "We are in the food web. We are killers, if only of plants."[2]

In addition, if human life, in the biblical words of Genesis, is to be "fruitful and multiply," it unavoidably becomes even more lethal than Hallie asserts. Human beings are thinkers and doers; they are political, social, and also religious creatures who plan, strive, and build. Scarcely any of humankind's initiatives can be pursued without dislocations and destructions of one kind or another. Even the most environmentally conscious projects that men and women carry out have lethal consequences for living creatures somewhere.

An absolute and unequivocal prohibition against killing is not what the sixth commandment can mean if it is coherent. With due qualification, human life depends on killing, but a corollary of that truth is that human existence and especially its *quality* also depend on careful discrimination between killing that is justifiable or excusable and killing that is not. Absent such discrimination, including laws and sanctions to implement the difference socially and politically, it is hard to imagine that human civilization could long endure. Instead, to use Thomas Hobbes's bleak description from 1651, human existence would likely be in "that condition which is called war, and such a war as is of every man against every man. . . . In such condition there is . . . continual fear and danger of violent death; and the life of man solitary, poor, nasty, brutish, and short."[3]

Not even the most thorough, rigorous, and truthful interpretation of the sixth commandment, however, may be able to provide a complete analysis of killing that is justifiable or excusable and killing that is not. After acknowledging that some kinds of killing are necessary for basic suste-

2. Philip Paul Hallie, "Cruelty: The Empirical Evil," in *Facing Evil: Light at the Core of Darkness,* ed. Paul Woodruff and Harry A. Wilmer (La Salle, Ill.: Open Court, 1988), p. 128.

3. Thomas Hobbes, *Leviathan* (Indianapolis: Bobbs-Merrill, 1958), pp. 106-7. To a considerable degree, human existence is perpetually in the state of war that Hobbes identified. The reason has much to do with humankind's repeated and escalating violations of the sixth commandment.

nance of human life, the category of killing may still remain larger than the category of murder. At least in many cases, if not ordinarily, murder is not the category into which one places killing in self-defense, for example, or killing to prevent the murder of another person or to combat warring aggression. Even when unjust war unleashes killing that is met with armed resistance, a gray zone of moral classification may exist, and it will be debatable whether all the killing done by the warring aggressor, wrong though it surely is, should be called murder. In short, there remain cases of killing, justifiable or unjustifiable, that are not necessarily cases of murder or at least not clearly so. That realization, however, does not cut slack for killing; at least it should not, because most killing can and should be found wrong and condemned without inevitably and always being classified as murder.

Perspectives

Much killing, but not all, is murder, but now two more questions must be addressed for the sixth commandment to make sense: When is killing murder? What constitutes murder? My response to those questions emerges from the perspectives that inform my thinking about the sixth commandment. My perspectives are those of a Protestant Christian philosopher/theologian whose work has concentrated for more than thirty years on the Holocaust, Nazi Germany's attempt to destroy the Jewish people, and on other genocides as well. This outlook reminds me, again and again, of an unmistakable instance of murder, namely, the murder that the Hebrew Bible identifies as the first one. Genesis 4 tells that story, which depicts Cain's slaying of his brother Abel.

When God favored Abel's offering but "had no regard" for Cain's, the latter's anger got the best of him. "Let us go out to the field," said Cain to the apparently unsuspecting Abel. "And when they were in the field," the biblical text continues, "Cain rose up against his brother Abel, and killed him." The story reports that God responded: "What have you done? Listen; your brother's blood is crying out to me from the ground!" Cain's killing made him "a fugitive and a wanderer on the earth," one who "went away from the presence of the Lord," but God spared Cain's life, marking him "so that no one who came upon him would kill him."

At rock bottom, murder takes place when one person kills another intentionally, deliberately, and unjustifiably. (Much hinges on the latter term in particular, a point to which we will return in due course.) Cain's killing of Abel was murder — *homicide* — or nothing could be. Moreover, like the sixth commandment itself, the Genesis narrative leaves no doubt that murder is wrong. That same account, however, raises as many questions as it answers. For instance, was Cain's killing of Abel clearly premeditated? Genesis does not say so explicitly, although far from being excluded, the text definitely invites such an inference. Furthermore, when Cain "rose up against his brother," was that action murderous from the outset? Again, the text allows for the possibility that it might not have been that way, although Cain's "rising up" resulted in killing that was unlikely to have been accidental. Otherwise, Cain probably would not have tried to fend off God's question — "Where is your brother Abel?" — by denial and evasion: "I do not know; am I my brother's keeper?"

The ambiguities do not end there. When Cain questioned whether he should be held accountable as his brother's keeper, was he implying that creation did not yet have a moral structure that condemned murder as the sixth commandment would do explicitly later on? Cain's defense might have been that he unfairly received an ex post facto judgment from God. Who says, and where and when was it said, Cain might have protested, that I am to be Abel's keeper? However, if Cain made a legalistic move of this kind, Genesis shows that God had none of it. Prior to Cain's murdering Abel, the biblical account in Genesis brims with language about what is good, about the knowledge of good and evil, about obedience and disobedience. The Genesis tradition, moreover, makes clear not only that God "created humankind in his image, in the image of God he created them; male and female he created them," but also that "God blessed them." Could it make any good sense for God to create human beings in God's image, bless them, and then permit them with impunity to slaughter one another intentionally? At the end of the day, ambiguity notwithstanding, no credible reading could interpret Genesis as doing less than defining murder quintessentially or as doing anything other than finding murder wrong — period.

The clarity notwithstanding, a troubling shadow still lurks in the questions and responses above. It will need revisiting. Meanwhile, a basic point is maintained within Jewish tradition, which, among other things, holds that when God gave Moses the Ten Commandments at Sinai, those imperatives were etched on two stone tablets, five commandments on each. The first five identified human duties to God; the second five underscored obligations that persons have to one another. Tradition holds further that there are parallels between the two sets of five commandments. Thus, the sixth commandment, "You shall not murder," is especially linked to the first commandment, "I am the Lord your God, who brought you out of the land of Egypt, out of the house of slavery; you shall have no other gods before me." Murder — the intentional, deliberate, and unjustifiable killing of one human being by another — is wrong for reasons that go deep down because they violate the first commandment.

God created human life in God's image. In God's sight, and surely in ours, that act was good. It was also awesome, even sacred, for in the ultimate sense no human being has the power to create human life — not even the wonders of twenty-first-century science contradict that fact — and murder destroys human life in ways that are beyond our repair and recovery. God may or may not resurrect the dead, but human beings utterly lack the power to do so. The result is that no human act rivals murder in defying, disrespecting, and denying God. The Christian philosopher Stephen Davis succinctly sums up the primary point: "Murder, then, is a crime both against the victim and his family and friends, and also (and most importantly) against God."[4]

Here it is worth noting that, according to the biblical scholar David Flusser, the Christian New Testament "does not use the term 'Ten Commandments' even once," but the injunction against murder is emphasized in multiple instances, and especially by Jesus in ways that are thoroughly consistent with the Jewish tradition he observed.[5] In Matthew 19:16-22, Mark 10:17-22, and Luke 18:18-23, for example, Jesus stresses the importance of obeying God's commandments and explicitly condemns murder. Paul does the same in Romans 13:9, adding that the sixth commandment and those prohibiting adultery, theft, and coveting "are summed up in this word, 'Love your neighbor as yourself.'"

Meanwhile, for one reason or another, and here lurks another troubling problem related to the sixth commandment, Cain, who did not have

4. Stephen T. Davis, "Genocide, Despair, and Religious Hope: An Essay on Human Nature," in *Genocide and Human Rights: A Philosophical Guide*, ed. John K. Roth (New York: Palgrave Macmillan, 2005), p. 38.
5. David Flusser, "The Decalogue in the New Testament," in *The Ten Commandments in History and Tradition*, ed. Ben-Zion Segal and Gershon Levi (Jerusalem: Magnes Press, Hebrew University of Jerusalem, 1990), p. 221.

the advantage of reading Genesis or Exodus, let alone the New Testament, may not have known as clearly as the readers of those texts that killing Abel was wrong. Genesis says little about the moral upbringing that Cain and Abel received from Adam and Eve, their biblical parents. Nor does it indicate much about what the brothers knew about God and God's expectations, except that they understood enough "in the course of time" to bring offerings to God. Abel, apparently, knew better than Cain what would please God. Whether Cain's misjudgment resulted from ignorance or from a disrespectful holding back of what he should have given to God, the result was the introduction of murder, which ever since has bloodied and scarred creation almost beyond belief. To illustrate the latter point, consider two further episodes. Linked to Cain's murder of Abel even though they are millennia removed from that act, these examples also help to shape my perspectives on the sixth commandment.

Two Episodes

Richard Rhodes's *Masters of Death: The SS-Einsatzgruppen and the Invention of the Holocaust* details how Nazi Germany's mobile killing units murdered more than 1.3 million Jews in eastern Europe during World War II. "Maps in Jewish museums from Riga to Odessa," writes Rhodes, "confirm that almost every village and town in the entire sweep of the Eastern territories has a killing site nearby."[6] Gratuitous and sadistic violence accompanied the slaughter. Rhodes describes one instance as follows: "A woman in a small town near Minsk saw a young German soldier walking down the street with a year-old baby impaled on his bayonet. 'The baby was still crying weakly,' she would remember. 'And the German was singing. He was so engrossed in what he was doing that he did not notice me.'"[7]

Although such brutal murder should rightly leave one speechless, there are many things that ought to be said about it. One of them is that if such action is not an example of unjustifiable killing, nothing could be. Of course, the young German and his Nazi superiors, SS leader Heinrich Himmler and Adolf Hitler himself first and foremost among them, would

6. Richard Rhodes, *Masters of Death: The SS-Einsatzgruppen and the Invention of the Holocaust* (New York: Knopf, 2002), p. 121.

7. Rhodes, *Masters of Death*, p. 140.

have argued differently. In their Nazi eyes, the mass killing of Jews was not only justifiable but also imperative. To them, Jews were such an unrelenting, pestilential threat to the "superior" German *Volk* that Jewish life — including, significantly, the Jewish tradition that emphasized the sixth commandment — must be eradicated root and branch. Himmler was not, however, an advocate of gratuitous and sadistic violence. He would have disapproved young Germans who found joy in impaling infants on their bayonets. He wanted "decent" killers instead.

Hitler, Himmler, and the young German soldier in Rhodes's account were neither insane nor completely irrational. They had a worldview that made sense to them, and they acted on it.[8] Nevertheless, rational and ethical scrutiny far better and deeper than theirs underscores how much the Nazis' reasoning, planning, and acting were misguided and immoral. For no matter how sincerely Hitler and his followers held their beliefs or how valid they took them to be, those convictions and the mass murder that flowed from them were based on error and terror, on deceit and delusion, on theft and tyranny, on falsehood and aggression, on hate and disrespect for human life other than their own. That catalogue does not exhaust the criteria that brand killing unjustifiable, but no killing arising from those conditions, dispositions, or motivations can reasonably be justified.

Unjustified and unjustifiable, so much of the killing done by Nazi Germany and its collaborators was not only murder but also *mass murder*. In 1944 Raphael Lemkin, a Jewish lawyer who fled from Poland during the Holocaust, named such crimes when he coined the term "genocide," which derives from the Greek word *genos* (race) and the Latin suffix *-cide* (killing). It refers to instances of mass murder, such as Nazi Germany's assault on the Jews, that do not target individuals alone but aim at entire groups. Owing considerably to Lemkin's dogged persistence, the United Nations adopted the 1948 Convention on the Prevention and Punishment of the Crime of Genocide, which defined that crime in terms of "acts committed with intent to destroy, in whole or in part, a national, ethnical, racial, or religious group, as such."[9]

Cain committed homicide and fratricide but not genocide. The

8. On this point see Claudia Koonz, *The Nazi Conscience* (Cambridge: Harvard University Press, 2003).

9. For more detail on these matters, see Carol Rittner, John K. Roth, and James M. Smith, eds., *Will Genocide Ever End?* (St. Paul, Minn.: Paragon House, 2002).

United Nations' definition indicates that genocide can take place without direct murder, but typically genocide is no less an occasion for murder than are homicide and fratricide. Granting some genocidal exceptions, all three are instances of murder; all three involve the intended, deliberate, but unjustifiable taking of individual lives. In genocide, however, the murderous aim is immensely escalated, and a person's life is at risk not for anything in particular that he or she has done but simply because the person exists at all as a member of a targeted group. The fact that the group is targeted is crucial, because all human individuals are fundamentally defined by factors of group identity of one kind or another. Indeed, there can be no individual human life without such identities. Unfortunately, not even genocide is the end of the matter where mass murder is concerned, and thus we come to the second episode that influences my wrestling with the sixth commandment. It involves calculations of time and distance.

In 1994 the political scientist R. J. Rummel, a demographer of what he calls "democide," published an important book called *Death by Government*. Writing before he could have taken account of the late twentieth-century genocidal atrocities in Bosnia, Rwanda, and Kosovo or the twenty-first-century genocide that continues in the Darfur region of Sudan at the time of this writing in June 2005, Rummel estimated that "the human cost of war and democide" — which he defined as "the murder of any person or people by a government, including genocide, politicide, and mass murder" — was more than "203 million people in [the twentieth] century."[10] (What the precise figure would be today, God only knows.)

"If one were to sit at a table," Rummel went on to say, "and have this many people come in one door, walk at three miles per hour across the room with three feet between them (assume generously that each person is also one foot thick, navel to spine), and exit an opposite door, it would take over *five years and nine months* for them all to pass, twenty-four hours a day, 365 days a year. If the dead were laid out head to toe, assuming each to be an average of 5 feet tall, they would reach from Honolulu, Hawaii, across the

10. R. J. Rummel, *Death by Government* (New Brunswick, N.J.: Transaction Publishers, 1997), pp. 13, 31. Observations about Rummel's data by the Holocaust historian Yehuda Bauer are worth noting: "Rummel has been criticized for exaggerating the losses. Even if the criticisms were valid, a figure lower by 10 or 20 or even 30 percent would make absolutely no difference to the general conclusions that Rummel draws." See Yehuda Bauer, *Rethinking the Holocaust* (New Haven: Yale University Press, 2001), pp. 12-13, 277 n. 17.

vast Pacific and then the huge continental United States to Washington, D.C. on the East coast, *and then back again almost twenty times.*"[11]

While Rummel may have thought that such calculations would make the abstraction of huge numbers more concrete, it is not clear that he convinced even himself, for he placed an endnote number at his calculation's conclusion. Note 14 reads as follows: "Back and forth, over 4,838 miles one way, near twenty times? This is so incredible that I would not believe the calculation and had to redo it several times."[12]

The Slaughter Bench of History

As we turn to the first of the four questions I identified at the outset, consider that the philosopher G. W. F. Hegel called history a slaughter bench.[13] Although he may not have acknowledged the point explicitly, he did so largely because the sixth commandment has neither functioned nor fared nearly as well as God and humankind should desire. Things could always be worse, even to the point of "omnicide," the total extinction of life that may now be within the willful killing and murderous prowess of human beings, but humanity's murderous ways lend all too much credence to the point made by the Holocaust survivor Elie Wiesel when he said, "At Auschwitz, not only man died, but also the idea of man. . . . It was its own heart the world incinerated at Auschwitz."[14]

Meanwhile the sixth commandment has had normative status, and it probably has had some braking effect on humankind's propensity for violence. Arguably, however, an honest historical appraisal leads to the conclusion that the most distinctive quality about the sixth commandment is the extent to which it has been violated — disregarded, dismissed, and disrespected. Along with those characteristics, one must add that the sixth commandment has never been backed sufficiently by credible sanctions, divine or human, that would ensure full respect for and obedience to it.[15]

11. Rummel, *Death by Government,* pp. 13, 31.

12. Rummel, *Death by Government,* p. 28.

13. See G. W. F. Hegel, *Introduction to the Philosophy of History,* trans. Leo Rauch (Indianapolis: Hackett, 1988), p. 24.

14. Elie Wiesel, *Legends of Our Time* (New York: Avon Books, 1972), p. 230.

15. If there is life beyond death, God's judgment may provide sanctions that condemn murder beyond all doubt and without remainder. Unfortunately, that outcome comes too

What Have You Done?

"What have you done?" God asked Cain after he murdered Abel. The slaughter-bench history of homicide, genocide, and democide, plus the potential of omnicide, calls into question the functional status of the sixth commandment. A commandment that is not obeyed may still be a commandment, but its functional status depends on obedience and credible sanctions against disobedience. An injunction that is not heeded lacks credibility. When Nazi Germany unleashed the Holocaust, the force of the injunction "You shall not murder" was impugned to the degree that millions of Jews were slaughtered. It took the violence of a massive world war, which left tens of millions more corpses in its wake, before the Third Reich was crushed and the Holocaust's genocidal killing centers were shut down. At least in biblical terms and in the Jewish and Christian traditions, God is the source and the ultimate vindicator of the sixth commandment. If God is not acknowledged and obeyed, God's existence is not necessarily eliminated, but God's authority is curtailed. And if God's authority lacks credibility, then the nature of God's existence is affected too. How has the sixth commandment functioned and fared in history? Two of the words that must be used in response to that question are "poorly" and "badly."

Disagreement

What does the sixth commandment reveal about humankind? Beyond the fact that human beings have often been what Richard Rhodes calls "masters of death" who flagrantly and repeatedly disobey the prohibition against murder, the commandment against murder can also make us contentious, confident, and confused. Those three qualities make an ill-fitting package.

A few weeks before writing this essay, I drove across the United States from Washington, D.C., to my home in California. I had spent the 2004-5 academic year at the United States Holocaust Memorial Museum, where I wrote a book about ethics during and after the Holocaust. On my way west, somewhere outside of Little Rock, Arkansas, a billboard caught my

---

late to be effective in history, for neither the murdered nor their murderers have returned to tell what God may have done with them. Nor has God made that situation crystal clear. Meanwhile, within history, murder is sometimes punished but not with sufficiently credible deterring impact. History's mounds of murdered dead grow larger and larger.

attention. Not the only one of its kind in the United States, it said: "You call it abortion. God calls it murder."

What about abortion? Few issues are more vexed than whether God calls abortion murder and how human beings know God's mind on that matter. More than once in this area, violence has eclipsed dialogue. What about euthanasia, another issue that pitted Americans, families even, against one another in 2005 in the media-hyped "right to die" case involving Terri Schiavo? Absent the sixth commandment and contention over the Decalogue, including wrangles over the relationship between civic displays of Exodus 20:1-17 and American constitutional requirements about the separation of church and state, it is hard to imagine that the Schiavo case would have riveted and ripped the republic as it did.[16]

The sixth commandment creates confidence, although not necessarily confidence that is warranted and wise, when people think they know exactly what it means and precisely to what it applies. But such claims, including their assumptions about "God's will," rarely produce more agreement than disagreement. Whether intended or unintended, one consequence of confidence about the meaning of the sixth commandment is often disagreement, frequently contentious disagreement. Typically, confusion — recognized and acknowledged or not — accompanies disagreement of that kind. It remains to be seen whether even the most careful inquiry can produce the clarity and insight that are needed, but such wrestling should be one of the sixth commandment's most critical byproducts.

Unmistakably, the sixth commandment declares that homicide is wrong. It requires us to find genocide and democide wrong as well. How it applies in other acts that take life away — along with war and capital punishment, abortion and euthanasia are two of the most crucial examples in our time — may not be as clear, but at the very least respect for the sixth commandment should make us deliberate thoughtfully and humbly as we wrestle with the silence, and therefore the need for interpretation, that is embedded in its unmistakable clarity that murder is forbidden.

16. It is not even clear that the disputes about the Schiavo case have been entirely laid to rest by the autopsy report released on June 15, 2005, which found that her collapse in 1990 had not been caused by physical abuse or poison but had left her with irreversible brain damage and in a condition that could properly be described as a persistent vegetative state. See, for example, Timothy Williams, "Schiavo's Brain Was Severely Deteriorated, Autopsy Says," *New York Times*, June 15, 2005.

What Has God Done?

In wrestling with the sixth commandment, God's question to Cain — "What have you done?" — can be put to God as well. God's prohibition of murder is clear, but arguably not clear enough because the commandment's meaning is neither completely self-evident nor as thoroughly detailed as it might be. Even if the taking of any life is in some sense wrong, and such a case can be made, God's specific positions — to the extent that they exist — on war, capital punishment, abortion, and euthanasia appear not to be entirely free of ambiguity, leaving men and women to contend for and about the interpretations that make the best sense. The complications, however, are not restricted to matters of interpretation. They also involve God's relation to murder, which is made the more troublesome because of the sixth commandment.

Could it be that the sixth commandment is violated by God, the very One who established it? That question does not imply, God forbid, that God is a murderer, but it does raise the possibility that God can be found wanting for failing to intervene against murderers and, to that extent, for being a bystander if not an accomplice when murder takes place.

When that possibility is raised, theology usually offers justifications or excuses for God in an exercise called *theodicy.* Where murder is concerned, theodicy typically gives God a pass by arguing that human beings and they alone are responsible for their actions because God gave them freedom to choose. Freedom's defense for God, however, is more problematic than it seems.[17] As homicide, genocide, and democide make clear, God's gift of freedom has taken an immensely murderous toll. History shows that human beings can and will use their freedom to murder wantonly and to a large extent with impunity because the murdering is never stopped soon enough. Auschwitz makes us ask, "Where was humanity?" Auschwitz can also make us ask, "Where is God?" and it does so because of the sixth commandment.

"You shall not murder" — this commandment reveals much about God. The revelation is awesome, but not only because God's commanding moral voice resounds within it. The revelation is also awesome because

---

17. For elaborations of my views on these matters, see, for example, my contributions to Stephen T. Davis, ed., *Encountering Evil: Live Options in Theodicy,* rev. ed. (Louisville: Westminster John Knox, 2001).

God's refusal or inability to prevent human beings from murdering one another ramps up humankind's responsibility for itself. The sixth commandment reveals God to be One who takes human accountability far more seriously than men and women are likely to do.

The Sixth Commandment and the Future

The sixth commandment will continue to be what I called it at the outset: the imperative that is the most necessary, although not sufficient, condition for human civilization. No less clear is the fact that this commandment will continue to be violated, often immensely and with a large measure of impunity. Furthermore, the God who prohibits murder is also the One who will do relatively little, if anything, to stop human beings from committing homicide, genocide, democide, and perhaps even omnicide.

The Jewish philosopher Emmanuel Levinas, who lost much of his family in the Holocaust, insisted that "You shall not murder" means nothing less than "you shall defend the life of the other."[18] The sixth commandment and the task Levinas rightly identifies as following from it show that nothing human, natural, or divine guarantees respect for either of those imperatives, but nothing is more important than making them our key responsibility, for they remain as fundamental as they are in jeopardy, as vitally important as they are threatened by humankind's murderous destructiveness and indifference.

18. Emmanuel Levinas, "In the Name of the Other," trans. Maureen V. Gedney, in *Is It Righteous to Be? Interviews with Emmanuel Levinas,* ed. Jill Robbins (Stanford: Stanford University Press, 2001), p. 192.

Response

Roger Brooks

I begin with deep appreciation for John Roth's essay. By proposing categories of historical action and definition, Roth provides a context for understanding the sixth commandment, "You shall not murder." Roth arranges human behavior along a line of prohibited acts, from most general — homicide — to most universal — omnicide.

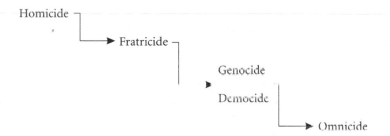

Roth's continuum is sophisticated because it compresses so many indices in one. *Number:* begin with a crime that targets an individual, then the family, then a nation or people, and finally all of humankind. *Purpose:* homicide and fratricide presumably target an individual for some perceived slight or wrongdoing; Cain killed Abel, for example, because God preferred the latter's sacrifice. Further down the continuum, though, the purpose is more conceptual: kill all the Jews, or annihilate all the enemies of a nation, or (most frighteningly) begin the nuclear exchange that might end human habitation of the planet. *Culpability:* although Roth doesn't move in this direction, common usage does. Somehow war crimes — genocide or democide — turn out to be more severe than "mere" homicide, and fratricide is so common as to scarcely warrant the evening news. Indeed, Roth's typology allows us to interrogate the sixth commandment deeply, both its followers and transgressors, and its commander, God himself.

This particular typology, with attention to the Holocaust as the exemplar of genocide, likewise reflects John Roth's entire career as philosopher, ethicist, and theologian. Through essays, books, and collections, he has proposed ways of approaching the terrible, and has allowed innumerable students and readers some conceptual clarity on the most troubling of human behavior: the Nazi mass murders of Jews during the Holocaust.

The utility of Roth's context, of course, suggests that we might profitably linger in other contexts as well. Indeed, Roth himself alludes to a midrashic context that likens the sixth commandment to the first. In what follows, I'll take Roth's lead and try to situate the sixth commandment more deeply in rabbinic dialogue.

Context I: What Could Be More Important?

Rabbinic literature links the Ten Commandments in a variety of ways, first to itself, and then to the great liturgical collection of biblical verses known as the Shema (Deut. 6:4-9; 11:13-21; Num. 15:37-41; it begins, "Hear, O Israel: The LORD is our God, the LORD alone!"). Each of these pairings reveals a critical bit of a larger understanding about "You shall not murder."

Consider the following text, which explains that committing murder diminishes God, citing Genesis's clear statement that we humans are stamped in God's image.

Mekilta Bahodesh Chapter Eight

In what arrangement were the Ten Commandments given? There were five on one tablet, and five on the other.

I. On the one was written, *"I the Lord am your God,"* and opposite it, *"You shall not murder"* — Scripture thus teaches that whoever sheds blood is regarded by Torah as if he had diminished the image of the divine King.

The matter may be compared to a human king who entered a city, where the people set up icons, made statues, and minted coins in his honor. Some time later, they overturned his icons, broke his statues, and mutilated his coins, thereby diminishing the image of the king. So, whoever sheds blood is regarded by Torah as if he had diminished the image of the divine King, for it is said, *"Whoever sheds the blood of human, [by humanity shall his blood be shed;] for in [God's] image did God make man"* (Gen. 9:6). . . .

It could not be more clear just how strongly linked we are to God himself, and not merely as recipients of the divine commandment. The rabbis' deep assertion, following Genesis, is that in our own essence we share in the divinity of God. Following the sixth commandment, then, is a powerful way of recognizing God's rule; and by contrast, the transgression of murder is a statement of unbelief that humanity shares anything with God, if not a denial of God himself.

A second text claims that by reciting the Shema prayer, Jews discharge their duty to recall the miraculous exodus from Egypt, since the Shema, line by line, contains references to each of the Ten Commandments, including "You shall not murder":

Jerusalem Talmud, *Berakhot* 1:5

Why should Jews recite the portions [that make up the Shema] two [times] each and every day?

. . . Rabbi Levi said, "[Jews should recite the Shema two times daily] because the Ten Commandments are contained within them. . . .

"(6) *'You shall not murder'* (Exodus 20:13a) — [corresponds to] *'and you will soon perish [from the good land that the Lord is assigning to you]'* (Deut. 11:17b), for anyone who murders will be murdered. . . ."

In Rabbi Levi's opinion, each word or phrase in the Shema prayer corresponds directly to one of the commandments. So recitation of that prayer was considered tantamount to reading and studying the Ten Commandments themselves. But, given his opinion, why recite the Shema twice daily (the question that prompted this entire passage)? The answer is implicit, supplied by the surrounding context in the Talmud. The first recitation of the Shema, in the morning, is to be taken at face value: each Jew proclaims the absolute monotheism of God, and restates the fundamentals of the covenant that binds the Jewish people to God alone. The evening recitation of the Shema, however, fulfills a separate duty incumbent upon all Jews, namely, remembrance of the exodus from Egypt during the evening prayers. The worshiper does this by reciting scriptural passages — the Shema — reminiscent of the Ten Commandments and the entire Sinaitic cycle.

As we have seen, this tightly and carefully constructed talmudic passage elegantly connects two great literary pieces of Jewish prayer. But it further indicates a theological position that reveals a paramount rabbinic conviction: the Ten Commandments are quintessential to Judaism. They are as basic and foundational as the simple assertion that there is but one God and that we should not murder one another. The rabbis, in short, were careful and attentive interpreters of Scripture and its injunctions. Just as the Ten Commandments stood as the highlight of God's Sinaitic revelation, and as the pinnacle of the entire story of the Israelites in Egypt, so rabbinic literature placed these laws at the heart of all Judaism.

Yet in rabbinic thought there was no actual daily reading of the Ten Commandments or of the rule "You shall not murder." Why? Precisely to underscore that rabbinic theology embraces the notion that God revealed the *entire* Pentateuch for Moses to record upon Mount Sinai. Each and every part of the written Scripture equally represents God's eternal law, God's Torah. The written law, Judaism holds, was accompanied by oral supplementary and complementary rules (later codified in the Mishnah). This belief in the integrity of the dual Torah — both written and oral — is the reason for the exclusion of the Ten Commandments from daily worship rites. If a single portion of the Torah were recited — especially a passage so central to the narrative of the Sinaitic theophany — people might be led to believe falsely that only that passage, the Ten Commandments, in fact was revealed at Mount Sinai, that the remainder was a later creation of lesser authority. The incisive rabbinic legislation prevents this type of exclusive importance being attached to the Ten Commandments.

Rabbinic literature, then, allows an apparent contradiction in its opinion to stand. The Ten Commandments represent the heart of all Judaic theology. But they are no more important than any other bit of the revealed law of Judaism.

Context II: Three Unforgivable Transgressions

Perhaps of equal interest, and addressing murder explicitly, is the epitome of the Torah's most serious laws: idolatry, fornication, and murder. These three are considered so serious that even force majeure offers no defense.

Bavli Sanhedrin 74a-b

Said Rabbi Jacob bar Zavedi, "I once asked Rabbi Abbahu, 'Didn't Zeira and Rabbi Yohanan say in the name of Rabbi Yannai, [or] Rabbi Yohanan in the name of Rabbi Simeon ben Yehozedeq:

"'They voted in the upper room of the house of Nitzeh in Lydda: "In regard to the Torah, how do we know that, if an idolater should force an Israelite to transgress one of the religious duties stated in the Torah, the [Israelite] should do so without incurring the death penalty, with the exception of idolatry, fornication, and murder? [Scripture states, *'You shall keep My laws and My rules, by the pursuit of which man shall live'* (Lev. 18:5)].""

These three sins cut to the heart of the rabbinic system, with its emphasis on holiness in matters of cult, family, and society: idolaters deny God's existence and sole sovereignty, thus destabilizing the Israelite religious world; fornicators and adulterers ignore normal familial ties, thereby destroying and tearing apart families; and most relevant to our context, murderers break the most basic social aspects of the covenant, making normal life in community next to impossible. So damaging are these three sins that, whether in public or private, no matter what type of duress is applied, a Jew may not be forgiven for such transgressions.

Conclusion

What do the rabbinic contexts add to John Roth's essay? Two things, I think. First, the seriousness with which rabbinic literature takes murder — one of three unforgivable sins — underscores Roth's continuum in definition of homicide. This is no simple crime. Homicide destabilizes everything from society to divinity. In each of the more extreme forms of which Roth reminds us, the destabilization is even worse. Roth's impulse to read human history as scarred by transgression of the sixth commandment corresponds to rabbinic impulses to see the same within the structure of the revealed law.

Second, the rabbis' equation of murder with diminishment of God himself neatly adjoins Roth's idea that there is something of a nexus here, in the sixth commandment, between humanity and God. Roth proposes questions directly aimed at lessons about us and about God, and he sees that parallel in the commandment's very existence; the rabbis do the same by equating victim and deity.

Response

Jean Bethke Elshtain

John K. Roth's "What Have You Done?" condenses centuries of history and theology into a pithy and provocative essay. Most helpfully, he reminds us at the outset of the great mischief unwittingly wrought by those who brought us that masterwork of English prose, the King James Version of the Bible. For the sixth commandment is best translated "Thou shalt not murder" rather than "Thou shalt not kill." If only . . . one ponders. If only . . . perhaps it wouldn't have been so difficult for Christians in the English-speaking world to sort things out in the matter of killing versus *wrongful death*, i.e., murder, if the commandment had been more accurately translated in the first instance. But then again, perhaps not. Given the person of Jesus the Christ, it is inevitable that Christians must think long and hard about killing. Period. The pity is that this has often been done so indiscriminately.

One example I sometimes give my students goes something like this: You are a moral philosopher and you happen upon a body lying facedown on a stone walk in a garden. It is clear that the hapless person is dead. Dried blood has oozed forth from some sort of wound. You must ponder the possibilities. Did the person slip, fall, strike his head and die as a result of the blow? We call this an accident, and no one is culpable. Or perhaps the person was jolted accidentally by another walker, tripped, and fell. What then? Well, it remains an accident. The other walker did not *intend* the man's death. But a degree of culpability may remain, especially so in this instance because no one stepped forward to get assistance when the accident occurred. Leaving the scene of an accident is actionable, and if the accident victim dies the culpability rises correlatively. But still, we do not charge anyone with murder. There is a third possibility. You look closer and notice a knife sticking out of the victim's back. He has been murdered, i.e., he is a victim of wrongful killing. Full culpability is assumed on the part of the agent. (Of course, once the law kicks in, it may be that there are extenuating circumstances; it may be that the perpetrator is mentally deranged, etc. But the central point remains.)

Why does the difference between intentional and unintentional death seem too difficult for so many to sort out? In part, I suspect, it flows from the handiness of being in possession of a trump card: I throw down the sixth commandment and put you on the defensive immediately — if you are trying to make a case for a justified war, or for capital punishment, or for restriction on abortion-on-demand. None of us wishes to be deprived of a guaranteed trump in a debate. To leave it at this, however, would be reductionistic. Surely there are other, and better, reasons at work. What might some of these misunderstandings flow from?

First, many Christians embrace the view that the early Christians, the first Christians, were full and unambiguous pacifists. The question of killing animals may not have been joined, but certainly any killing of human beings was ruled out, and this they practiced. The fact that the historical record is far more ambiguous than such a repristination narrative suggests does little to shake loose this conviction. It follows that all of Christian history, save for the clusters of perfectionist souls along the way, is a tale of decline, and many of the greats in the tradition — Augustine, Aquinas, Luther, Calvin — are part of the problem.

Second, many Christians consider themselves under a strong obligation to offer on this earth a kind of foreshadowing of the peace of the kingdom to come. This means Christian practice should come as close as humanly possible to what that peace means — that the lion lies down with the lamb, swords are beat into plowshares, and nations and peoples know war no more. Nor any sort of violence. This is a powerful and, in many ways, a noble ideal. The problem enters when the ideal turns into a rigid ideology and stirs its advocates to cry "peace, peace" when there is no peace — as, for example, in the run-up to World War II when so many Christian pastors and ministers advocated a form of isolationism and preached a moral equivalence between embattled Great Britain and Hitler's Third Reich. Surely, however, concern with the kingdom should mean concern with what is happening to what Dietrich Bonhoeffer called "the bleeding brothers and sisters of Jesus Christ," his reference point being the Jewish people suffering under Hitler's brutal regime.

Third, there is undoubtedly a theodicy at work in the advocacy of many who disdain any distinction between killing and murder. It probably runs along lines that require casting out from memory those moments in Scripture when God calls for the use of coercive force and imposes a harsh justice on his enemies. What I reference here is, in other words, a kind of New Testament exclusivism, as if it was a mistake for Christianity to be saddled with the story of the people of Israel and the God of the Old Testament. Now, admittedly, few own up to this explicitly, but I suspect it is at work rather often. We resist mightily this God of justice in favor of what we take to be the New Testament advocacy of mercy. We then weld a vision of justice onto this vision of mercy and call it "peace" — but justice in any meaningful sense really falls away.

There can be no sort of earthly justice, save in small circles of friends and family and in one's church family (hopefully), without coercive force. One needs to *execute* laws, not just pass them. Force was called upon to enforce *Brown v. Board*. Martin Luther King and the Southern Christian Leadership Conference used militant nonviolence to call down the violence of others upon them, triggering thereby the full enforcement arm of the federal government, including federalizing the National Guard in a number of southern states. It is a chimera to assume one can have any measure of justice in a polity that neglects the power of enforcement. We want God's hands to be pristine, and we think the use of force somehow precludes this.

Many find they cannot put together the often fierce God of justice with the Christ of the New Testament. But the complexity of Christianity requires precisely that. Roth's challenging essay prods us to raise these questions all over again, and in so doing, performs an essential service.

Sexuality and Marriage

Carl E. Braaten

You shall not commit adultery.

In this chapter I will follow the lead of Martin Luther, who interpreted the seventh commandment of the Decalogue, "You shall not commit adultery," as applicable to every kind of unchastity in thought, word, and deed. Of course, here Luther was being guided by the example of Jesus, as reported in Matthew 5:28: "But I say to you that everyone who looks at a woman with lust has already committed adultery with her in his heart." In the same vein we will emulate the pattern of the Judeo-Christian ethical tradition that does not limit the explanation of this commandment to adultery as the specific form of unchastity that occurs by either partner in marriage. Related issues bearing on sexuality and marriage will also be considered.

The rabbit has become the symbol of contemporary America's obsession with sex. It was the founding trademark of the Playboy philosophy. As a symbol, it intends to commend not only the sexual behavior for which the bunny gained its reputation, but also an attitude that, like the bunny's, is frolicsome and sportive, morally unreflective and spontaneous in matters of sex. A widespread conviction prevails that traditional moral codes cannot cope with the magnitude of the sexual revolution that has swept American society in recent decades. Loud and frequent are the calls for a new morality suitable for these postmodern times — which to those who cling to traditional morality seem more like a cover for plain old-fashioned immorality.

This is an essay in Christian theological ethics. I define Christian ethics as disciplined reflection on the question of what we ought to do here and now on the basis of God's creative and redemptive activity as revealed through the Holy Scriptures. As such we will make statements on sexuality and marriage of a different order than those we find in textbooks of biology, psychology, or sociology. Science deals with what is; ethics deals with what ought to be. The two modes of discourse should never be confused. To be sure, theological ethics should take pains to be informed by the scientific disciplines, but it may very well assert things that directly conflict with current views about sex and marriage that claim the authority of modern science.

Human Sexuality in the Order of Creation

In the book of Genesis (1:27) we read: "So God created man (singular) in his image, in the image of God he created them (plural); male and female he created them." This passage is the *locus classicus* for the biblical affirmation of the dignity and goodness of human sexuality. The humanity God created in his own image is not a solitary individual but precisely male and female in their complementary sexual differences. A single human being cannot reflect the image of God, for God has revealed himself as essentially love. Love implies a relationship between a lover and the beloved. Human sexuality is the means that God built into man and woman to draw them toward each other. God saw that it would not be good for man to live alone, for alone man could not give and receive love. And without love there would be no human analogy for the love of God, no imprint in humanity of the divine essence.

The bipolarity of the sexes belongs to the basic structure of human existence. There is no one who is not either male or female, a fact inherent in the way God created humans and one that is unmistakably visible in our anatomies. The fact of sexuality cannot be explained as a result of humanity's fall into sin. The idea that human sexuality is part of the original design of the Creator has not always been clearly supported by the Christian tradition. Christian ethics must therefore affirm today, on the basis of the integral part of sex in God's creative intention for humanity, that any religiously motivated contempt for one's sexuality is a blasphemy of the Creator. Sexuality is not a source of sin.

136

Sex and the Dimensions of Love

Sexuality is a profound element in the mystery of human love that reaches its highest goal in the "one flesh" union of man and woman. When it reaches this goal, human love becomes a parable of God's love for his people Israel and Christ's love for his church. Sex and love find their fulfillment within the framework of marriage. Of course, they also exist and seek expression prior to and outside the marital situation. Human beings become sexually vital in their early teens and fall romantically in love perhaps several times before becoming totally committed in marriage. Before taking up the Christian doctrine of marriage, it is useful to analyze the nature and meaning of sex in relation to the various dimensions of love.

As the saying goes, love is a many-splendored thing. Humans are endowed with a basic sexual urge, a phenomenon they share with all other animals. We will use the Latin word *libido* — which Freud made popular — to designate this type of love. The *libido* drives man and woman to unite sexually with each other. This *libido*-love is part of the scheme of God's creation, and is therefore natural and good. The sexual act expresses the desire for self-fulfillment in the abandonment of oneself to another person. This is the way it ought to be, the very way God made humans. However, because *libido* has become perverted by sin, it expresses itself instead as an egocentric impulse toward an infinite experience of pleasure for its own sake. *Libido* is a surging power driving humans in a frantic chase for ecstasy. The ecstasy of sex, however, lasts but a few seconds. *Libido* is insatiable; its thirst for pleasure is unquenchable.

The *libido* is not only fleeting, but also fickle. It fastens on to no special person. Anybody will do — even prostitutes and animals. The other person is an exchangeable commodity in the economy of libido. Who the other person is does not matter so long as the *libido* uses the other person as an instrument to fill a biological need or to get rid of some tensions. This is a description of *libido* in the state of perversion. The inherent purpose of *libido* to drive the self into union with the other self is frustrated as the *libido* becomes self-seeking and autonomous; it becomes a law unto itself. The *libido* takes over and leaves in its wake a wreckage of every personal relationship. Literature is replete with examples of Don Juans and Casanovas.

The self-destructive tendency of a fleeting, fickle, and frustrative *libido* raises the question of its possible personalization. The answer is that the *libido* is rarely by itself. Usually it is incorporated into another dimension of love, which we will call *eros* — to use Plato's term. *Eros* is the type of love that is attracted by the inherent beauty and loveliness of the other person. *Eros* is usually spoken of as romantic love; it includes but transcends sexual desire. Two lovers want each other as whole persons and not only to be the stimulus of the other's sexual glands.

Western culture has made romantic love its ideal and the basis for the grand march of couples into marriage — and out of it. As falling in love becomes the sufficient reason for getting married, falling out of love then becomes the adequate excuse for getting a divorce. While romantic *eros* helps to personalize the *libido*, it shares the same fickle and fleeting character. It is one thing to get a man and a woman together, quite another to keep them together. Two persons head over heels in love possess the irrational belief that their love will last forever. When the glow of the romance fades away, they realize that *eros* gives them no power to keep the promises they made while under its spell.

Where is the love capable of sustaining the personal union of a man and a woman after the *libido* has cooled off and the emotions of *eros* lose their spontaneity? There is such a love, which Aristotle called *philia*. Two persons unite when they are driven by *libido* and attracted by *eros;* but the quality of this union depends on whether they can grow in the love of friendship — *philia*. The frailties of *libido* and *eros* need the strength of companionship that generates the altruistic virtues of constancy, fidelity, and loyalty. *Philia*-love is absolutely essential in order that the inherent purpose of *libido* and *eros* might be realized, namely, profound union with the other partner and ever-increasing penetration of the mystery of selfhood. This is the type of love involved between aged couples who have long since outlived their earlier libidinous and erotic attractions for each other. *Philia*-love offers a profound analogy of divine love, for it is blessed with the virtue of faithfulness.

All the types of love we have portrayed are poisoned by the unrelenting egoism that lies in the depths of human experience. Even the best of friends at times have a falling out. There is another dimension of love that makes it possible to forgive the humanly unforgivable. The New Testament writers chose the Greek word *agape* to name this type of love. It is a forgiving, self-sacrificing, and suffering love, whose paradigmatic occurrence took place, according to the Christian message, in the passion of Christ.

Agape-love has a concrete application in the dimension of sexual relations. It expresses itself in the interest of the other person; it is unselfish and other-directed. When the other types of love break down, it perseveres. It stands at the extremity opposite *libido*. *Libido* is primarily interested in filling its own need, *agape* in filling the need of the other. *Libido* is impatient; it demands immediate satisfaction. *Agape* is disciplined and patiently accepts the challenge of pleasing the other person, even when at times the task seems hopeless. Paradoxically, even the *libido* is satisfied only when *agape* has its way, for in a real sense the *libido* cannot be satisfied, except in the most superficial physiological sense, until the other person shares in the joy of sexual ecstasy.

The progression in the stages of love from *libido* to *agape* can be completed only in marriage and finally only in a monogamous marriage. The point is this: if one consults the instincts of one's own *libido*, one would scarcely opt for marriage, let alone a monogamous marriage. But if the other person in the love affair is consulted, he or she will want to be "the only one." Even *eros* will tolerate no third party; it is basically monistic. Lovers feel that "two is company, three is a crowd." *Philia* in this progression is even more narrowing, for a profound development of a marital companionship is a task that can be realized only in a lifelong one-to-one relationship. Sharing certain intimacies of one's life with many persons would mean that they lose all significance for any. And finally the dimension of *agape*-love gains its deepest meaning from the marriage symbolism that discloses the mystery of Yahweh's monogamous love for his people Israel and Christ's faithful love for his one bride, the church.

Deviations of Sexual Behavior

We have affirmed that marriage is the goal but not the only medium of sex and love. It is obvious that members of both sexes, single and married, enter into daily relations that have sexual and erotic undertones. What are the ethical limit and criterion of erotic interplay that goes on outside of marriage? To answer this question we will need to invoke the nature of love in all its dimensions, the dignity of personhood, and the integrity of marriage. One could say with Karl Barth that "in this matter everything is good which in the full and strict sense is compatible with marriage, and everything is bad which is not so compatible" (Karl Barth, *Church Dogmatics* III/4, p. 140). The ultimate criterion of sex is marriage, and not only love, because marriage is the telos of love.

In this limited study we will bypass certain forms of sexual abnormality against which there has been not only a clear ethical consensus but also a weighty body of medical, sociological, and psychological opinion. We have in mind such deviations as exhibitionism, rape, incest, and zoophilia. There are numerous prohibitions against such practices in the Bible, in the Judeo-Christian tradition, in the codes of other societies and present-day legal systems. Few if any would champion the removal of the traditional taboos against such behaviors. The matter is somewhat different with prostitution and homosexuality. Whereas the negative verdict of the biblical-Christian tradition is equally clear on these things, society today is in the process of revising some of its attitudes as a result of modern scientific studies, the moral relativism of the dominant secular anthropologies, the demise of religious authority in the public realm, and the decline of moral standards within the churches. In this state of flux and oscillating opinions on moral questions, Christian ethics will need to address those patterns of sexual behavior that abrogate the divine intention embedded in the structures of love and marriage.

The specifically Christian point of view on prostitution may be said to be the reverse of the legal point of view — compassion for the prostitute and a harsh judgment on the one who visits her. This stems from Jesus' attitude toward prostitutes. Of course, prostitution is clearly recognized as sinful, but in Jesus' estimate the sins of pride and of the spirit are much more treacherous, and these sins often afflict most those who sit in judgment on the prostitutes. Harlots will go into the kingdom of God before the chief priests and the elders of the people (Matt. 21:31). The point Jesus is making is that the prostitute knew that she was a sinner in need of forgiveness. When the woman caught in the act of adultery was dragged before Jesus, he said, "Neither do I condemn you. Go your way, and from now on do not sin again" (John 8:11). The sin is not condoned, but the sinner is offered forgiving love.

The person who has sexual intercourse with a prostitute, however, is doing something that has negative consequences for his relation to Christ. Saint Paul in 1 Corinthians 6 argues that the Christian is faced with a clear alternative: union with Christ or union with a prostitute. "Do you not know that he that is joined to a harlot is one body?" Sexual intercourse brings about a union that leaves an indelible imprint on the persons involved. The sexual act cannot be divorced from the center of one's selfhood, the heart of a person. In uniting with a prostitute the person is affecting (perhaps also infecting) the very depths of his being and revealing where his ultimate loyalty lies. The sexual act can never be a neutral and ephemeral occurrence. Involved in it, willy-nilly, is an expression of one's interior life and its relation to God and other persons. The whole meaning of sex in the progression of love that leads to a permanent and profound relationship with another person in marriage is emasculated by prostitution.

It is still a matter of scientific debate whether homosexuality has a biological basis or is the result of cultural conditioning traceable to early childhood experiences. Christian ethics is in no position to take sides on this psychological question. Its chief concern is not to explain homosexuality but to lay the theological basis for the pastoral care of homosexuals. Yet, the psychological question does have direct social consequences. The widespread acceptance of the biological explanation of homosexuality is behind current attempts to justify it and to make it socially acceptable. If homosexuals are made that way, the reasoning goes, they have a moral right to express what is natural to them. Within recent decades this way of thinking has been gaining ground not only in society at large but also among theologians and within Christian circles.

On the basis of the Christian view of the polarity of the sexes grounded in the "image of God," homosexuality must be regarded as contrary to the divine intention for human sexuality. This statement is ethically normative even though one might accept the biological theory of homosexuality. The mere fact that some homosexuals may be born with such a predisposition does not necessarily mean that it is God's design for humanity. What we often call "natural" is the good creation in the state of its fallen condition. Homosexuality, however natural it might seem in the biological sense, is not rooted in the order of creation in the theological sense. It was not as a biologist but as a theologian that the apostle Paul regarded homosexuality as absolutely contrary to the ordering of human relations intended by God. On account of sin God's intention is being frustrated in the sexual dimension as well as everywhere else.

It is much easier to demonstrate that homosexuality is physiologically, psychologically, socially, and ethically abnormal than to heal the condition. It is, moreover, not merely a question of healing the homosexual; society itself needs to be healed. Many homosexuals would not think of going to their pastor, for instance, for fear of being rejected by moralistic indignation. Most homosexuals have already accepted the fact of their abnormality; their life is a continual round of struggle and defeat; they know they need help. Because of traditional repugnance of homosexuality, widespread ignorance of the problem, moralistic attitudes in the church, and legal hazards in society, the homosexual is often far removed from easy access to the ministrations of healing.

For Christians the ethical problem soon becomes a matter of pastoral care. How can the church help homosexuals to be "cured" so far as that is possible, to accept their condition for what it is, to sublimate their sexual urges, and to live by forgiveness in this aspect of life too? Homosexuals are not helped at all by anyone pretending that their condition is normal after all. The burden on the church today is not so much to revise its belief that homosexuality is a deviation from the divine purpose of sex, to which the Scriptures abundantly testify, but more to change its attitude toward those afflicted by this condition and to open up channels to help them. From the point of view of the church's ministry of healing, it makes no real difference whether homosexual practice is theologically spoken of as "sin" or psychiatrically spoken of as "sickness." The grace of love and compassion is needed in either case.

A Theological Perspective on Marriage

Marriage as a basic institution of society is believed by Christians to be a mandate and gift of God to his children. The biological and personal drives of sex and love are the means God uses to pressure persons to enter into marriage. God's creative work is done in this entirely natural way. God's word is heard not so much as a voice from above but as a pressure from below that is universally effective, even among people who know not God. People may do God's will even against their will because God is a living, active power in every nerve and sinew of their being.

Christians thus do not understand marriage to be a specifically Christian phenomenon in the order of redemption. Luther spoke of it as a "worldly thing." What he meant is that marriage is as much a part of God's intention for man and woman as for the lilies to grow in the field or for the birds to fly in the sky. As divinely instituted, each marriage in its concrete particularity is from the hand of God. Those who enter into marriage involve themselves in a state that God himself has ordained and over which he rules. Marriage is thus not merely a contract between two persons who just happen to be in love. Whether married persons know it or not, God has built certain demands and gifts into marriage and exerts his will through them. All people are involved with the living God and participate in the same structures of creation and are accountable to the same law of God. The facts of life — of sex, love, and marriage — are the same for believers and nonbelievers alike.

Marriage takes on a special meaning for those who view it biblically as an earthly reality that points to the mystery of God's covenant love. In the Bible God's relation to his covenant people Israel and Christ's relation to his church are symbolized by the love between a husband and a wife (Eph. 5:25-33). The choice of marital love as a parable of divine love does not elevate marriage into a supernatural order; instead it consecrates and sanctifies marriage in all its true naturalness. There is a reciprocal action between the symbol and that which it symbolizes. If marital love, say, the love of Hosea for his faithless wife Gomer (Hos. 3:1ff.), gives us a glimpse of God's love for Israel and Christ's love for his church, then this divine love in turn becomes the prototype of how a husband and wife ought to love each other. The order of marriage in the realm of creation is thus connected with the history of God's redemptive action in Christ. The power of God's love makes it possible to realize more fully the meaning of marriage under the conditions of sin. The gospel does not bring a new kind of marriage but a new insight and a new power to live responsibly within the order that comes from God's creative and providential activity.

The Structure of Marriage

In the Christian view marriage is a union of one man and one woman in a lifelong partnership of mutual love and help. Marriage is intended to be a lifelong union. According to God's design, it is indissoluble. The biblical expression of this conviction is that "the two shall become one flesh." No one has the right to sunder what God has put together (Matt. 19:5-6). The marriage covenant made by a couple is unconditionally valid — no strings attached. It is for better or worse as long as the two shall live. The entire meaning of marriage is vitiated when it is regarded as a temporary expedient or social convenience to be dissolved when either of the partners wants out.

Marriage can attain its most perfect state only if it is monogamous. Many people today seem to doubt this and take great delight in proving

143

that monogamy is only a relative social datum. It just happens to be our marriage custom, our preferred convention. Any notion that it is better than polygamy or polyandry is supposedly only a case of ethnocentrism. Besides, polygamy was commonly practiced in ancient Israel and is nowhere explicitly condemned in the early church.

Cultural anthropologists are surely right in showing that monogamy was not the most primitive, universal, or dominant institution of ancient societies. Despite this, Christian theology would still assert that monogamy is God's intention for marriage. Christians are ultimately persuaded by the fact that the New Testament picture of marital love as a parable of Christ's love for his church presupposes monogamy. The love that husbands and wives are exhorted to show toward each other precludes multilateral relations with other persons.

Although the ideal of monogamy arose only gradually in the course of history, Christians see in this development a revelation of God's will. The strong conviction that monogamy is God's standard for marriage arose among Gentile Christians in connection with the apostolic preaching of the gospel of love. The bride and groom are fully devoted to each other as Christ and his church are bound to each other. There is no room in this relationship for another lover and no toleration of marriage as a part-time partnership. Therefore, biblical Christians will always maintain the ideal of monogamy. It alone makes sense of everything else they know about sex and love in light of God's revelation. Just as the love between a man and a woman must be less than full if it is not lifelong, so must it be less than perfect if it is shared with a third party. Indissolubility and monogamy are interdependent.

Premarital and Extramarital Intercourse

Traditional proscriptions against premarital intercourse have been exploded by precautionary measures invented by modern science. Parents who counseled their teenagers against premarital sex relied on the triple threat of "conception, infection, detection." Modern methods of contraception and public education on sex and venereal disease have, however, deprived this triple threat of any real force.

God's command regarding sex and marriage is valid in spite of the none too glamorous statistics gathered by pollsters about the sexual misbehavior of American men and women. But they say, "Everybody is doing it." That does not make it right. Statistics do not alter the specifically ethical dimension of the problem. In expounding the seventh commandment against adultery, we have inquired into the will and law of God mediated more broadly through the very structures of sex, love, and marriage, that is, through natural life and the echoes of that commandment in the human conscience (natural law). All persons, Bible-believing or not, may gain a partial knowledge of the inherent meaning of sex and love through their moral conscience, and share the biblical prohibitions against sexual activity outside of marriage. The Christian understanding of sex as an inseparable dimension of the totality of love that can attain its consummate fulfillment in marriage alone provides the basis of the church's teaching ruling out venereal experiences before and outside of marriage. There is thus no ethical basis for distinguishing between premarital and extramarital sex. In either case it is inconsistent with genuine love involving commitment and obligation between two persons in an enduring relationship.

The refusal of sexual adventure outside of marriage may be expressed further by the fact that the Bible uses the word "know" *(yadah)* as a symbol for the act of sexual intercourse. This suggests a personal involvement of two persons totally committed to each other, and if totally, then not only for a few fleeting moments. Further, a total commitment to the other person in love means that the erotic element may not be disconnected from the dimension of agape and the sworn fidelity that it engenders. This agape-love makes an egocentric person allocentric, that is to say, more solicitous of the other person.

An encounter in depth between two persons in love demands continuity of expression. The sexual act is not to be the end of an urge but the beginning of a new relationship in which the various dimensions of love can find fulfillment only within the institution of marriage. Premarital intercourse is immoral because it appropriates a privilege without accepting a correlative responsibility for the ensuing well-being of the other person.

Marriage and Celibacy

Marriage is a vocation, a calling from God. It is not the only possible calling, however. Celibacy may also be accepted as a divine summons. This has been largely forgotten in the Protestant tradition. Being single is often viewed as a pitiable fate rather than as a possible vocation within the scope of Christian freedom. The Reformation did not make marriage a binding law for all Christians, but it aimed to liberate religious people from the widespread belief that virginity was superior to marriage. The Council of Trent even pronounced an anathema against those who deny that it is better to remain a virgin or celibate than to get married. For Luther the reformer, marriage was a holy estate, pleasing to God, and by no means inferior to the ideal of celibacy. In the order of redemption Christians are free to remain single or to marry as a matter of choice. What matters is that, whether married or single, Christians live out their calling by grace through faith.

Divorce and Remarriage

Marriage as a lifelong fellowship between one man and one woman is an institution subject to the destructive powers of sin and death at work in human existence. In the Christian view a marriage ends with the death of one of the persons, and the surviving partner is free to marry again. But a marriage can also be destroyed by the power of sin. It can end in a legal divorce that confirms the radically spiritual alienation of two persons. The New Testament understands divorce as sin. When divorce is permitted, it is never condoned. According to Matthew 19:8, divorce has become a necessary expedient on account of the "hardness of heart." It is not sufficient to speak of divorce merely in terms of an "error of judgment" or a "bad mistake."

Most modern scholars agree that Jesus' word against divorce was originally given without any qualifications whatsoever, such as we find in Mark 10:11 and Luke 16:18. In these passages it is said that whoever divorces and remarries commits adultery. However, in the Matthew parallel to these passages (19:9), Jesus is made to introduce one qualification — "except for fornication." This is generally now considered to be an instance of the later church adjusting the absolute form of Jesus' teaching to meet the emergency situations of daily life. The absolutes of Jesus, inseparable from his radical eschatological outlook, had to be reshaped to meet the practical needs of church members. Later Paul adds another qualification to the absolute rule against divorce, namely, when the unbeliever in a marriage takes the initiative to break up the marriage (1 Cor. 7:15).

The Christian church must clearly teach that basically there are no grounds for divorce that can excuse it or atone for its sin and guilt. Divorce must always be considered an emergency measure, a rescue operation, to be encouraged only when the marriage has been shattered beyond repair. When a marriage is filled with bitterness and the atmosphere is so charged with hostility that the life and health of parents or children are threatened, whoever is at fault, Christian counselors must not flinch from trying to work out the best solution for the well-being of all concerned.

In view of the fact that the content and scope of the church's discipline have had an increasingly diminishing significance in the lives of Christian people, it is a rather idle question to ask whether divorced persons may remarry. Christians, like others, do remarry, usually at the first opportunity. In light of the church's double-barreled message of God's law and his forgiving love, the church's pastoral approach should be determined not by the guilt or innocence of the persons involved, but rather in accordance with readiness to enter into a new relationship, fully aware of God's infinite mercy to make all things new, in spite of their sin and guilt. Above all, an evangelical approach in pastoral ministry regards it as an unjustifiable restriction on the unlimited scope of God's grace to excommunicate divorced persons who remarry. God's grace is sufficient not only to forgive past sins but also to open the door to new possibilities.

Response

Elliot N. Dorff

Dr. Braaten has done us all a great favor in clearly articulating a Christian perspective not only on adultery, but on sex and marriage generally. Because I have written extensively on the Jewish tradition's perception of sex and marriage in my book *Love Your Neighbor and Yourself: A Jewish Approach to Personal Ethics* (Philadelphia: Jewish Publication Society, 2003), instead of repeating that here I will use the order of Dr. Braaten's paper to respond to some of his points from a Jewish perspective.

I say *a* Jewish perspective and not *the* Jewish perspective because as soon as one becomes familiar with the Jewish tradition, one recognizes that it is a very feisty tradition that revels in argument. One standard Jewish joke, in fact, is that wherever there are two Jews, there are at least three opinions — but someone asked me recently whether you really need two Jews to have three opinions! Moreover, since the demise of the Sanhedrin (Supreme Court) in 361 c.e., there has been no central Jewish authority to define official Jewish belief or practice. These facts do not make Judaism incoherent; in fact, I will describe below mainstream Jewish beliefs about the topics Dr. Braaten addresses, indicating where I disagree with them. This active, argumentative approach to life, though, means that on some of these issues, at least, individual Jews may well have a different opinion.

The Seventh Commandment

One can see immediately that Judaism and Christianity are indeed different religions in that Jews understand the Ten Commandments as part of a much larger structure of 613 commandments in the Torah (= the five books of Moses). Although the Torah singles out these commandments as "the ten words" (literally, Decalogue; Exod. 34:28; Deut. 4:13; 10:4) and depicts their announcement amid thunder, lightning, and earthquakes on Mount Sinai (Exod. 19–20), these commandments have no greater authority in Jewish law than do any of the other 603.

This context is important because the classical rabbis — the teachers and interpreters of the Jewish tradition whose thought is contained in the Mishnah (edited ca. 200 C.E.), Talmud (edited ca. 500 C.E.), and other works of rabbinic literature — had many other commandments on which to base a Jewish view of sex and marriage. The tradition therefore understood this commandment as referring specifically and exclusively to *adultery*. This did *not* include, as it did for Jesus, a prohibition against having sexual desires for people other than one's spouse, as long as one did not act on them. Thus when President Jimmy Carter confessed that he "lusted in his heart," I remember saying to myself, "So what else is new?" After all, we all have such inner feelings and cannot be held responsible for controlling them. What we can and must control is what we do with such feelings.

Even with regard to the physical act of adultery, the rabbis narrowed the prohibition to cover only a married man having sex with a woman married to someone else or a married woman having sex with a man other than her husband. It did not include a man (married or not) having sex with a single woman. That was because polygamy, although discouraged, was still legal in those times. The Torah's rule protecting the primogeniture rights of the unloved wife's firstborn son (Deut. 21:15-17) and its stories about the conflicts among Abraham's and Jacob's wives (Gen. 21:9-21; 30:1-22) already indicate that it saw polygamy as less than ideal, and the rabbis imposed a number of burdens on the husband (e.g., to support them in separate dwellings, to have sex with each of them a minimal number of times per week) to make it distasteful, if not impossible, for a man to do within the bounds of the law. Still, because it was legal at that time, a man who had sex with a single woman had not committed adultery. If she was a prostitute, she would be flogged for that (Deut. 23:18), the punishment based on the rabbis' application of Deuteronomy 25:1-3 to all negative commandments where some other punishment was not specified (*Sifre* on Lev. 25:2; Babylonian Talmud, *Sanhedrin* 10a; *Makkot* 2b), but lashes are far short of the death penalty prescribed for adultery (Lev. 20:10). If she was not a prostitute and he later married her, that was simply a first or second marriage, but he is punished for his act of premarital sex by never being allowed to divorce her; if he did not marry her, he had to pay a fine (Deut. 22:28-29) and could be flogged by the court for indecent behavior, but, again, all these consequences are far short of execution. Finally, sexual behavior short of intercourse did not qualify as adultery; one became liable only when penetration occurred (Maimonides, *Mishneh Torah, Laws of Forbidden Intercourse* 1:10). The rabbis narrowed the commandment in these ways not only because of the legitimacy of polygamy at the time but also because they were squeamish about the death penalty and wanted to apply it as rarely as possible. So for Jews the seventh commandment is really only about adultery and only as defined above.

Human Sexuality in the Order of Creation

In this section Dr. Braaten takes a courageous stand in rejecting those elements of the Christian tradition that defined sex as a product and producer of sin. The Jewish tradition never saw sex that way. The Torah, first of all, says that when God created human beings — and that includes the sexual parts of human beings — he declared his new creation "very good" (Gen. 1:31). Judaism understands sex as it understands all our other human faculties (body, mind, emotions, will, the ability to interact with others, etc.) — namely, that these are all morally neutral abilities we have; what makes any one of them morally good or bad is how we use them. The Torah, then, is, as its name literally means, a book of instruction whose commandments, beliefs, and stories define for us what constitutes a good and bad use of these powers.

The Jewish tradition very much believes, as the Torah states, that "it is not good for a man to live alone," and therefore marriage is the ideal. In fact, that is so much the case that Judaism does *not* uphold a divine calling — or even the permission — to remain celibate. The second chapter in Genesis (2:18) describes the human being as needing a spouse, and the first chapter commands humans to "be fruitful and multiply" (Gen. 1:28; see also 9:1, 7); celibacy obviously precludes fulfilling that need and that commandment. Furthermore, sex is a major source of pleasure and as such is a gift from God. Therefore the rabbis note that the Torah instructs a Nazirite, who takes a vow to abstain from wine and cutting his or her hair for a period of time, to bring a sin offering at the end of that period (Num. 6:14); on the basis of that, the rabbis maintain that it is actually a sin to abstain from the pleasures of life that God has provided for us within the bounds of the law (*Sifre Numbers* 30; Babylonian Talmud, *Ta'anit* 11a-11b), for that is an act of ingratitude to God. As a result, the Talmud actually looks down upon rabbis who are not married (*Kiddushin* 29b-30a) and asserts that "A man is forbidden to remain single even if he has children from a previous marriage" (*Yevamot* 61b). This is not just an ancient attitude. When I was in rabbinical school (1966-70), at a time when the Conservative movement ordained only men, we were told that if we were not married by the time we were ordained, we should be aware that the women of the congregation's sisterhood would do everything in their power to get us married fast! And this is not true for men alone; the Talmud already states several times over that a widowed woman would much prefer to remarry than to remain alone (*Yevamot* 118b; *Ketubbot* 75a; *Kiddushin* 7a, 41a) — and so the Jewish community has historically seen it as its duty to help women as well as men find suitable mates through the agency of the matchmaker *(shadhan).*

The Torah actually prescribes two commandments that apply to sex, and so it sees sex as fulfilling two independent functions in the order of creation. One, as we have seen, is procreation. The other is based on Exodus 21:10, according to which, as the rabbis understood that verse, when a man marries a woman "her food, her clothing, and her conjugal rights he may not diminish." In most cultures to our own day, the presumption is that only men want to have sex; women tolerate the sexual advances of their husbands because they want children and financial security. The rabbis eighteen hundred years ago, however, presume that women want the pleasures of sex just as much as men do, and so in explicating this verse they assert that a man has the duty to offer to have sex with his wife as often as his line of work will allow him to be home at night (Mishnah, *Ketubbot* 5:6). Conversely, he too has a right to sex within marriage. He may never, however, force himself upon his wife; the rabbis recognized and forbade marital rape (Babylonian Talmud, *Eruvin* 100b; Maimonides, *Laws of Forbidden Intercourse* 21:11; Joseph Karo, *Shulhan Arukh, Orah Hayyim* 240:10, *Even Ha'ezer* 25:2). In addition to procreation, then, sex is seen as a source of physical pleasure to which each member of the couple has a right.

At the same time, the Jewish tradition does *not* maintain that "A single human being cannot reflect the image of God." Marriage is the ideal, but every person is created in the image of God and must be respected for that. With a very high proportion of Jews in our day going to college and graduate school and thus postponing marriage, rabbis these days must strike a delicate balance between encouraging marriage and yet reaffirming the divine worth of each and every human being, married or not.

Finally, that a person should not be left alone is not just a fact motivating marriage. It also explains the Jewish commandment to visit the sick. The rabbis knew that illness is not only debilitating, but isolating, and so they maintained that visitors actually help people get well (*Nedarim* 39b-40a).

Sex and the Dimensions of Love

Dr. Braaten asserts that "*libido*-love is part of the scheme of God's creation, and is therefore natural and good." It is certainly natural, but for Judaism whether it is morally good or not depends on how and where we express it. It is likely to be misused, and thus the rabbis call it the *yetzer ha-ra*, the evil inclination. On the other hand, though, our self-directed *libido* can be not only good, but very good. Thus the rabbis, in noting that God declares the creation of all other things "good" but the creation of the human being "very good," say the following: "'It was very good' (Genesis 1:31). Rabbi Nahman, son of Samuel, said: This is the evil inclination. But is the evil inclination very good? Yes, for if it were not for the evil inclination, a man would not build a house, or take a wife, or beget a child, or engage in business, as it says, 'All labor and skillful enterprise come from men's rivalry with each other' (Ecclesiastes 4:4)" (*Genesis Rabbah* 9:7). Thus, while self-directed energy, including self-directed sexual energy, is definitely not sufficient for either individuals or society at large, it is necessary and can even be very good.

Romantic love *(eros)* is also not sufficient. I often like to illustrate the difference between the popular American vision of marriage with that of Judaism by pointing to two songs in Broadway plays. In *South Pacific*, we are told that "some enchanted evening you will meet a stranger across a crowded room, and somehow you'll know, you'll know even then, that somehow you'll meet her again and again." Marriage, in this view, is one enchanted evening after another. Marriage in reality does indeed have some enchanted evenings, but most are emotionally bland and some are downright unenchanting. As a result, when Americans find that their marriage is not producing one enchanted evening after another, they think that something is wrong with their marriage and all too often seek a divorce. Contrast that view with the one in *Fiddler on the Roof,* where Golda and Tevye talk about their twenty-five-year marriage as doing the tasks of life together without ever thinking about love, but now, after twenty-five years, "it's nice to know" that they love each other! Love, on this view, is not the reason you get married; it is a product of a life of caring for each other. This is at least *philia* and perhaps *agape* as well. People who get married understanding marriage to be a companionship to navigate life come into marriage with very different — and much more realistic — expectations, and are therefore much less likely to divorce. Enchanted evenings, then — and they surely have them — are frosting on the cake.

Homosexual Sex

Although the Jewish tradition, like the Christian tradition, prohibits all the "deviations" that Dr. Braaten lists, the contemporary Jewish community, like the contemporary Christian community, is reconsidering the ban on homosexuality. The most lenient Orthodox position draws a distinction between the sin and the sinner, asserting that engaging in homosexual sex is a sin, but a Jew who does it is still a Jew and must be welcomed into the community along with all the rest of us sinning Jews. On the other end of the spectrum, the Reform and Reconstructionist movements now ordain openly homosexual Jews as rabbis and endorse those of their rabbis who choose to officiate at commitment ceremonies. It is in the Conservative movement, of which I am a part, that the controversy continues unabated, for it is the middle movement, committed at once to seeing Jewish law as binding but also changing over time.

The issues are not nearly as neat as Dr. Braaten paints them. First, as Kinsey demonstrated more than fifty years ago, people do not fit into neat boxes of either heterosexual or homosexual; there is a range of sexual orientations (Kinsey counted seven), from completely heterosexual in desires, fantasies, and behaviors to completely homosexual in all three of those ways. Furthermore, homosexuals can now procreate and raise children — women through artificial insemination or adoption and men through surrogate motherhood or adoption. That robs the argument against homosexuality of one of its strongest claims. Moreover, as the recent record of thousands of people seeking to get married in Holland, Belgium, Spain,

Canada, and several American states and cities proves, homosexuals are not, as the stereotype asserts, always promiscuous and uncaring about the social values of becoming part of a stable couple raising children. Furthermore, it is definitely in society's best interests pragmatically to confirm such unions, both to diminish the spread of sexually transmitted diseases and to have more stable couples in our midst who are caring for themselves and possibly children as well so that society does not have that burden. Ontologically, it appears that God has created most of us as heterosexual but some of us as homosexual. If God is indeed, as the psalmist asserts, "good to everything, and his mercies are over all his works" (Ps. 145:9), one senses a divine command to apply our new knowledge about sexual orientation to redefining what that means vis-à-vis homosexuals.

It is surely the case that promiscuous, cultic, or abusive sex flows from sin, but contrary to Dr. Braaten's assertion, it is not at all clear that loving, monogamous, and socially responsible sex does. In fact, it seems that such sex flows from exactly the same reservoirs of love and social concern that marriage does. Furthermore, the truth status of Dr. Braaten's claim that homosexuality is "abnormal" depends upon what he means. If he simply means the descriptive statement that most people are not homosexual — that homosexuality is not the statistical norm — then he is surely correct. But if he means to make a normative judgment — that homosexuality violates what *should be* our moral norms — then he has to justify that judgment, and I, for one, think he has failed to do so. Finally, he is just wrong in claiming that homosexuality is a "sickness"; since 1973 all of the professional mental health organizations in North America — and now the American Medical Association too — have denied that that is so.

I would go further. That is, I would not only remove the ban against homosexual sex, but publicly celebrate and consecrate homosexual unions. Among other things, heterosexual marriage is society's way of publicly saying to a couple that they should be faithful to, and caring of, each other. Marriage does not prevent adultery or divorce, but it does diminish the probability of either. Given society's interest in pairing people off in units of couples who take responsibility for caring for each other and the children they raise, it seems to me — but certainly not to all Jews — that we *should* consecrate homosexual unions to say publicly to gays and lesbians that we want them to be faithful to, and caring for, each other too.

The Theological Meaning of Marriage and Divorce

In Judaism marriage is a threefold phenomenon: it is contractual, social, and religious. Because it is contractual between the parties, divorce is not a sin. The Torah, in fact, specifically allows it (Deut. 24:1-4). This means, of course, that the Jewish tradition did *not* understand Genesis, as much of Christianity has, to mean that a married couple "becomes one flesh" (Gen. 2:24) in an ontological sense, such that they become one being that physically and legally cannot be severed. Judaism instead understood that phrase simply as a description of the fact that when a couple marries, they become "one flesh" in the act of sexual intercourse — and become intertwined in each other's lives in a whole host of other ways as well. They remain, however, two distinct people, and as the Torah itself prescribes, divorce is legal. The rabbis (Mishnah, *Gittin* 9:10) interpret Deuteronomy 24 to allow a couple to divorce simply for what we would call "irreconcilable differences," with no requirement to demonstrate any grounds to the court.

Even if divorce is not a sin, it is always sad, for it ends the dreams of the couple to live their lives together. As a result, until very recent times divorce was very rare among Jews, in part because the Jewish community did everything in its power to help the couple get along. The University of Judaism, where I teach, created a modern version of that when it instituted a Preparation for Marriage course in 1975, consisting of ten sessions for ten couples at a time. In 2000 the university conducted a survey in which it found that instead of the prevailing divorce rate in America of close to 50 percent, the divorce rate among those who had gone through that program was 8 percent. As a result, I will not officiate at a marriage in Los Angeles unless the couple has taken that program; I actually think it is rabbinic malpractice to do so. But while we should do everything possible to give couples the tools to make sure they are right for each other before they marry and to sustain their marriage throughout life, if such efforts fail, we need to allow the couple to dissolve their marriage without adding guilt to their disappointment and misery.

The social element of Jewish marriage is twofold. Marriage is, first of all, a social event, in which the community is actually required to make sure sufficient people attend the wedding to help the bride and groom rejoice. It is, secondly, a social phenomenon in that society in the form of Jewish law delineates not only the forms of marriage (and divorce), but also the responsibilities of spouses, parents, and children to each other.

Finally, marriage is a sacred event, for it represents the beginning of the relationship in which the couple will carry out the two divine commandments cited above — namely, procreation and fulfilling each other's sexual needs. It is also sacred in that blessings of God are invoked in the wedding ceremony. From Isaiah and Hosea to Rabbi Akiba's interpretation of the love poetry of the biblical book Song of Songs to the medieval Kabbalists, it is also sacred because it is modeled after, and reminds us of, the marital relationship between God and the people Israel. As such, celibacy is frowned upon, and although single individuals are to be respected as retaining their divine imprint, marriage remains the ideal.

Calvin and the "Stewardship of Love"

Allen Verhey

You shall not steal.

Let's be honest. The eighth commandment has always been the favorite commandment of the propertied class. The rich cherish both the authorization it seems to afford to their possessions and the protection it evidently provides against any who would take them away — including (and especially) the poor. The economically powerful have frequently read the commandment in self-serving ways, defending their tightfisted grip on their own prosperity and security as a faithful performance of the law of God.

John Calvin's account of the eighth commandment provides an alternative reading, a reading it is the burden of this essay to discover and describe.

But let's be honest again. Calvinism has sometimes pronounced a priestly benediction upon those readings of the commandment favored by those who would use it to protect their possessions and to keep them from the poor. Whatever the merits of Weber's thesis that Calvinism provided the "spirit of capitalism,"[1] Calvinists have sometimes been overtaken and

---

1. Max Weber, *The Protestant Ethic and the Spirit of Capitalism,* trans. Talcott Parsons (New York: Scribner, 1958). In brief the Weber thesis is that Calvinism legitimated the transition to modern industrial and capitalist societies by its opposition to traditionalism, its "inner-worldly asceticism," its doctrine of vocation, and its "practical syllogism," which (in his view) allowed the Puritans to infer an assurance of their election from their financial success. It has evoked, of course, an enormous controversy that still continues. Jan Rohls, "Reformed Theology and Modern Culture," in *Reformed Theology for the Third Christian Millennium: The 2001 Sprunt Lectures,* ed. B. A. Gerrish (Louisville: Westminster John Knox,

possessed by the spirit of Mammon. Calvinists have accommodated themselves to an economic culture that insists that more is better, that equates
wealth with virtue and poverty with vice,[2] that delights in conspicuous
consumption, and that anxiously strives to secure its future by its possessions. And whatever the merits of Nick Wolterstorff's account of Calvinism as "world-formative Christianity,"[3] honesty requires the admission
that we Calvinists have been too much "conformed to this world," accommodated to a "Christianity-formative world." We need ever again to be reformed, indeed to be "transformed by the renewing of [our] minds, so that
[we] may discern what is the will of God — what is good and acceptable
and perfect" (Rom. 12:2).

Calvin's reading of the eighth commandment stands in the service of
that transformation and discernment. Like Paul's appeal for transformation, the basis for his reading of the commandment is "the mercies of
God" (Rom. 12:1), or our knowledge of God as "the fountain of every
good" (*Institutes* 1.2.1). The basic image for Calvin and for his reading of
the law is not God as Lawgiver but God as the gracious "Author of every
good" (1.2.1). The God who is the author of the law is the very God who
authors every good. The God who gives the law is the very God who delights to give his children good gifts, and the law is to be counted among
the good gifts of this gracious God. The law begins with good news, with
gospel, and the gospel when it is fully revealed in Christ holds us to the law.
Indeed, "the law of God contains in itself that newness by which his image
can be restored in us" (3.6.1). The appropriate human response to God is
gratitude, and it is gratitude that prompts us to read and to perform the
law. It is the gospel as law and the law as gospel that should move us to offer our hearts and lives — including our economic lives — as "living sacrifices" and as our "spiritual worship" (Rom. 12:1).

But let's be honest still. Calvin's reading of the eighth commandment
is not without ambiguity. When he says, for example, that "what every

---

2003), pp. 45-59, rejects the thesis. The best defense and development of Weber's thesis is still
David Little, *Religion, Order, and Law: A Study in Pre-Revolutionary England* (New York:
Harper Torchbooks, 1969). Little emphasized the transition from traditional authority to
"legal-rational" authority.

2. This identification may be regarded as a secular version of Weber's "practical syllogism."

3. Nicholas Wolterstorff, *Until Justice and Peace Embrace* (Grand Rapids: Eerdmans,
1983), p. 3.

man possesses has not come to him by mere chance but by the distribution of the supreme Lord of all" (2.8.45), the appeal to a "providential distribution" sounds like a justification of the economic status quo. And when he suggests that each "consider what, in his rank and station, he owes to his neighbors" (2.8.46), it sounds like a license for social and economic inequalities. We will have to acknowledge the difficulties and ambiguities along the way, but we will make little progress in discovering and describing Calvin's account of the eighth commandment unless we set it in the context of Calvin's account of the knowledge of God in the *Institutes*. For Calvin, after all, when we read and respond to the commandment, we respond to God, who is the Lawgiver.

There are two other reasons to set Calvin's reading of the eighth commandment in the context of the *Institutes*. First, it is too often overlooked that Calvin presented the *Institutes of the Christian Religion* to the reader as a hermeneutical tool, to help the reader "to determine what he ought especially to seek in Scripture, and to what end he ought to relate its contents."[4] If we would ask how Calvin reads any part of Scripture, including the eighth commandment, we should take this advice to the reader seriously. And second, it is also too often overlooked that the *Institutes* was "public theology." The Prefatory Address to King Francis I, which was published with the first edition of the *Institutes*, makes that plain.[5] Although Calvin defended the persecuted evangelicals against the charge of sedition, he also defended the sovereignty of God over public life, over politics and economics, over the king. He wrote to Francis that "a true king" is "a minister of God in governing his kingdom," but he warned him that "that king who in ruling over his realm does not serve God's glory exercises not kingly rule but brigandage."[6] God's rule — and the commandment against theft — extends to the secular and civil realm.

---

4. "John Calvin to the Reader," in *Institutes of the Christian Religion*, ed. John T. McNeill, trans. Ford Lewis Battles (Philadelphia: Westminster, 1960), p. 4. See also Calvin's "Subject Matter of the Present Work," p. 7: "[I]t can be a key to open a way for all children of God into good and right understanding of Holy Scripture."

5. Note also, of course, that the concluding chapter of the *Institutes* (4.20) deals with civil government.

6. "Prefatory Address to King Francis I of France," in *Institutes*, p. 12.

I

We read Scripture that we might know both God and ourselves. This knowledge of God we seek in Scripture is not the stuff of "idle speculations" (1.2.2; see also 1.5.9; 3.2.36; and 3.6.4). It is "piety," the acknowledgment that God is God and not us, the readiness to delight in God as the "fountain of every good" (1.2.1) and gratefully to do his will.

It is not that the knowledge of God is unnatural to us. We are created, after all, to know God. Moreover, God is inescapable — and inescapably known — in the world God has made and preserves. There is in every human being a *sensus divinitatis,* an awareness of a divine presence and power, and with it a conscience, some inkling of what life should be like in a world made by God (1.3; see also commentary on John 1:5). But we are dull and arrogant (2.8.1). The *sensus divinitatis* becomes for us a "factory of idols" (1.11.8; see also 1.5.12), and conscience "is miserably subject to vanity" (2.2.25). "The pious mind does not dream up for itself any god it pleases, but contemplates the one and only true God," God "as he manifests himself" (1.2.2; see also 1.4.3). God manifests himself, to be sure, in the creation, but decisively in Scripture. There we may learn to know God and ourselves. There God not only teaches us "to look upon a god, but also shows himself as the God upon whom [we] are to look" (1.6.1).

If God is the creator, then nothing God made is God. The prohibition of idolatry is given with the disclosure of God as creator. We may not make a god of our possessions, trusting them rather than God. And if God is the creator, then all that God made is good. Evil does "not spring from nature, but from the corruption of nature" (1.14.3). The inference permits and requires "pious delight" in things God has made, including the things God has given to us. So we ought to be mindful that "wherever we cast our eyes, all things they meet are works of God, and at the same time to ponder with pious meditation to what end God created them" (1.14.20; see also 3.10.2). That "end" is not simply utility or necessity; God gives food for "good cheer" and wine "that gladdens the heart" (3.10.2). But neither, of course, does he give these blessings for the sake of gluttony or drunkenness. The God who blesses us with abundance does not intend that we should hoard his blessing; the end for which God gives us possessions is mutual helpfulness. So Calvin urges a course between "bare necessity" and "intemperance" (3.10.1), and calls, first, for a certain detachment from our possessions (a certain nonchalance concerning them, lest we be tempted to idolatry), second, for moderation in the desire for and use of them, but thirdly and decisively, for stewardship (3.10.4-5). This stewardship is a "stewardship of love," for God "approves no other distribution of good things than one joined with love" (3.10.5; see also 3.7.5). Such sharing is the purpose for which God confers God's blessings upon us.

The readiness to distribute goods according to a stewardship of love has its formation in piety, in the knowledge that the Creator is the author of every good and can be trusted. And so it is "great ingratitude . . . to doubt whether this most gracious Father has us in his care" and "impious . . . to tremble for fear that his kindness might at any time fail us in our need" (1.14.22). Such anxiety prompts a tightfisted hoarding of our possessions, as if our life depended on them rather than on God. And so it is great ingratitude — and idolatry — to fail to share the blessings of God when a neighbor is in need.

We do not properly confess God as Creator unless we also acknowledge God's providence (1.16.1), for God's work as Creator is not simply past or finished. God would not allow his creation to be destroyed by human sin. By his providence God governs and preserves the world God has made, "sustains, nourishes, and cares for" it (1.16.2). Things happen not by chance, nor by fate, but by the constant care of God. The doctrine is complex, but it is not idle speculation. Piety knows God as Creator and Provider and is formed by this knowledge to gratitude, patience, and "an incredible freedom from worry about the future" (1.17.7-11; see also 3.7.8-9).

Thus we must understand Calvin's reference to a providential distribution of possessions when he comments on the eighth commandment. When he says, "What every man possesses has not come to him by mere chance but by the distribution of the supreme Lord of all" (2.8.45), he is not providing a justification for the economic status quo. Providence is not fatalism. Providence names the care of God that preserves the world and the cause of God in the world against the chaos toward which human self-love always tilts it. Piety acknowledges that we owe everything to God, that we are not our own, and that our possessions are not our own. The knowledge of God the provider is a call to gratitude in prosperity, not a license for a tightfisted sense of entitlement. To be sure, it is also a call to patience in adversity. But decisively it is a call to be not anxious. Piety knows that we do — and that we can — depend on God. And that freedom from anxiety is freedom for using God's gifts and our possessions to help a neighbor in need, freedom for the stewardship of love.[7]

With this knowledge of God the Creator comes knowledge of ourselves. First, we know that we are the cherished children of God, dependent on God, having "nothing of our own" but receiving God's care and gifts (2.1.1). Moreover, we know that our neighbors are the cherished children of God! We may and we must "look upon the image of God in all men, to which we owe all honor and love. . . . Therefore, whatever man you meet who needs your aid, you have no reason to refuse to help him" (3.7.6). We are created for fellowship not only with God but also with each other (commentary on Genesis 2:18). We are created for "mutual communication."[8] "Since God has united men amongst themselves by a certain bond of fellowship, hence they must mutually communicate with each other by good offices. Here then it is required that the rich succour the poor and offer bread to the hungry."[9]

Second, however, we know that we are fallen, that our sin has made us both guilty, liable to God's judgment, and corrupt, prone to sin, inclined to selfishness (2.1.8). We are estranged from God and from our true nature, from our fellowship and "mutual communication" with our neighbors. Such self-knowledge, too, is not mere speculation. It takes root in our heart as humility (2.2.11). Humility does not disparage the good gifts of God that God preserves, including human understanding and will. But it knows that we can neither fully understand nor choose the good without the grace of God.

We may also know, however, that we are *not* without the grace of God. We may know that the triune God is not only the Creator but also the Redeemer. This knowledge of God as Redeemer is first made known under the law, as the title of book 2 of the *Institutes* says, and then to us in the gos-

---

7. See also Calvin's commentary, *The Second Epistle of Paul to the Corinthians and the Epistles to Timothy, Titus and Philemon*, trans. T. A. Smail (Grand Rapids: Eerdmans, 1964), p. 107, on 2 Cor. 8:2, where, after identifying "the thing that makes us more close-fisted with our money than we should be" as our anxiety about the future, he says, "But the man who depends on the Lord's blessing has his mind set free from these vexatious cares and at the same time his hand set free for beneficence."

8. See Ronald Wallace, *Calvin's Doctrine of the Christian Life* (Grand Rapids: Eerdmans, 1959), pp. 148-56.

9. Sermon on 1 Tim. 6:9-11, in *Johannis Calvini Opera*, 53:582; cited by Wallace, *Calvin's Doctrine*, p. 153.

pel (see also 2.9.10). God would redeem the good creation God made from the hold that sin has on it, renew the image of God in humanity, restore our fellowship and mutual communication, including our use of our possessions. And when we know God as Redeemer, then we know ourselves as redeemed, as justified and sanctified.

Calvin reads the law, that is, the Torah, as the account of God's gracious covenant with Israel. It starts — and continues — with promise (2.7.1). The Torah is not to be reduced to the commandments, and the commandments are not given to abrogate the promises to Abraham but to "renew" the gracious covenant (2.7.1). They point us toward the fulfillment of the promise, to the righteousness of God, to Christ. That is the fundamental purpose of the law, and it is fundamental to Calvin's reading of the commandments. The commandments are not properly read as "bare law in a narrow sense" (2.7.2), but as clothed with the gospel. Thus Calvin's three uses of "the moral law" are hermeneutically sealed. The "bare law" can only condemn (2.7.6-9) and restrain (2.7.10). Even those uses, however, must be seen in the light of the gospel, as "tutelage to Christ" by humbling the proud and retraining others "from so slackening the reins on the lust of the flesh as to fall clean away from all pursuit of righteousness" (2.7.11). They are fulfilled in "the third and principal use" of the law (2.7.12), the "better and more excellent use" (2.7.13), when humble and hungry for righteousness, those who know the grace of God read the law "to learn more thoroughly . . . the Lord's will" and "to be aroused to obedience" by delight in the law clothed in the gospel (2.7.12). In its third use the law points toward its fulfillment in the restored image of God; it "points out the goal toward which throughout life we are to strive" (2.7.13).

The commandments, however, are evidently prohibitions (or binding prescriptions), not goals. How does one get from a prohibition like "you shall not steal" to a goal, to a telos? We may begin with Calvin by acknowledging that the commandment always means more than it says. The commandments always involve synecdoche, referring to a part to suggest the whole. Indeed, "there are such manifest synecdoches that he who would confine his understanding of the law within the narrowness of the words deserves to be laughed at" (2.8.8). We may not be content with the moral minimalism that attends only to the prohibition of, for example, theft by violence. Such moral minimalism stands in the service of self-righteousness, not the righteousness of God.

Calvin begins, then, by acknowledging synecdoche, that each commandment is part of a whole. But lest we "twist Scripture . . . thus making anything we please out of anything" (2.8.8), Calvin identifies additional principles for moving from prohibition to the goal of the commandments, and the most important is that we "ponder why [the commandment] was given to us" (2.8.8). That is, we must consider the purpose of God, the intention of the Creator and Redeemer God, who is also the Lawgiver, in giving the commandment. We must "look to the Lawgiver, by whose character the nature of the law also is to be appraised" (2.8.6). That, of course, requires a knowledge of God's work and character, a knowledge that the *Institutes* as a whole attempts to summarize. We are to read the commandment in the light of the knowledge of God as Creator and Redeemer of this world.

We will read the commandments well, according to Calvin, when we read them as clothed in the gospel. The commandments form human life not just to external obedience but to an "inward and spiritual righteousness" (2.8.6). Christ's revelation of the righteousness of God helps us understand the purpose of the law, including the law against theft.

Finally, Calvin calls attention to the principle of contraries. By forbidding something, God commands the opposite (2.8.8). These rules, synecdoche, purpose, and contraries, are "common sense" rules (2.8.9) for interpreting the commandments, and they allow us to move from prohibition to the "goal" of the commandments. They are neglected or violated when we want to render the law manageable and self-serving. Given these hermeneutical rules, "it will not be difficult to decide the purpose of the whole law," to grasp the goal of all the laws: "the fulfillment of righteousness," the love of God and the neighbor, "all the duties of piety and love" (2.8.51). And the love of God and the neighbor, in turn, governs our interpretation of each of the commandments; it provides another hermeneutical rule. "Here, therefore, let us stand fast: our life shall best conform to God's will and the prescription of the law when it is in every respect most fruitful for our brethren" (2.8.54).

There is one more hermeneutical rule. The first table is first. The worship of God is the "foundation of righteousness" (2.8.11; see also 2.8.50), and not just any old God, but the God who identifies himself in the preface as the "author of [our] freedom" (2.8.15), the covenant God who makes and keeps promises, the Creator and Redeemer to whom gratitude is due.

This is the context for Calvin's reading of the eighth commandment, and it is high time to turn to it.

II

We may begin again with synecdoche. The commandment prohibits "theft, which all naturally abhor as disgraceful."[10] It is, however, but a part for the whole. Calvin warns against the moral minimalism that would prohibit theft by violence while it calls "prudent" the one "who takes in the simple, and insidiously oppresses the poor" (p. 111). Such moral minimalism serves self-righteousness, not the righteousness of God, but God "pronounces all unjust means of gain to be so many thefts" (p. 111). Theft by violence, at least the sort of violence that the poor and powerless have access to, receives little emphasis in the *Institutes*. "There are many kinds of theft," he says (*Institutes* 2.8.45), and he begins to list them: theft by violence, theft by fraud, theft through craftiness, theft through flatteries, but he stops his list-making to generalize. The commandment prohibits "all those arts" whereby we take what is our neighbors'. And "all those arts" include legal means, court action of one sort or another. What is due another is not simply a matter of legal entitlement, and there can be legal theft. God "sees the intricate deceptions with which a crafty man sets out to snare one of simpler mind. . . . He sees the hard and inhuman laws with which the more powerful oppresses and crushes the weaker person" (2.8.45).

Synecdoche points not only beyond theft by violence but also beyond possessions toward all the rights of another. The law prohibits any failure to give others what is their due. Here Calvin refers especially to the responsibilities of one's calling and of one's "rank and station." It is theft when one does not carry out what he owes to others according to one's calling (2.8.45; see also 3.10.6). Calvin provides a table of duties for rulers and citizens, for ministers and laity, for parents and children, for the young and the aged, for servants and masters. There are things due another that are associated with these roles, and Calvin regards the withholding or the appropriation for oneself of what is due another as a form of theft. "Let each man consider what, in his rank and station, he owes to another, and pay what he owes" (2.8.46). But lest we conclude that Calvin's treatment of the command licenses the economic status quo marked

---

10. John Calvin, *Commentaries on the Four Last Books of Moses Arranged in the Form of a Harmony*, trans. Charles William Bingham, vol. 3 (Grand Rapids: Ferdmans, 1950), p. 111; hereafter cited as *Comm*. References to this volume will be cited parenthetically in the text.

by "rank and station," we need only remember the emphasis above on oppression as a form of theft. Different occupations and different social roles are a part of "mutual communication," a division of labor by which we may serve each other and the common good. The emphasis does not fall so much on the "vocation" itself or on the social role as it does on serving God and the neighbor *through* that vocation and position.[11] Calvin's account of "calling" and even of "rank and station" is marked by a fundamental mutuality and equality. The emphasis is not on the rights that are mine by my rank and station but on the duties to my neighbor that are mine by both my rank and station and my neighbor's.[12]

Calvin begins his treatment of the eighth commandment in the *Institutes* by calling attention to "the purpose" of the commandment. As we have said, to understand God's intention with the commandments, we have to understand something of God's character. Here the inference is explicit. "Since injustice is an abomination to God, we should render to each man what belongs to him" (2.8.45). The commandment itself, of course, or for that matter the Decalogue, does not mention justice. But Calvin confidently reports that the purpose of the command is nothing other than justice. How could it be otherwise if God, "the Lawgiver, by whose character the nature of the law also is to be appraised" (2.8.6), is a lover of justice? But what sort of "justice" is this? Calvin's "to each what is due" is an ancient but formal principle of justice. It does not yet say what is due another or how we would determine what is due another. We have already seen that it is not simply legal entitlement. We have seen that Calvin's reference to a providential distribution of wealth (2.8.45) is not a justification for the

---

11. Ernst Troeltsch, *The Social Teaching of the Christian Churches,* trans. Olive Wyon (New York: Macmillan, 1931), distinguished the Lutheran and Calvinist conceptions of "calling" along these lines. Lutherans sought obedience to God *in vocatione,* but Calvinists sought obedience to God *per vocationem.* The Calvinist emphasis on serving God and the neighbor through one's calling, moreover, made it possible to be suspicious of some "callings" as unfitting to the Christian's service of God, whether as generally unserviceable to the cause of God or as individually unsuited to one's gifts and talents. Thus was broken the assumption that one would be a farmer because one's father was a farmer. Calvin himself observed that "it would be asking for too much, if a tailor were not permitted to learn another trade, or a merchant to change to farming" (commentary on 1 Cor. 7:20). Moreover, it also made it possible to be suspicious of the particular vocational system of any society as marked by the fall, corrupt, and in need of correction so that we could all serve God and each other better in "mutual communication." See Wolterstorff, *Until Justice,* pp. 16-18.

12. See further Wallace, *Calvin's Doctrine,* pp. 157-69.

economic status quo or a license for a tightfisted sense of entitlement. And we have seen that justice is not simply determined by one's rank and station; rather, justice is normative for the performance of the duties that belong to different roles. Justice is not simply identified with the system of vocations and social roles but is to be sought through them. But what is this justice?

We begin to make some progress toward understanding what Calvin means by justice when we look at his use of the principle of contraries here. To be sure, one inference warranted by the principle of contraries is contentment. "We will duly obey this commandment, then, if content with our lot, we are zealous to make only honest and lawful gain; if we do not seek to become wealthy through injustice, nor attempt to deprive our neighbor of his goods to increase our own; if we do not strive to heap up riches cruelly wrung from the blood of others; if we do not madly scrape together from everywhere, by fair means or foul, whatever will feed our avarice or satisfy our prodigality" (2.8.46). The long list of the prohibitions entailed by the eighth commandment in that quotation must not be allowed to hide the positive command to be content. It is a contentment gained by faith in God as the author of every good. It is the nonchalance, the freedom from anxiety that Jesus, the best interpreter of the law, exhorted us to as the course of wisdom and faith. That contentment enables us to be patient in adversity and grateful and generous in abundance. But Calvin continues to work with the principle of contraries until he reaches this conclusion: "Let us share the necessity of those whom we see pressed by the difficulty of affairs, assisting them in their need with our abundance" (2.8.46). There is the principle of justice at work in Calvin's treatment of the eighth commandment. It is familiar enough as Paul's principle of equality in 2 Corinthians 8:14: "As a matter of equality your abundance at the present time should supply their want, so that their abundance may supply your want, that there may be equality" (RSV). In his commentary on this passage Calvin said, "Thus the Lord commends to us this fair proportioning of our resources that we may, in so far as funds allow, help those in difficulties that there may not be some in affluence and others in want." It is a manna economy. "All that we have is manna. . . . [T]here must be such an equality that nobody starves and nobody hordes his abundance at another's expense" (commentary on 2 Cor. 8:15). The justice that is the goal of the commandment is simply the restoration of "mutual communication" with those blessings with which God blesses humanity.

In his *Commentaries on the Four Last Books of Moses,* Calvin identifies the purpose of the eighth commandment by considering the purpose of the whole law, namely, love (*Comm.,* p. 110). But love requires economic justice. Here the purpose is stated that "everyone's rights should be safely preserved." And using the principle of contraries in the *Commentaries,* Calvin concludes that "God, who has laid mankind under mutual obligation to each other, [requires in the commandment] that they may seek to benefit, care for, and succour their neighbours" (p. 111). The justice love requires is mutuality and equality, distributing to persons as they have needs unmet by their own resources.

One may still wonder, I suppose, whether Calvin "twists Scripture" in moving from the prohibition to such a notion of justice. Here the *Commentaries* may be especially helpful as Calvin arranges other texts with the eighth commandment and comments on them. Some are gathered according to the principle of synecdoche, as other forms of theft. So, for example, the prohibitions against deception and fraud and against holding back the wages of a hired hand (Lev. 19:11, 13; *Comm.,* pp. 111-13) are regarded as included under the eighth commandment. So, again, the prohibition against oppression of workers (Deut. 24:14-15; *Comm.,* pp. 113-15).[13] And, again, the prohibitions in Leviticus 19:35-36 and Deuteronomy 25:13-16 against false weights and measures and against the subversion of justice are "the most injurious thefts of all" and "the grossest violation of public justice" (p. 120).

But some of the passages disclose and defend the reading of justice we have suggested. When Exodus 22:21-24, Leviticus 19:33-34, and Deuteronomy 10:17-19 demand protection for the sojourner, for the poor, for widows and orphans, Calvin points out that the people were "commanded to cultivate equity without exception" (p. 116). Moreover, to demand that equity display a special care for the poor, for those who "are more exposed to violence and various oppressions" (p. 116), is not "twisting Scripture" but reading it in the light of the work and character of God the Redeemer who is the Lawgiver. Along with the text Calvin reminds his readers that God delivered Israel from their sojourn and slavery in Egypt. God has shown

---

13. In his sermon on this passage, Calvin condemns as theft the behavior of the employers who offer half wages to the worker desperate for a job. *The Sermons of M. Iohn Calvin vpon the Fifth Booke of Moses Called Deuteronomie,* trans. Arthur Golding (London: H. Middleton for George Bishop, 1583), p. 860, cited in Wolterstorff, *Until Justice,* p. 188 n. 17.

himself to be the sort of God who loves justice, to be sure, but also the sort of God whose justice attends to the cries of the poor and powerless (pp. 117, 119).

Again, in his comments on Exodus 22:26-27 and Deuteronomy 24:6, 10-18, a series of texts on loans, Calvin identifies as a "principle of equity" that one should not demand in pledge what the poor need for sustenance or what a workman needs to earn a living (pp. 122-23). Why does equity include this special concern for the poor? Along with the text Calvin cites the deliverance of Israel from their bondage in Egypt (p. 125). And in his comment on Exodus 22:25, Leviticus 25:35-36, and Deuteronomy 23:19-20, Calvin appeals to our creation in mutual dependence as a basis for his account of justice.

> [S]ince all men are born for the sake of each other, human society is
> not properly maintained, except by an interchange of good offices.
> Wherefore, that we may not defraud our neighbours, and so be ac-
> counted thieves in God's sight, let us learn . . . to be kind to those
> who need our help, for liberality is a part of righteousness, so that
> he must be deservedly held to be unrighteous who does not relieve
> the necessities of his brethren when he can. . . . [T]hose who have
> abundance do not enjoy their possessions as they ought, unless they
> communicate them to the poor for the relief of their poverty.
> (p. 126)

To give but one more example from many, Calvin's comment on a collection of passages on gleaning, Leviticus 19:9-10, 23:22, and Deuteronomy 24:19-23, calls for liberality from the wealthy that they may thus imitate God. It is "ingratitude" to withhold what we derive from God's blessing. So the rich are to supply the needs of the poor from their abundance, says Calvin, citing 2 Corinthians 8 (p. 152).

The *Commentaries*, finally, are helpful in another way. Calvin distinguishes the political aspect of a number of the laws he gathers with the eighth commandment from the moral aspect. The political aspect is provisional, related to Israel's particular historical and economic context. The content of the law may be adjusted to fit a different historical and economic context, but the purpose of the law is still normative — and normative also politically. One example of this is the legislation concerning the year of release in Deuteronomy 15:1-11. Calvin acknowledges that "we are not bound by this law at present," but he insists that "the object to which it tended ought still to be maintained." And that object, that purpose, is that the needy should be protected against too harsh a practice of demanding the repayment of loans and that the law restrain those with economic power who would oppress the poor in order to enrich themselves (p. 154).

The more famous example, of course, is Calvin's treatment of the prohibition of usury. He takes the issue up both in his *Commentaries* (pp. 125-33) and in his famous letter *De Usuris*.[14] Without wishing to oversimplify Calvin's careful argument,[15] it is sufficient here to say that once again Calvin takes the political aspect of the law to be provisional, related to Israel's particular historical and economic context. The context of sixteenth-century Geneva was quite different. Loans were no longer simply a matter of giving aid to a person who was in danger or desperate; they were part of a practice of creating a working capital. Calvin was among the first great leaders of public opinion to reject the traditional position that the Bible provided a perpetual rule against the lending of money with interest (and Aristotle's dictum that money does not produce money). The prohibition was provisional, and in the quite different context of Geneva he was ready to allow interest on loans. But again the purpose of the law was still normative — and normative also politically. And the purpose of the law was love and justice, and more particularly the sort of love and justice that protects the poor from the oppressive rich (pp. 126, 127). Little wonder, then, that Calvin hedges his approval of usury with a number of restrictions designed to protect the poor from the avaricious rich and the rich from avarice.[16]

Theft is any violation of economic justice, and economic justice is not a matter of individual entitlement but a matter of "mutual communication." Justice does not require that inequalities be eliminated, although the conviction that "enough" is best moves in that direction. But it does require that inequalities finally stand in the service of the poor, meeting their needs. Where the needs of the poor are not supplied, justice is not being done and the commandment is not being gratefully and gladly obeyed.

14. See John Calvin, "On Usury," in *From Christ to the World: Introductory Readings in Christian Ethics*, ed. Wayne G. Boulton, Thomas D. Kennedy, and Allen Verhey (Grand Rapids: Eerdmans, 1994), pp. 453-55.

15. For a fuller — and excellent — account of Calvin's argument concerning usury, see James B. Sauer, *Faithful Ethics according to John Calvin*, Toronto Studies in Theology, vol. 74 (Lewiston, N.Y.: Edwin Mellen Press, 1997), pp. 169-226.

16. See Calvin, "On Usury," p. 454.

III

Calvin has set the commandments in the context of the knowledge of God the Redeemer as made known in the law, but he is (and we are) not quite done. God the Redeemer is definitively disclosed in Jesus as the Christ, the righteousness of God, the restored image of God, the fulfillment of the law. And we must attend briefly to the renewal of "mutual communication" in the church.

We are united to Christ and so to his body, the church, by the Spirit and by faith, the "principal work of the Spirit" (*Institutes* 3.1.4). Faith is "a firm and certain knowledge of God's benevolence toward us" (3.2.7), but again this knowledge is not mere speculation. "[I]t is a doctrine not of the tongue but of life. It is not apprehended by the understanding and memory alone . . . , but it is received only when it possesses the whole soul, and finds a seat and resting place in the inmost affection of the heart. . . . [I]t must enter our heart and pass into our daily living, and so transform us into itself that it may not be unfruitful for us" (3.6.4). It transforms us into itself by sanctification, by the mortification of the old self-centered self and the vivification of a new self, the restored image of God (3.3.8). Calvin provides an account of this sanctified life in 3.7-10, the Golden Booklet of the Christian Life. It is, of course, in agreement with Calvin's account of the law (see 3.6.1 and 3.7.1), but Calvin starts here not from the commandments but from our union with Christ. He starts with character rather than conduct.

The sum of the Christian life here is self-denial. "We are not our own. . . . We are God's" (3.7.1). Neither are our possessions our own. Self-denial looks chiefly to God, prompting us to the service of God and to "seek not the things that are ours but those which are of the Lord's will and will serve to advance his glory" (3.7.2). But self-denial looks also to the neighbor, prompting humility and generosity. "Let this, therefore, be our rule . . . : We are the stewards of everything God has conferred upon us by which we are able to help our neighbor, and are required to give an account of our stewardship. Moreover the only right stewardship is that which is tested by the rule of love" (3.7.5). Such stewardship is not to be rendered contemptuously of the neighbor in need.[17] The "conceit of phi-

---

17. In Calvin there is no correspondence, contrary to both Weber's "practical syllogism" and to a bourgeois morality, between wealth and goodness or between poverty and immo-

lanthropy" is inappropriate where we are all the recipients of God's great kindness, and each is "a debtor to his neighbors" by the ties of human solidarity.[18] So kindness toward the poor should "set no other limit than the end of his resources." And these resources, what we call our own, "should have their limits set according to the rule of love" (3.7.7; see also 3.10.5). Self-denial will not look for "any other way of prospering than by the Lord's blessing" (3.7.8) and will "pursue only those enterprises which do not lead us away from innocence" (3.7.9). The rest is theft — and so is any violation of the "stewardship of love."

Having shown that faith is not "devoid of good works" (3.11.1), Calvin turns to the other effect of our union with Christ by the Spirit and by faith, namely, justification (3.11-18). By God's grace we are made free. The goal of God the Redeemer is our freedom no less than our righteousness, but also our righteousness no less than our freedom. We are not freed from the law as if it were suddenly "superfluous" (3.19.2). We are rather free from the condemnation of the law. We are free for righteousness, yielding glad and grateful obedience to the Creator and Redeemer (3.19.4-5). And we are free in things that are "indifferent" (3.19.7). Here Calvin is at pains to steer a course between license and legalism (3.19.7; see also 3.19.2 and especially 3.20.1), but echoing and citing the prophets, he condemns the conspicuous consumption of the wealthy (3.19.9). This remains the rule, "that we should use God's gifts for the purpose for which he gave them to us" (3.19.8; see also 3.20.2), and this remains the purpose, to display our piety and our gratitude by sharing God's good gifts — and especially with the neighbor in need.

One may not consider the Christian life in Calvin's thought without considering prayer, for prayer is "the chief exercise of faith" (3.20.1). The response of piety to the manifestation of God as Creator and Redeemer is "to seek in [God], and in prayers to ask of him, what we have learned to be in him" (3.20.1). To learn to pray reverently, earnestly, humbly, and confi-

---

rality. There is no legitimate inference from the datum of worldly prosperity to the conclusion that the prosperous are among the elect. Calvin notes, for example, the poverty and afflictions of the patriarchs (*Institutes* 2.10.11-12). In Calvin the assurance of salvation is never found either in speculation about some eternal decree (3.24.4) or in considering ourselves, whether our little faith or our worldly success, but always by attention to Christ, who makes known God the Redeemer (3.24.5).

18. Calvin here, and characteristically, identifies love of the neighbor with natural law. We are bound to each other by nature, and we owe each other mutual aid.

dently (the four "rules" for prayer, 3.20.4-16) is also to learn to live reverently, so that we may attend to God as God and to all else as related to God; earnestly, so that we gladly and zealously seek God's kingdom (3.20.7); humbly, so that we rest in God's grace and "aspire to godliness" (3.20.10); and hopefully. And in learning to pray for "our daily bread," we learn to be grateful for the gifts of God that sustain and delight both us and our neighbors. We learn to trust God and not to be anxious. We learn a manna economy in which the axiom is not "more is better" but "sufficient is best." To make this petition and then "to seek gain by unlawful devices" or to hoard "piled-up" riches is to mock the God to whom we pray (3.20.44). We learn, moreover, to make this petition in common, in community, when we say "our" bread; the bread, too, is common bread (3.20.47), and so we learn to share. When we pray that we not be led into temptation, we must be alert to both the temptation of too much and the temptation of too little (3.20.46).

The church is "the communion of the saints," for God gathers them into "the society of Christ on the principle that whatever benefits God confers upon them, they should in turn share with one another" (4.1.3). The church is the gracious instrument of God by which God gathers and nurtures the saints in their earthly condition (4.1.1), and this earthly condition requires attention to the poor. The church may not neglect the needs of the poor and still be the church, and Calvin identifies the office of "caring for the poor" as a permanent office in the church. He praises the practice of the ancient church that distributed its treasury to the poor (4.5.8), and he denounces those clergy of his own time who make themselves "rich by this booty," neglecting the poor. "[A]ll they eat and all they wear comes from theft" (4.5.17). The church's power to make law is limited on the one hand by the prohibition against usurping the freedom of either God or conscience (4.10.1) and on the other by the commandment of mutual love (4.10.30-31). Even laws that may claim biblical authority, like women covering their heads (4.10.31), are subject to these limits. The church's juridical power pertains to "the discipline of morals" (4.11.1), not by force but by the preaching of the word and by mutual admonition and correction (4.12.2). The church is a community of moral discourse, discernment, and discipline, and its discourse, discernment, and discipline properly reach into the world of our possessions.

The sacraments, too, may remind members of the church of their community with one another and nourish "a stewardship of love." The

Lord's Supper particularly reminds us that Christ "makes himself common to all" and "makes all of us one in himself" (4.17.38). Accordingly, "we ought not to allow a brother to be affected by any evil, without being touched with compassion for him" (4.17.38).

While the church is being renewed in "mutual communication" by its voluntary obedience to the preaching of the word and by its practice of mutual admonition, the world goes on. But neither God nor the faithful may abandon the larger society. Civil government has the vocation to establish and maintain "civil justice and outward morality" (4.20.1). With its coercive power, it is distinct from Christ's spiritual rule, but it is not antithetical to it. Indeed, as the vicars of God, civil rulers are charged to provide "some image of divine providence, protection, goodness, benevolence, and justice" (4.20.6). They are to protect and preserve some order in this world, an order that must itself approximate in outward morality the order that God is restoring. The state will have to be satisfied with something less than the "fruit of the spirit," but it should not be satisfied with injustice. The state cannot coerce contentment, moderation (although Geneva did have its sumptuary laws), or love. But although the state cannot coerce love, its laws "must be in conformity to that perpetual rule of love" (4.20.15). They need not agree precisely with the judicial laws of Moses, which were provisional, after all, but they must have the same purpose — equity (4.20.15-16). The state may and must intervene in economic matters to protect property (4.20.3) and to protect the poor from hoarders and monopolies, from false measures and deception, in a word, from theft. But that word, as we have seen, covers a lot of ground. Theft is any violation of economic justice, and economic justice is not a matter of individual entitlement but a matter of "mutual communication" and the "stewardship of love."

Response

Sue Ann Wasserman

Allen Verhey's essay on John Calvin and the eighth commandment has brought me to a whole new perspective on the theology of Calvin. What amazed me most was how much Calvin's utopian vision of our responsibility to create a just society parallels Jewish text and thinking. Snippets of Jewish liturgy, biblical text, and medieval and contemporary theology kept leaping to mind. Calvin's commentary breaks wide open the childhood understanding of "You shall not steal" as a simple exhortation against thievery.

Calvin employs four hermeneutical rules to interpret the eighth commandment, and each brings him to a deeper understanding of the text. Synecdoche requires that one understand each commandment in its greater context — there are limits to interpretation. Bringing the Gospels to bear elucidates the ultimate and spiritual purpose of the command. The principle of contraries — by forbidding something, God commands us to do the opposite — requires him to search out what it is that God does want us to do. Finally Calvin must interpret the text from the perspective that it was given by a God who intends that our service to God lead us to righteousness and to gratitude.

The hermeneutical rules Calvin utilizes are similar to a traditional Jewish method of studying and understanding biblical text known as *PaRDeS*. *PaRDeS* is an acronym for four Hebrew words that themselves represent four levels of interpretation: *P'shat*, meaning simple — a literal understanding; *Remez*, meaning hint — an allegorical understanding with references to other texts; *Drash*, meaning explanation — a moral or homiletic understanding; and *Sod*, meaning secret — a mystical understanding.

While the literal understanding of the text "Thou shall not steal" is self-evident, the question of "what" one may not steal is not. Traditional Jewish commentary interprets our text to refer specifically to the theft of human beings — kidnapping — understanding that the theft of property is prohibited in Leviticus 19:11. The wording in Hebrew, *lo tig'nov*, is the same in both Leviticus and Exodus, so the rabbis base their differing understandings on the context. In Exodus the commandment follows two capital crimes: murder and adultery. This leads them to the interpretation that in Exodus stealing is also a capital crime, meaning the stealing of a person.

As we look more deeply into the command over the centuries, the understandings broaden. In Jewish criminal law there are seven categories of theft: (1) deceit or fraud, which is viewed as stealing another person's mind; (2) falsifying weights and measures; (3) stealing useless objects, which isn't punishable; (4) misappropriating bills, lands, or consecrated property, for which one needs only to make restitution; (5) stealing chattels, for which the penalty is double payment; (6) stealing and selling or slaughtering oxen and sheep, which must be repaid four- or fivefold; and (7) kidnapping, which is punishable by death (*Mekchilta Mishpatim* 13; Tosefta, *Baba Qamma* 7:8-17).

Stealing is seen as so fundamentally wrong that with the exception of food that has already been consumed, there is no minimum amount of property that is allowed to go uncompensated. One can't even steal as a prank or only to grieve the one from whom one steals, intending all along to return the object. Nor can one steal so as to repay double, thereby giving a gift to another. Intellectual and emotional "property" is no less scrupulously guarded. Rabbi Richard N. Levy writes,

> The prohibition against stealing extends even to non-material thefts, which we hardly think of as stealing at all — to keep other people waiting, thus stealing their time; to forget to credit the author of an idea or a felicitous expression, thus stealing their creativity. In its most serious form, this is plagiarism. But even in its minor form, it violates the Talmudic injunction to speak an idea *beshem omro*, "in the name of its speaker." When we mislead someone or flatter a person dishonestly, we are guilty of *genevat da'at*, stealing a bit of their knowledge; and when we gossip, engaging in *lashon hara*, the language of hurt, we are stealing from someone's reputation.[1]

1. Richard N. Levy, quoted in *Broken Tablets: Restoring the Ten Commandments and Ourselves*, ed. Rachel S. Mikva (Woodstock, Vt.: Jewish Lights Publishing, 1999).

However much Judaism, like Calvin, protects the rights of ownership based on biblical injunctions and later generations of laws against stealing, there are clear limitations to the ownership of property. There is an abundance of biblical and postbiblical source texts that reinforce the theological assumption that in truth "ownership" is God's alone. Psalm 24:1 reads:

> The earth is the Eternal's, and the fullness thereof;
> The world, and they that dwell therein.

Nowhere is this perspective on ownership made clearer than in Leviticus 19:9-10, which is in the middle of the Holiness Code (Lev. 17–26). The verses read: "When you reap the harvest of your land, you shall not reap all the way to the edges of your field, or gather the gleanings of your harvest. You shall not pick your vineyard bare, or gather the fallen fruit of your vineyard; you shall leave them for the poor and the stranger: I the Eternal am your God."[2] The text confirms our role as mere stewards of the earth and God as the true owner with the authority to direct its usage. Rabbi Levy again connects this to the eighth commandment:

> Theft is wrong, *a priori*, because it takes from others and it takes from God, who has ordained a method for distributing Divine bounty. The Holy One apportions the land and wealth that belong to God to individuals who are commanded to share it with God's agents, the poor. The responsibility of the poor is to gather their portion — the corners of the fields and gleanings from fruit trees, vines, and grain. (When vines fall from the hired gatherers' arms, it is as though God causes them to fall, as though God accompanies the harvesters and harvests for the poor.) . . . Stealing is a serious crime in Jewish tradition. So is the sin of encouraging stealing by refusing to share the bounty God has temporarily entrusted to us.

The context of the command to leave the corners and some of the gleanings untouched is significant. This chapter and those surrounding it are meant to lead us to a life of holiness. Judaism teaches us that holiness is achieved through our actions — our ethical and moral behavior. The expectation is that we will attempt to imitate God. Just as we are God's stew-

---

2. Translation from *The Torah. A Modern Commentary*, ed. David E. S. Stein, rev. ed. (New York: Union for Reform Judaism, 2004).

ards of the land, we are also God's presence made tangible in the world. If God demands a just world where all are fed and clothed, treated with dignity and love, then we are the ones who must make it happen. The Hebrew word most commonly used for "charity" is *tzedakah;* but it's not an accurate translation. *Tzedakah* comes from the root letters *tzadi, dalet, koof,* meaning justice. Giving *tzedakah* is fulfilling our obligation to work toward a just world. It's not something we do out of the goodness of our hearts but rather in response to a divine command.

Dr. Meir Tamari (an economist, Jewish scholar, and founder of the Center for Business Ethics and Social Responsibility in Jerusalem) writes: "Jewish tradition insists that we are obligated both individually and collectively. By collectively I mean through the community or through the state apparatus, to help those people who are deprived, poor, weak, inefficient and even who are lazy. There is no such concept in Judaism of the 'deserving poor.' We must, however, quickly add that this is not an entitlement; this is an obligation on me, which is something different. A poor man is not entitled; I am obligated, which is different from what the modern world thinks."[3] The world was created with the potential for holiness and wholeness, but that potential can only be realized if we accept the responsibility of being God's partner. Dr. Verhey's closing sentence makes John Calvin's commitment to this abundantly clear: "Theft is any violation of economic justice, and economic justice is not a matter of individual entitlement but a matter of 'mutual communication' and the 'stewardship of love.'" Though the language is Christian, the meaning resonates for me as a modern Jew. True economic justice will be achieved only when we all accept our part in remedying the inequalities that now exist. Living in relationship with God means that we acknowledge our responsibility for caretaking all of humanity.

3. "In the Marketplace: Jewish Business Ethics," published by Targum/Feldheim at http://www.targum.com.

Bearing True Witness

Miroslav Volf with Linn Tonstad

You shall not bear false witness.

The commandment "You shall not bear false witness against your neighbor" belongs in the second table of the law, which is concerned with the social fabric of human existence. The commandments of the second table have traditionally been understood as offering guidelines for a way of life that is good for all people, regardless of religion or irreligion, although many theologians have been careful to emphasize that worshipers of God have special requirements laid on them that are drawn from but go beyond the letter of these laws.

The ninth commandment, about not bearing false witness, is concerned with speech about the other — the neighbor, the stranger, and God — though it also has implications for how we are to speak of ourselves. Commenting on the main thrust of the commandment, Thomas Aquinas, one of the greatest Christian thinkers from the thirteenth century, wrote, "The Lord has forbidden anyone to injure his neighbor by deed. In this Commandment he forbids us to injure him by word."[1] The commandment, then, is an answer to the question, How are we to speak about each other so as not to injure one another?

---

1. Thomas Aquinas, *God's Greatest Gifts: Commentaries on the Commandments and the Sacraments* (Manchester, N.H.: Sophia Institute Press, 1992), p. 65.

Truthful Speech, Neighbors, and God

The prohibition against false witness has generally and rightly been interpreted as ruling out all lying and all untruthfulness. The great church father from the fifth century, Augustine, for instance, wrote, "in the very Decalogue it is written 'Thou shall not bear false witness' under which general term it comprises all lying."[2] But though all untruthfulness is prohibited, the focus of the commandment is not on truth for truth's sake. The particular form in which the commandment is given — namely, its explicit prohibition of false *witness* — suggests that consequences of untruthfulness for other people in a more public setting are principally in view. It aims primarily at maintaining justice in society by not allowing people to use false witness to twist their relationships with each other for their own gain. Put differently, the commandment prohibits all lying, but it focuses on the damage that lying does. The social character of truth telling, and thus its importance in creating and maintaining reliable relationships and social structures, comes to the fore in this commandment.[3]

The prohibition against false witness is applicable in many settings, but two — twin obsessions of contemporary culture — are especially significant today: justice and difference. Though concern about justice and difference was present in the Hebrew Scriptures, today it has acquired a new form and possibly, in the case of difference, a new urgency. We will explicate the significance of the ninth commandment primarily in the light of these two issues, though its relevance is, obviously, much broader.

First, the question of *justice* has taken on particular importance in a time of movements for social justice, concern about international cooperation to bring war criminals to justice, and more recently, the fight against terrorism and the techniques used therein, among other issues. The demand for justice is heard from all parts of the globe and from all over the political spectrum, with widely differing ideas about what justice truly requires. This concern for justice ranges from the specific and local (e.g., what is the role of the judiciary?) to the general and universal (e.g., are there such things as universal human rights?).

2. Augustine, "On Lying," in *Nicene and Post-Nicene Fathers*, 1st ser., vol. 3, ed. P. Schaff (Grand Rapids: Eerdmans, 1956), p. 460.

3. See on this Walter Brueggemann, "Truth-Telling as Subversive Obedience," in *The Ten Commandments: The Reciprocity of Faithfulness*, ed. William P. Brown (Louisville: Westminster John Knox, 2004), p. 292.

The ninth commandment is mainly about truth telling and does not speak directly to the problem of justice. It contains nothing like the kernel of an answer to philosophical and legal questions about the nature of justice, nor does it suggest a particular judicial system. Then how is it related to the problem of justice? It sketches a way, grounded ultimately in the reality of the one true God, to act under any system of justice and most accounts of the nature of justice. For justice cannot be practiced without obedience to the ninth commandment.

Second, the question of *difference* is also pervasive in the modern world. How are we to deal with differences — whether between individual persons, broader cultures, or whole nations? How are religious people themselves, who may disagree vehemently on the most important questions in life, to get along with each other? How are they to interact with nonbelievers? The vituperative and even violent tone that sometimes characterizes interactions among religious people makes these questions pressing. Failures of religious people to get along with one another continue to be a source of suspicion against religious faith itself in the modern West.

Though the ninth commandment presupposes determinate beliefs about God and God's relation to the world, it doesn't offer a way to justify any particular religious perspective. Rather, it provides a guide for how all people, religious or not, ought to speak of each other in order to live together in ways that give others their due. The ninth commandment protects difference not by advocating a given content of belief or prescribing a substantive end for which we all should strive, but by demanding a mode of communication that will enhance a common life together, whatever convictions or ends persons, cultures, and nations arrive at through their decision-making procedures.

Historically, the ninth commandment has been taken to refer not just to truthful speech about human beings but to truthful speech about God as well. Believers in the God of Moses and in One whom Jesus Christ called "Father" are required to witness truthfully about God in their convictions about God no less than in their dealings with those around them. Just as false witness subverts relationships between people, false witness about God is a form of unfaithfulness to God and subverts religion even as it can appear to explicitly affirm and defend religion. Moreover, on the assumption that God is the foundation of all earthly good, false witness to God turns faith into a force that harms people and foments discord and possibly even hate.

The commandment is formulated negatively: "You shall *not* bear false witness against your neighbor." The Protestant tradition from which we write has historically read the commandment, however, as having a positive side as well. The negative side is a prohibition against misrepresentation, while the positive side is an injunction to present the other in the best possible light. Both the positive and negative sides of the commandment have implications for how to characterize each other and ourselves in the public sphere and in smaller communities, and most importantly for how to speak of God.

The Prohibition: Do Not Speak Falsely about the Other

The prohibition against lying in court is the paradigmatic application of the negative side of the commandment. The importance of truthful testimony in court can hardly be overstated, both with respect to the actual carrying out of justice and with respect to maintaining people's faith in the justice system itself. First, in and of itself, false witness is a form of injustice. The witness is false precisely in not "rendering" properly the character or actions of the person against whom it is uttered, in failing to give the person his or her due.[4] Second, because false witness fails to give the other his or her due, it forms a basis for miscarriage of justice. Finally, miscarriage of justice has negative consequences upon faith in the whole system of justice. If untruthful testimony is permitted, no system of justice will be trustworthy, no matter how Solonic or Solomonic it may be.

Martin Luther, the father of the Protestant Reformation, interpreted the commandment as pertaining primarily to the courts: "In the first and simplest meaning," he wrote in his *Large Catechism*, "as the words stand, this commandment pertains to public courts of justice, where one may accuse and malign a poor, innocent man and crush him by means of false witnesses, so that consequently he may suffer punishment in body, property, or honor."[5] Given the court setting, the commandment is intended to

4. For the idea of "rendering" with regard to truthfulness in history writing, see Paul Ricoeur, *The Reality of the Historical Past* (Milwaukee: Marquette University Press, 1984), pp. 26-27.

5. Luther, *Large Catechism*, in *The Book of Concord: The Confessions of the Evangelical Lutheran Church*, ed. Robert Kolb and Timothy Wengert (Minneapolis: Augsburg Fortress, 2000), p. 420.

ensure that "all people should help their neighbors maintain their legal rights. One must not allow these rights to be thwarted or distorted but should promote and resolutely guard them."[6]

Though the form of the prohibition is general and applies to all ("innocent man" or "neighbor"), Luther suggested that its main concern is with protecting the powerless against the powerful. He had in mind the likelihood that judges would be swayed by the power or privilege of some who came before the court and would allow truth to be bent and justice twisted. A special effort has to be made to protect the powerless. Those who judge must be "quite blind" to the power of those who come before them, and so do those who witness in court. The commandment is therefore a way to hedge against the all-too-easy corruption of procedures and of authority for the benefit of those in power.

Truth telling requires fairness in court toward the powerful, not just toward the powerless, of course. As Friedrich Nietzsche noted, the powerless have their own way of making false witness plausible and thus distorting justice,[7] though maybe less so in court than in other settings. To the extent, however, that human beings tend to favor the powerful and that the powerful have means to ensure that they are favored, the commandment can be fulfilled only if we are particularly vigilant that false witness is not employed against the powerless.

In a sense, this is a pragmatic approach to the justice and authority of a legal system. Instead of worrying mainly about the transcendental foundation of justice and how to access it through legal procedures, the command forbids undermining the rule of law in ways that will be harmful to others by pretending to submit to it. False witness doesn't do only direct and concrete — material — harm to the neighbor who is its victim. It also undermines the reliability of the legal system overall as well as more generally tearing the bonds between people. Healthy bonds are the precondition for the correction of any legal system as well as a consequence of its proper functioning.

As we suggested earlier, the commandment does not just forbid false witness in the court of law. Its application is broader and covers all false

6. Luther, *Large Catechism*, p. 421.

7. See his account of resentment in Friedrich Nietzsche, *On the Genealogy of Morality*, ed. Keith Ansell-Pearson, trans. Carol Diethe (Cambridge: Cambridge University Press, 1994).

witness borne against another, indeed all forms of lying. Consider stereotyping based on prejudice as a form of false witness. We rarely think of stereotyping as a form of false witness. But it is such; it's false speech about the other. *The Presbyterian Study Catechism* makes this point well: "In forbidding false witness against my neighbor, God forbids me to be prejudiced against people who belong to any vulnerable, different or disfavored social group. Jews, women, homosexuals, racial and ethnic minorities, and national enemies are among those who have suffered terribly from being subjected to the slurs of social prejudice."[8]

True, we are often not aware of our prejudices. They are false and injurious judgments we have slipped into making without even thinking whether they are based on sufficient knowledge or justified grounds. In such cases we are not deliberately bearing false witness. But since we are required to be truthful, we have the responsibility to acquire sufficient knowledge so as to make correct judgments. And true, it's not just people from dominant groups who have prejudices. Think of various conspiracy theories generated by minority church groups against "the Vatican" or of the facile imputation of excessive greed or lust for power to any successful CEO or politician! Prejudice is a form of false witness no matter where it comes from. And yet here too the false witness of the powerful is more injurious than the false witness of the powerless, and that holds true whether the powerful are in the minority or the majority. In any case, prejudice constitutes an injury as well as invites injurious actions on the part of others.

There are two other culturally important forms of injurious false witness that bear mentioning: false advertising and propaganda. These distortions of truth have negative consequences for the general population. People are misled into believing what they would not have believed otherwise and into acting as they would not have acted had they not been the objects of manipulation and misinformation. In advertising, care should be taken to avoid misrepresentation, overselling, false impressions, or even the creation of a false sense of need for the product advertised. Similarly, the commandment implies governmental responsibility for giving its citizens reliable information rather than "spin" to convince them of some course of action the government has already decided on. Certainly, it prohibits any type of the Orwellian "renaming" and "renarrating" to which totalitar-

---

8. *The Presbyterian Study Catechism*, 1998, Presbyterian Church, USA, September 15, 2005, available at http://www.pcusa.org/catech/studycat.htm.

ian and authoritarian regimes often take recourse to give a veneer of legitimacy to their abusive power. If we find ourselves resisting the suggestion to apply the commandment to such forms of distorted speech as stereotyping, false advertising, and propaganda, it may be wise to examine whether that is because it is easy to overlook subtle and yet pervasive ways in which we are untruthful, injure one another, and corrupt the fabric of society as a whole by false speech.

There is another level at which the prohibition against giving false witness is relevant — in speaking about oneself. Clearly, this is the case if we understand the commandment broadly, as prohibiting all lying. We should speak truthfully no less of ourselves than of our neighbors. But even if we understand the commandment more narrowly as referring simply to false witness about others, it still contains implications for truthfulness about ourselves. When we bear false witness and thus create an image of reality that is in accordance with what we find convenient to be true instead of conforming our speech to the order of things, we engage in hypocrisy. The favorable reception of our witness depends on the assumption that we are trying to name reality truthfully rather than speaking in blatant disregard of the truth. False witness about our neighbors *is* false witness about ourselves because to bear false witness against neighbors we must present ourselves as bearing true witness.

In sum, the negative aspect of the commandment against false witness functions paradigmatically in the courts, which is to say, in the public system of justice. By extension, it also forbids all lying, including stereotyping, false advertising, and propaganda. Finally, it prohibits giving a false account of oneself in the way that hypocrites do.

Though it may be easy for us to agree that we should not bear false witness in the domains mentioned above as well as in others, it is often not easy to tell when we are bearing false witness. Sometimes we do so in full awareness of what we are doing, of course. More often, however, we may speak untruthfully even when we want to speak the truth. Prejudice frequently functions that way, as we have seen. But we also distort truth in other settings without knowing it. Sometimes the line is hard to draw between "false" and "true," as it is on occasion hard to know when advertisers are justly praising their product and when they are overselling it.

Moreover, all our knowledge is situated, and when we bear witness, we bear it "from somewhere" rather than "from nowhere" or "from everywhere": we understand the world as finite human beings, occupying a particular social location, and pursuing particular interests, and each of these things puts blinders on us. The consequence is often more or less serious distortion of truth. The commandment not to bear false witness does not demand of us what we as inescapably finite, fallible, and failing human beings cannot do, namely, to transcend finitude and speak the absolutely uncontestable truth in the way the all-knowing God would. But it does urge us to make an honest and serious commitment to plain speaking and to resist the pull of personally and socially injurious falsehood.

The Injunction: Speak Only the Best of the Other

The prohibition against distorted speech is the negative side of the commandment and provides a minimal condition for justice. But for societies to flourish, more is needed: active protection and promotion of the other through speech, even the other with whom we disagree or with whom we are in conflict. In the Christian tradition the prohibition against false witness has been often interpreted as demanding not only that we avoid harming others with distorted speech but that we positively help them with loving speech. This is the broader and less obvious meaning of the commandment.

Seeking to express what he took to be the spirit of the commandment rather than its mere letter, Luther insisted that we cannot fulfill the ninth commandment just by abstaining from injurious false witness. What fulfills the ninth commandment, he insisted, is not just "a peaceful and beneficial manner of speech which harms no one." It is rather the kind of speech that "benefits everyone, reconciles the discordant, excuses and defends the maligned, that is, a manner of speech which is truthful and sincere."[9] Put in terminology used by the letter to the Ephesians, to fulfill the commandment we must speak "the truth in love" (Eph. 4:15).

The positive side of the ninth commandment has two aspects. First, we should *protest when others bear false witness.* We break the command not just by bearing false witness but by not defending our neighbors when we know that false witness is being borne against them. This was Calvin's view. He used Exodus 23:1 (read by him as "Thou shalt not receive a false

9. Martin Luther, *Luther's Works* (hereafter *LW*), vol. 43, ed. Harold J. Grimm (Philadelphia: Fortress, 1957), p. 23.

report") to demand that we refuse to endorse falsehoods implicitly by receiving them without correction.[10] We must give the other the benefit of the doubt. Instead of assuming the worst, or just thoughtlessly passing on what we hear, the command urges us to discernment in both listening and talking.

Second, we should *portray the neighbor in the best light.* Luther wrote: "You shall speak the best about your neighbor, in the market, in conversation, and elsewhere, and likewise in court."[11] In fact, he went so far as to demand that one place one's own reputation on the line not just to defend the neighbor from slander but, surprisingly, "to cover the sins and infirmities of our neighbors."[12] He, rightly, limited such "covering up" to private relationships between individuals. In the official capacity as a judge, for instance, a person has the responsibility to expose and condemn wrongdoing, whereas in the capacity as a private person who has suffered wrongdoing, she has the responsibility to forgive it and cover it up. "Hiding" sins is one particular and carefully circumscribed instance of a more general injunction to speak well of a neighbor in a way that reconciles and heals persons and relationships.

For Luther, the basic idea behind the demand is that human beings are "as much responsible for being as vigilant for their neighbor's interest as they are for their own!"[13] The real difficulty of keeping the commandment starts here. It cannot be fulfilled without giving up false self-interest — the desire for one's own benefit at the expense of the other, and indeed, the desire for one's own benefit more than that of the other. And yet that's what Christian life offers and demands: in all our dealings with our neighbors, God empowers and commands us to love them as ourselves. Even more, we should love them as Christ, who laid down his life for them, loved them. As Luther put it, we should be "Christs" to our neighbors.[14]

---

10. John Calvin, *Commentaries on the Last Four Books of Moses,* vol. 3 (Grand Rapids: Eerdmans, 1950), pp. 179-81.

11. Luther, "The 7th, 8th & 9th Commandments," in *LW* 51:158.

12. Luther, *Large Catechism,* p. 424. On multiple ways to "hide" sins, see Søren Kierkegaard, *Works of Love,* trans. Howard V. Hong and Edna H. Hong (Princeton: Princeton University Press, 1995), pp. 280ff., and Søren Kierkegaard, *Eighteen Upbuilding Discourses,* trans. Howard V. Hong and Edna H. Hong (Princeton: Princeton University Press, 1990), pp. 55-78.

13. Martin Luther, "Treatise on Good Works," in *LW* 44:110-11.

14. Martin Luther, "Freedom of the Christian," in *LW* 31:368.

On this second reading, the meaning of the ninth commandment goes far beyond a scrupulous adherence to truth in the avoidance of injury through falsehood. In addition, it requires that we further the good of others as we speak of them. All speaking about others is to take place with care for the reputation of the neighbor in a way that goes not only beyond a parsimonious truthfulness that would feel itself justified in speaking any evil of the other if it could plausibly be thought to be true, but also beyond even avoidance of all distorted speech to active care for and promotion of the welfare of the other. The Heidelberg Catechism's final requirement with regard to the ninth commandment is that "I should do what I can to guard and advance my neighbor's good name."[15] What is demanded is benevolent and beneficent speech, not just noninjurious speech. Such speech is not limited to private settings but should characterize public communication as well.

The positive dimension of this commandment offers an image of a society that deals with difference better than is currently the case, or, for that matter, better than was the case throughout human history. The effort to speak and hear good of others would foster negotiation of differences without canceling them. It would nudge us, for instance, to practice "double vision" — to view our neighbors not just from our perspective but from their perspective too — and would help us not only to understand them more truthfully but to appreciate them more generously even if, ultimately, we end up significantly disagreeing with them.[16] The focus on benevolence in representation makes this commandment essential to life in a pluralistic world.

In its positive aspect, the commandment urges us to make the activity of communication an occasion to practice grace. That's what the positive side of the commandment is all about. While the negative side represents a requirement of strict justice in rendering others their due, the positive injunction goes beyond what a strict construal of justice would require and demands that we show grace to others. Graceful speech is a way of fostering flourishing relations between people as they think and speak of one another.

Both on the broad public level and in the local community, trying to

15. *The Heidelberg Catechism* (Grand Rapids: Board of Publications of the Christian Reformed Church, 1973), p. 55 (q. 112).

16. See Miroslav Volf, *Exclusion and Embrace: A Theological Exploration of Identity, Otherness, and Reconciliation* (Nashville: Abingdon, 1996), pp. 233-73.

speak the best of each other is unusual. Just as the courts were the paradigmatic setting for the prohibition against bearing false witness, the church ought to be the paradigmatic setting for the positive injunction to tell the truth in love. The church itself is constituted by God's grace to be an embodiment of grace and therefore ought to practice grace in all its actions, including its speech. Though that is often not the case, the church ought to be an institution in which loving speech about others is valued, nurtured, and practiced. When we find churches and church members sniffing out the wrongdoing of others and giving a distorted account of the motives and characters of people with whom they disagree, the church is acting in a way untrue to itself.

The positive injunction in the commandment can be extended to include one more requirement of individuals. Beyond speaking well of their neighbors, they are also urged to speak well of themselves. The commandment, which functions negatively as a prohibition against hypocrisy in self-presentation, functions positively as a discouragement of false modesty, whatever its causes may be. Just as we are forbidden to make ourselves out to be better than we are, we are also discouraged from undercutting ourselves in dealing with others, even as we do seek to foster their well-being and promote their interests in a way equal to or greater than our own. Human beings were created in God's image (Gen. 1:27) and redeemed on account of God's inestimable love (John 3:16). To speak about ourselves as though we were of little value — say, when we have failed to reach goals we have set for ourselves or when we have wronged others — is to speak falsely about God's beloved creatures.

There are difficulties with the positive aspect of the ninth commandment. What does speaking well of others mean exactly? Why isn't it a form of false witness? Clearly, we should not speak well of one person if we are thereby papering over the wrongdoing she has committed toward another person. That would be like stealing from Peter to be generous to Paul. And yet there are ways of speaking well even of a wrongdoer while simultaneously pursuing the demands of justice. However, the primary application for the positive side of the command not to bear false witness is not in relation to wrongdoers but in relation to our ordinary neighbors, especially to those who are different from us, with whom we disagree, or with whom we are in conflict. Speaking well of them is a gift we give them — the gift of being seen with a loving gaze, heard with a loving ear, and described with a loving word.

Are we untruthful and unjust when we do that? In a sense, we are. But the name of that generous "untruthfulness" and "injustice" is loving grace. To exhibit such loving grace to all is what we are created and called to do by the same God who prohibits false witness. Moreover, an argument can be made that such grace toward the other will help us eschew bearing false witness when it is in our interest to do so and therefore enable us to keep the negative aspect of the commandment.[17]

Speaking of and with God

We have seen the negative and positive functions of the commandment applied on the level of the individual, the local community, and public society as a whole. The result of obeying the commandment would be a just and grace-filled society — a society in which we would find ourselves not only speaking the truth even when it is not in our interests but also defending those with whom we disagree and being defended by them. The antagonistic character of many conflicts would be greatly lessened. Yet the observance of the commandment would in no way deny the real differences between people and between their understandings of what is true and good. Instead, it would regulate the negotiation of those differences in truth and grace.

Beyond the practical betterment of society, for believers the observance of the ninth commandment is a matter of faithfulness to God. We owe it to God and not just to other people to speak rightly of them. Prohibition against false witness is *God's commandment,* after all. But we also owe it to God to speak rightly of *God,* our radically transcendent and yet most intimate neighbor. The God of justice who is at the same time the God of grace is the God to whom believers witness both when they speak directly of God and when they promote the welfare of their neighbors in light of this commandment.

In speaking of God, the commandment can once more be read as having both negative and positive aspects. In a polemical Reformation setting, Luther drew attention to the way adequate witness to God can easily be subverted by the very leaders who were to safeguard that witness in the first place. "All the great ones would oppose [the gospel] and grow furious"

17. See Volf, *Exclusion and Embrace,* pp. 233-73.

if it were to be preached again, he wrote.[18] That opposition to the gospel and the accompanying embrace of its substitutes constitute the false witness about God that the negative aspect of the commandment prohibits. The negative aspect, however, is but the obverse of the positive, which is to witness to "the gospel and the truth of faith."[19] The one who keeps the ninth commandment will risk "life and limb, property and reputation, friends and all that he has,"[20] Luther claimed, in order to speak rightly of God. In his mind the most important neighbor about whom the believer should witness truthfully is God.

An instance of false witness about God is found as early as the story of the fall in the Garden of Eden, the paradigmatic instance of such false witness. The serpent says to Eve, "Did God really say, 'You must not eat from any tree in the garden'?" (Gen. 3:1). The temptation functioned by insinuating a distorted picture of God. It suggested that God is arbitrary and excessively demanding (prohibition against eating the fruit of one tree), rather than generous (gift of all other trees, and indeed of the whole creation).[21] This is, however, the very opposite of who God truly is. Adam and Eve in fact did avoid saying what was untrue of God, so it seemed that they were safe in what they said and implied. And yet they were not. They did not take the further step of giving expression to God's unsurpassable goodness and speaking of God as someone whose actions and motives are to be interpreted in the best light.

Two ways of witnessing truthfully about God — positive and negative — can be done directly as well as indirectly. The direct way is exemplified in the apostle Paul's discussion of God's faithfulness to Abraham and Abraham's faith in God. The apostle said of Abraham, "He did not waver through unbelief regarding the promise of God, but was strengthened in his faith and gave glory to God, being fully persuaded that God had power to do what he had promised" (Rom. 4:20-21). As an act of trust and an affirmation of belief, faith is a form of direct witness to God. Indeed, it is the most proper form of direct witness to God, all other forms being derivative from it (whether they consist in speaking to God in gratitude or praise or speaking of God in theologically reflected speech). Why? Because faith is a

18. Luther, "Treatise on Good Works," in *LW* 44:112.
19. Luther, "Treatise on Good Works," in *LW* 44:111.
20. Luther, "Treatise on Good Works," in *LW* 44:110.
21. See Miroslav Volf, *Free of Charge: Giving and Forgiving in a Culture Stripped of Grace* (Grand Rapids: Zondervan, 2006).

mode of relating to God as God truly is, namely, the one who is faithful and whose nature is unconditionally loving. That's why it takes faith to give God glory, as the apostle Paul implied and as Luther argued.[22]

The second and indirect mode of faithful witness to God is required of the believer in relation to other people and flows naturally from the direct faithful witness to God. Witnessing rightly about God to others is not only and maybe not even primarily a matter of what we say to them about God — although that is important as well. It is more than anything a form of life lived as an alternative to a false life, which bears witness to the presence of God within it. This is once more why the church ought to be the space in which truth telling in the way this commandment requires it is passionately practiced. In their life in the church, in their character, activities, and speech in society, believers ought to witness truthfully about the God who has been faithful to them. Since church is the community of those whose lives have been marked by grace, members of that community should act in such a way that they show grace to one another and to those outside the community. The experience of grace is never a private affair, and it is never something that can rightfully be kept for ourselves. The parable of the unmerciful servant (see Matt. 18:23-35) is a reminder that grace hoarded is grace squandered.

To witness truthfully about God is to witness to the one who, in the Christian account of reality, gives authority to and makes possible the reasonable obedience of the command not to bear false witness. Ultimately, we refrain from false speech and we show grace in our speech as individuals, members of local communities, and participants in the public arena because we believe in God, creator, redeemer, and consummator of the world, who is a God of truth and love — a God of loving truth and truthful love. While pragmatic arguments about the benefits to society of dealing with each other in truthful ways can convincingly be made, the requirement for believers who have experienced the grace of God is absolute. They should not speak falsely but show grace to others, and in so doing they will witness truthfully to God. Just as faith toward God is the most basic form of direct truthful witness to God, so love of the neighbor borne of that faith is the most basic form of indirect truthful witness about God.

In conclusion, the ninth commandment urges us to make the nature of the speech with which people characterize one another and God the ob-

---

22. See Luther, "Freedom of the Christian," in *LW* 31:353.

ject of attention. At minimum, it demands what strict justice requires: not to speak *falsely*, whether in court, in the marketplace and halls of power, or in church and family. Beyond that, it urges us to speak of others in the most generous way compatible with not speaking falsely. In both of these ways, it functions as a safeguard against allowing legitimate disagreements about wrongdoing suffered or endured or about comprehensive interpretations of life or the shape of social arrangements to escalate into bloody wars. And most importantly, the commandment also guards our speech about the One for whose sake we seek to honor this commandment and thus contribute to human flourishing.

Response

David Patterson

Professors Miroslav Volf and Linn Tonstad offer a great deal of insight into the meaning of the ninth commandment. In keeping with the Christian understanding they present, from a Jewish perspective, too, this commandment is about doing injury to our fellow human beings, and therefore to God and to ourselves, with our words. As it is written, "Death and life are in the power of the tongue" (Prov. 18:21). In response to these authors' understanding of the commandment from a Christian perspective, I would like to add a Jewish view of the commandment, as well as raise a question concerning a Christian perspective on it.

A good place to begin a Jewish approach to the ninth commandment is with the Hebrew: *Lo-taaneh vereakha ed shaker* (Exod. 20:16). The verb *lo-taaneh*, "You shall not bear. . . ," is *anah*, a word that means to "answer" or to "respond" in the light of having heard a summons or a question. Which means: our neighbor cries out to us, asking us, as God asked the first human being, "Where are you?" Therefore, in order to answer *Hineni!* — "Here I am for you!" — we must answer *in truth*, that is, with the truth of who we are, children of God subject to his commandments. To speak lies about our neighbor is to fail to be who we are by failing to be present before the other human being. And the failure to be present before the other human being is a failure to be present before God.

"False witness about our neighbors," then, "*is* false witness about ourselves," as Volf and Tonstad maintain, but perhaps for an even deeper reason. For among the greatest commandments of Torah is *Veahavta lereakha kamokha*, "And you shall love your neighbor as yourself" (Lev. 19:18). Contrary to a common misconception, this commandment does not mean "I know how much you love yourself, and that is how much I want you to

194

love your neighbor." No, given the meanings for the word *kamokha*, "as yourself," as well the *le-* in *lereakha*, a better translation would be: "you shall show love *toward* your neighbor, for that loving *is* your self": the soul and substance of who you are lie in that loving approach toward the neighbor, with hands ready to *give* to the neighbor. For the root of the verb to "love," *veahavta*, is *hav*, which means to "give." Like the failure to speak the truth with regard to our neighbor, the failure to love our neighbor is a failure to be who we are, a failure to *give* who we are. Therefore living in a caring relation and answering truthfully to our neighbor are of a piece.

Volf and Tonstad point out that social justice is impossible without a caring relation to one another, which in turn is impossible without a testimony contrary to *ed shaker*, to "false testimony." True "testimony" or *ed* is at the root of *edah*, "community," and social justice is necessary to any human community that is indeed a community. Also essential to human community or *dwelling* in the world is the divine Presence, the *Shekhinah*, which is the "Indwelling Presence" of God. Volf and Tonstad sense this connection in their insistence that the ninth commandment pertains to false testimony against the divine Neighbor, as well as against the human neighbor. If the commandment does not include false testimony against God, then it loses its truth and authority, as Volf and Tonstad suggest when they write, "We refrain from false speech . . . because we believe in God, creator, redeemer, and consummator of the world."

Therefore the substance of this commandment regarding our relation to our neighbor lies in the substance of the commandments regarding our relation to God. Here too the Jewish tradition may add some depth to our understanding. The midrash, for example, teaches that the first five commandments (on the human-to-God relation) parallel the second five (on the human-to-human relation) (see *Mekilta de-Rabbi Ishmael, Bachodesh* 8). Thus, when the tablets are held side by side, the fourth commandment, which concerns the observance of the Sabbath, parallels the ninth commandment. Just as our Sabbath observance opens a portal for the Holy One to enter the world, so do the lies we speak close that portal. And when that portal is closed, we lose our humanity.

Hence, as Volk and Tonstad state, "the focus of the commandment is not on truth for truth's sake"; it's on truth for the sake of the Holy One and the human being created in his image. The commandment is a response to the question of how we speak about each other so as not to injure one another. Jewishly speaking, it is about *lashon hara*, or the "evil tongue." So serious is *lashon hara* that the Talmud compares it to the sins of idolatry, adultery, and murder (*Arakhin* 15b), the three sins a Jew must refuse even on pain of death (*Sanhedrin* 74a). *Lashon hara,* says the Talmud, kills three people — the speaker, the listener, and the subject — and is equivalent to atheism (*Arakhin* 15b). Here too Volk and Tonstad are right on target in their argument that the commandment pertains not only to the one who speaks false witness but also to the one who hears it, maintaining that "we should *protest when others bear false witness.*" If we do not protest, then we become an accomplice to the violation of the commandment.

The Talmud relates in this connection that when Rabbi Alexandrai was asked about the source of life, he answered by quoting the Psalms: "Who is the man who longs for life and loves days, that he may see the good? Guard your tongue from evil and your lips from speaking deceit (Psalms 34:13-14)" (*Avodah Zarah* 19b). Therefore, every day observant Jews repeatedly pray to God, "Guard my tongue from evil and my lips from speaking deceit." The evil of the "evil tongue" lies in the harm we cause our neighbor when we speak or listen to false witness or negative statements about our neighbor — *even if they are true.* And yet in the best-known work on the topic, the Chofetz Chayim makes no mention of the ninth commandment in his list of the thirty-one commandments pertaining to *lashon hara*. Nor does the Talmud link false witness with the evil tongue.[1] Instead, the evil tongue is associated with the commandment "You shall not be a gossipmonger among your people" (Lev. 19:16). There are, however, other sacred texts that link *lashon hara* with bearing false witness. Examples include the midrash on Proverbs 25:4 and the section called "The Path of the Tongue" in the *Netivot Olam* (chap. 7, p. 79). Further, in the Otzar Midrash King Solomon maintains that the ninth commandment includes the prohibition against *lashon hara* (Otzar Midrash, *Aseret Hadibrot* 18).[2]

The key to the connection between the ninth commandment and the evil tongue lies in the bond between word and meaning, which is the bond between human and human. The prohibition against bearing false witness against our neighbor is a prohibition against tearing word from meaning. At stake in our observance of the commandment is the meaning of the

---

1. Chofetz Chayim, *Guard Your Tongue,* adapted by Zelig Pliskin (Jerusalem: Tzur-Ot Press, 1975), pp. 13-26.

2. See *Judaic Classics,* CD-ROM, Davka Corporation, 1995.

word "human being." A lie is an assault on the word, which in turn is an assault on the human being. According to Jewish tradition, the deadly nature of a lie is at the heart of the Tower of Babel. Commenting on the phrase *navlah sham sfatam*, "let us confuse their tongues" (Gen. 11:7), the eighteenth-century sage Rabbi Yaakov Culi explains that *navlah* may also be read as *nevelah,* which means "corpse." Read in this way, says Rabbi Culi, the verse means "let us make their speech produce corpses."[3] Which is to say: in the lie that tears word from meaning people lose their memory of what "person" means. And when we forget what a person is, people die, violently and indiscriminately.

Recall in this connection the midrash that when a man fell to his death during the construction of the tower, no one even noticed; but when a brick was dropped and broken, a great lamentation went up and a cry of "Oh, woe! Where shall we find another like it?" (*Pirqe Rabbi Eliezer* 24). This confusion began when they attempted to "make themselves a name" by creating their own dimension of height, the tower, rather than live in a relation to the Most High, from whom their name derives. When, through our false witness, we lose the dimension of height and holiness, words lose their meaning and humans lose their holiness. The mending of the bond between word and meaning is attained in the pursuit of truth and justice that Volk and Tonstad describe in their essay. And it has never been more needful than now, at the onset of the twenty-first century, when murderers pass as martyrs. Despite our philosophical concern with language, we have lost the link between word and meaning. Which means: we have lost the link between human and human.

Volk and Tonstad have astutely demonstrated how and why the ninth commandment is essential to the bond between human and human, between God and humanity. As a Jew, however, I must express a concern over a few lines in their essay. Quoting Paul, they assert that "to fulfill the commandment we must speak 'the truth in love' (Eph. 4:15)." Isn't "the truth in love" the truth of the new covenant of salvation through the blood of Jesus Christ, the Son and incarnation of God? The authors maintain that the "opposition to the gospel" constitutes "the false witness about God that the negative aspect of the commandment prohibits. The negative aspect, however, is but the obverse of the positive, which is to witness to 'the gos-

---

3. Yaakov Culi, *The Torah Anthology: MeAm Lo'ez,* vol. 1, trans. Aryeh Kaplan (New York: Maznaim, 1977), p. 420.

pel and the truth of faith.'" It would seem, then, that the Jews, who consci-
entiously reject the gospel, are in violation of the ninth commandment.

But perhaps "the gospel and the truth of faith" is not so much about
the content of doctrine as about human relation. From a Jewish stand-
point, true testimony lies far more in actions than in words or even in beliefs. Recall that the Hebrew term for "bearing" witness suggests that to
bear witness is to respond to a question; if it is God who commands, it is
also God who asks. He asks about our testimony to and for our neighbor,
putting to us the questions he put to Cain: "Where is your brother?" (Gen.
4:9) and "What have you done?" (4:10). God does not ask, "What do you
believe?" or "Are you saved?" Nor does he ask because he does not know:
"The voice of your brother's blood," he declares, "cries out to me" (4:10).
No, he asks because if Cain is to be Cain, a human being created in the image of the Holy One, then he must answer, not with an affirmation of faith
but with a demonstration of deeds.

To bear witness to the truth is to say to God *Hineni!* by saying it to our
fellow human being. We bear that witness more with our hands than with
our mouth. To bear false witness, then, is not only to speak falsely but also
to act falsely. And acting falsely has little to do with professing a doctrine
or a belief; it has everything to do with answering the cry of our fellow human being with a piece of bread or a loving embrace. The terrorist fanati-
cism that plagues our world demonstrates what happens when we understand the prohibition against bearing false witness in terms of professing a
doctrine, and not in terms of loving-kindness toward every human being,
despite the differences of doctrine. If we are content to recite, "I believe, I
believe," then we bear false witness against God and neighbor. How, then,
shall we observe the ninth commandment? By answering *in truth* the questions put to Cain: Where is your brother? And what have you done? — lest
we become a Cain to our brother.

God or Mammon

R. R. Reno

You shall not covet.

"Do not lay up for yourselves treasures on earth, where moth and rust consume and where thieves break in and steal," Jesus advises us, "but lay up for yourselves treasures in heaven" (Matt. 6:19-20). Echoing the spiritual diagnosis that animates so much of the Old Testament, Jesus links covetousness to adultery and idolatry as he completes the thought, "For where your treasure is, there will be your heart also" (v. 21). Just as a man cannot vow himself to a woman and chase skirts; just as he cannot fast to purify his soul and parade his sanctity before others; so also, he cannot seek the treasure of heaven while turning his heart and mind to acquiring the treasures of this world. "No one can serve two masters," Jesus teaches, "for either he will hate the one and love the other, or he will be devoted to the one and despise the other. You cannot serve God and mammon" (v. 24).

It is telling that Jesus does not say that we cannot serve God and Baal, or God and Caesar, or God and Dionysius, though quite obviously he could have because we cannot. This is fitting. Priests and theologians are most often servants of Baal. Few lust for power and surrender to Caesar. Most suffer from the wandering eye of sexual desire, but it is notoriously fickle. In contrast, the eye of greed is widespread, and it can become fixed, constant, and dominant. The keen moral psychologist John Chrysostom saw how avarice can trump. "So tyrannical is the passion" for wealth, he notes, "that it sometimes prevails over lust." For this reason the strict taskmaster Mammon can create the illusion of virtue. As Chrysostom observes, "to spare their money, many indeed have bridled their unchastity."[1] The expense of the swinging life may be its greatest deterrent, and the ability of greed to restrain lust shows the power of Mammon.

Greed is cruel as well. Chrysostom observes in the same homily that the desires of the body admit of temporary satisfaction, but the avaricious soul always wants more. Quoting from Sirach and exploiting the tradition that draws on the tripartite scheme of 1 John 2:16 ("lust of the flesh, desire of the eyes, and pride of life"), Chrysostom places greed among the sins of the eyes. As Chrysostom observes of the greedy soul: "He sees with his eyes and groans as a eunuch groans when embracing a girl" (Sir. 30:20). The image of unconsummated — unconsummatible — desire reflects the literal meaning of avarice. It comes from the Latin verb *aveo*, "to crave." The term translates the Greek term *pleonexia*, the desire to have more. Both words suggest a state of desire that, unlike lust and gluttony, seeks no specific object of pleasure and admits of no satiated satisfaction. Instead, avarice aches ever for more. Like a perverse reflection of the love of God that is happily without limit, greed seeks an infinite goal. The murderer may be satisfied with sweet revenge, but the servant of Mammon will pile treasure to ever greater heights.

The great tradition of Christian moral reflection sees still further implications. Basil links avarice to theft and false testimony: "Who is the father of lying? Who is the maker of forgeries? Who brings forth perjury? Is it not wealth? Not a zeal for wealth?"[2] Others list violence and murder as fruits of greed. Chrysostom observes that often men do not honor their fathers and mothers. As they covet their inheritances, they resent the financial liabilities that arise from aging parents. Not only are the fifth and sixth commandments violated by greed, but the second as well. As Chrysostom continues, many possess wealth and dare not use it, "but consecrate it, handling it untouched, not daring to touch it, as though it were some dedicated thing."[3]

Thus does the reign of Mammon involve a wholesale violation of the

---

1. *Homilies on Matthew* 83.2. My use of patristic sources throughout this essay is deeply indebted to Richard Newhauser's invaluable monograph, *The Early History of Greed: The Sin of Avarice in Early Medieval Thought and Literature* (Cambridge: Cambridge University Press, 2000).

2. Patrologia Graeca 31:297. I draw this quote from Newhauser, *Early History of Greed*, p. 65.

3. Chrysostom, *Homilies on John*, Homily 65, par. 3.

Ten Commandments. The plenary wickedness of covetousness is summed up in the most common images of greed in Christian literature, ancient and medieval. Avarice is pictured as a transfixed eye that is bewitched by the luster of gold and a gaping mouth that consumes the poor. The former symbolizes an idolatrous transgression of the first table of the Decalogue, and the latter a systematic transgression of the second table.

Can we see the dangers of serving Mammon? Do our contemporary moral sensibilities allow us to see the expansive, spiritual nature of covetousness? For many, social ethics and questions of economic justice have come to predominate. We tend to follow 1 Timothy 6:10: "Love of money is the root of all evil." And this shift in focus may be a proper reading of the signs of the times. Our middle-class society is defined far less by honor — the dry tinder that the sparks of pride can turn into a raging fire — than by wealth. The dangers we face are many, but the danger most pressing may be Mammon's command over our lives. However, to see the symptoms does not guarantee accurate diagnosis and appropriate treatment. We do well to consult the treasure of Christian moral teaching on the dangers of greed, for in this tradition the social realities of greed are subordinated to its spiritual dangers. The final commandment of the Decalogue is clearly linked to the first, and we ignore this link at our peril.

I

For Marxists and Leftist fellow travelers, the luster of coins is a purely social construct that has no intrinsic beauty. We need only smash the idols of capitalism by abolishing private property, and the charm will be broken. This promise is the key to the enduring appeal of Leftist thought. Even though historical materialism is an utterly failed theory of history, and actually existing socialist countries were and continue to be moral and economic failures, the dream lives: put an end to the acquisitive marketplace, and greed will die.

Most do not renounce commerce altogether. Nonetheless, contemporary Leftists of various stripes worry about income inequality, condemn conspicuous consumption, and work hard to minimize the influence of markets over our lives. In general, the activist is strategizing to find a way for society as a whole to minimize incentives toward commercial gain and maximize social relations free from the base metals of gold and silver. The assumption is not unlike that of iconoclasts. If we eliminate the objects of vicious desire, especially the tempting conventions of private property, then we will free ourselves from the reign of Mammon.

But is this so? Will smashing stained glass windows prevent us from giving our hearts to false gods? Will eliminating or minimizing the role of private property tame our covetous desires? I have never found the Marxist moral analysis of wealth and its grip on the human soul persuasive. I have not been edified by the many sermons I have heard (few self-consciously Marxist, but all shaped by a general Leftist sentiment) that have attempted to shift the dangers of our desire for wealth onto the supposed injustices of our economic system. I have found Boethius, the fifth-century Christian philosopher, more persuasive.

Boethius wrote his influential treatise *The Consolation of Philosophy* in the dungeon of Alvanzano, where he had been sent by the emperor Theodoric and from which he would not emerge until the time of his execution. The substance of his reflections concerns misfortune and the saving power of true wisdom. The treatise begins with Boethius bewailing his circumstances, the injustice of his imprisonment, and the ill fortune he has suffered. It is in this mournful state that a woman appears before him, the beautiful and commanding countenance of Lady Philosophy.

In the course of his discussion with Lady Philosophy, Boethius laments that the world is against us, for Fortune spreads her benefits in a fickle and unjust fashion. The wicked prosper and the righteous often suffer defeat. Wealth and honors go to those who do not deserve them, while the meritorious receive no reward. Boethius's complaint is parallel to the social moralism of the Left. The structures of society are unjust. Honest labor is exploited and human needs are neglected, while the accidents of birth and accumulative desire are rewarded. But for these unjust structures, virtue would flourish and human relations would be properly ordered toward the common good.

Lady Philosophy defends the vagaries of Fortune against Boethius's complaint, and by extension, against the complaints of so many social critics in our day. True, she says, wealth and honors are spread unevenly and without consistency. But, she continues, our complaints are based upon spiritual fantasies. We imagine that Fortune should solve our problems by being more evenhanded. Against this dream, Dame Philosophy points out that just distribution of worldly goods will not quench our bitter complaints. "Wild greed," she says, "swallows what it has sought, and still gapes wide for more."[4] Those of us who think a meritocratic system will bring us to a greater social comity and personal satisfaction are as deluded as those who seek a more egalitarian system, and the utopians who imagine a world of plenty in which none hanker for more are most deluded of all. "What bit or bridle," Lady Philosophy asks, "will hold within its course this headlong lust, when, whetted by abundance of rich gifts, the thirst for possessions burns?"[5] The answer is clear. As Dame Philosophy teaches throughout her conversation with Boethius, we can conquer vice only with virtue. Spiritual diseases require spiritual cures.

The wisdom of Dame Philosophy is simple, yet in so much of our thinking about wealth and its capacity to distort and destroy human life, we often ignore it. When Mammon beckons and controls, no social reform will do the trick. One needs little experience in life to see that few will be happy with what they have, whether distributed according to merit, equally, or according to need. We are no more cured of our avarice by the banishment of money and the reform of social injustices than the idolatrous heart is transformed by the destruction of graven images. Even if we socialize capital, ban usury, and redistribute wealth, we cannot escape the dangerous temptations of avarice. Mammon has many methods of temptation at his disposal. He is not limited to the lure of gold and silver coins, or the conventions of inheritance, or economies that protect private property and use markets to allocate capital. Greed is not a vice that stems from the social phenomena of money and the marketplace, and it cannot be overcome by destroying those social practices. As Jesus' teaching in the Sermon on the Mount makes clear, avarice is spiritual, and when we violate the first commandment it flourishes, no matter how elaborate the dams and levies of social justice.

II

If modern socialism has tempted us to fantasize that we can defeat Mammon by limiting the role of private property in social life, and in so tempting us has unwittingly served Mammon by distracting us from the deeper, spiritual sources of our greed, then an opposite modern sentiment has

---

4. Boethius, *The Consolation of Philosophy* (New York: Modern Library, 1943), p. 24.
5. Boethius, *The Consolation of Philosophy*, p. 24.

produced a similar complacency. The social realist argues that greed is inevitable. Can life be lived any other way? A modern man or woman who has read a book or two in economic or political theory might well think that ambition and desire for reward are not just inevitable but are positively necessary for any productive society. As Adam Smith suggests, when harnessed to the marketplace, greed has the paradoxical effect of contributing to the common good. In this way, private vice can put on the mien of public virtue, and Mammon can claim valid title to his realm.

To illuminate the lure of this way of thinking, I turn to William Langland, a late medieval poet and contemporary of Chaucer, who wrote a strange and beautiful poem called *Piers Plowman*.[6] His extended and complex work vividly portrays social problems. It is rich with the injustices brought on by the emerging mercantile, money-based economies of Europe. Langland dramatizes the social situation with an allegorical dream in which Meed the Maiden ("meed" is an old English word that denotes reward, wage, or recompense for labor, but it can also mean bribe) wreaks havoc with her alluring beauty. Clergy fall victim to simony. Knights and noblemen neglect their duties and chase after her. Merchants regret their losses more than their sins. Justice can be bought and sold. Usury, avarice, theft, lying, envy, and richly decorated pride flourish. Everyone ogles Meed the Maiden with corrupting desire.

In the framework of the allegory, Meed the Maiden is captured and brought before the king. Like all worldly rulers, the king would like to harness this lovely lady to the task of just governance. To bring Meed the Maiden under the sway of justice, he urges Conscience to marry her. But Conscience is too wise to the ways of such a woman, for she is fickle and has ruined many men. It appears that the blandishments of Meed the Maiden cannot be domesticated. But what, then, is the king to do? Here Langland seems to anticipate a modern approach to social problems. Should the king not banish Meed the Maiden from his kingdom? Should he not root out the profit motive, ensure income equality, socialize the means of production?

---

6. My reading of *Piers Plowman* follows the helpful analysis found in chapter 4 of Donald R. Howard, *The Three Temptations: Medieval Man in Search of the World* (Princeton: Princeton University Press, 1966). See also David Aers, *Chaucer, Langland, and the Creative Imagination* (London: Routledge and Kegan Paul, 1980), especially chapter 1, "Imagination and Traditional Ideologies in *Piers Plowman*," pp. 1-37. Citation of the poem follows passus and line from the "C" text according to my translation.

At this point Langland allows Meed the Maiden to speak in her own defense. She offers what in present terms might be called neoconservative observations about society:

> It becomes for a king that shall keep a realm
> To give men meed that meekly him serves,
> To aliens and to all men, to honor him with gifts;
> Meed makes him be beloved and held as a man.
> Emperors and earls and all manner lords
> Through gifts have servants to run and ride.
> The pope and all prelates presents accept
> And give meed to men to maintain their laws.
> Servants for their service meed they ask
> And take meed of their masters as by agreed accord.
> Both beggars and beadsmen crave meed for their prayers;
> Minstrels for their minstrelsy ask for their meed;
> Masters that teach clerks crave their meed
> Priests that preach and the people teach
> Ask for meed and masspennies and their meals as well.
> All craftsmen crave meed for their apprentices
> Merchandise and meed must go together.
> There is no lad that lives that loves not meed
> And glad to grasp her, great lord or poor.
>
> (3.264-82)

Needless to say, the king, who is the allegorical voice of social authority, is taken aback. "By Christ," he says. "Meed is worthy, me thinks, her mastery to have" (3.283-84). But this is not the final word. The elaborate allegorical dream concludes as Conscience goes to get Reason, who puts Wrong on trial while Meed winks at the lawyers and sows corruption and confusion. The king is exasperated. Like a utopian revolutionary, he dismisses the entire machinery of the legal system and installs Reason as his chief chancellor and Conscience as the king's justice in all the courts.

The allegorical dream ends, but as the poem continues it becomes clear that Langland rejects utopian strategies for expelling Lady Meed and her temptations from social relations. He does not think one can sweep away a social system occupied by finite, fallen men and women and animated by vice by installing Reason and Conscience as omnipotent legislator and judge. In a poignant scene of good intentions brought to grief by human failings, Langland concludes that we must deploy the attractions of Lady Meed (and the punishments of Sir Hunger!) to motivate the greedy (and discipline the lazy). Thus, in the larger context of the poem, Lady Meed's speech would seem to win the day. It is not true that love makes the world go 'round. In general, it makes the world stop in its tracks — or go off its rails. For men and women tainted by original sin, meed makes the world go 'round.

If I am right about my interpretation of the social philosophy implicit in *Piers Plowman* (and it is a very complex and difficult poem to interpret), then it highlights an important aspect of our struggle with Mammon. If we join Langland in rejecting the Leftist hope that we can build a society that banishes temptation, then we must shape our social policies in such a way that our all-too-real vices are restrained and disciplined to serve useful ends. But Langland's social conclusions dramatize the deepest temptation of Mammon, a temptation we have already seen in the Leftist utopian dreams. It is the temptation to believe that there is no difference between spiritual and worldly life. For the Leftist, vice is a social phenomenon. If we would but change the structures of society, we can cure the souls of citizens. For the social realist, the collapse of the spiritual into the worldly is not based in the hope that social change will bring virtue. Instead, the collapse is based on the false inference from the inevitable and necessary role of avarice in worldly life to the conclusion that it is not a vice.

Although the paths are very different, the destination is the same. We can redefine virtue to accommodate economic necessities, or we can insist that economic necessities are the sources of vice. We can celebrate the dynamic and wealth-generating economies of democratic capitalism as providential gifts, or we can rally in the streets to smash capitalism and establish a social system in which it will be impossible to be greedy. In both cases, we want our decisions about political parties or social policies to be spiritually pure. In both cases, and this is the crux of the problem, we raise the god of the worldly life — Mammon — to the level of the God of heaven and earth, either to insure comity or to initiate combat.

We should resist this deification of Mammon with all our might, for at root it entails transgression of the first commandment, because it presumes that the god of this world has the power to define good and evil. Here Langland offers clear guidance. Meed the Maiden is not an independent actor or sui generis principle of wrong. She wreaks havoc because she brings out our base desires. She is an accelerant or precipitant who exposes weakness of character. Or to shift metaphors, she is nothing more than the gold of merit or just reward that the alchemy of vice turns into the lead of luxury and bribery. Not surprisingly, then, the poem turns from the dream about Meed the Maiden to a second dream in which Reason preaches a long sermon that calls the seven deadly sins to repentance. Just as Lady Philosophy teaches that spiritual problems require spiritual solutions, Langland sees that avarice cannot be defeated in the world. Vice must be overturned in the heart. One can concede that the world is dominated by Mammon, but one should never allow the world to dominate one's soul.

III

Can we follow the wisdom of Boethius and Langland, a wisdom representative of the wider Christian tradition? With a simple inference I think we can. If Mammon is the god of this world, then we can escape his clutches only if we renounce the world. While it does not always formulate the antecedent (perhaps pride and not love of money is the root of all evil), the great bulk of the premodern Christian tradition consistently affirms the consequent. Consider the advice that Saint Paul gives to those of us whose duties and vocations necessarily involve us in the "necessities" of life — marriage and procreation, as well as commerce and governance. He tells us to "deal with the world as though [you] have no dealings with it. For the present form of the world is passing away" (1 Cor. 7:31). We may not be able to withdraw from the world. In fact, God may call us to an even greater involvement in the world. Yet, it should be an involvement as though it were no involvement, an acknowledgment of certain worldly necessities that is, at the same time, a recognition that such necessities are passing away.

The implications for avarice are clear. One need not serve Mammon if one is willing to renounce citizenship in his kingdom and live as a resident alien. We can acknowledge the necessity of meed and yet escape the vice of avarice, if we will not define our lives in terms of the worldly affairs that Mammon inevitably dominates. For this reason, in one way or another, the Christian tradition has taught *contemptus mundi,* contempt for the world, as the basic strategy for overcoming avarice. To live a life of action and responsibility is the vocation of most Christians. Few of us are called into the desert or cloister. Yet, such a life must be lived with the knowledge that this world we are called to serve, sustain, and improve is passing away.

This is easily said, but how can it be done? There are many strategies. One thinks, for example, of the haughty nobility of the chivalrous ideal in medieval poetry. The deep shame that the poet ascribes to Sir Gawain when the Green Knight exposes his secret cowardice and covetousness, a cowardice and covetousness based on no shameful thing, but rather a love of life, testifies to the medieval ideal of contempt for the world.[7] But we do not live in a world in which chivalrous ideals can function (though the success of the Tolkien movies may suggest otherwise), so I turn to three other spiritual strategies for resisting greed, each of which is widely commended by the old writers of the tradition, and each of which creates a contempt for the world that allows us to develop a proper love for God.

In late medieval and Renaissance culture, contempt for the world is expressed in the popular image of the saint or nobleman contemplating a skull in order to overcome the bewitchment of the world by bringing to mind the reality of death. This contemplation of death — *memento mori* — remains a useful spiritual exercise. A common piece of contemporary wisdom reiterates this ancient truth. We are told that in our dying moments we will not regret that we did not spend more time at the office. To know the ubiquity of death makes us sensible of the absurdity of putting our trust and hope in wealth and worldly achievement. Is it an accident that our society, which so wants our loyalty, hides death from view and wishes to protect us from this harsh reality?

In his *Divine Comedy,* Dante depicts the Mountain of Purgatory with seven ledges, one for each of the seven deadly sins. On the ledge of avarice the souls lie facedown, adhered to the pavement. Dante stoops down to speak with one soul. He explains to Dante his punishment: "Even as our eyes fixed upon earthly things, were not lifted on high, so justice here has sunk them to the earth . . ." (*Purgatorio* 19.118-120). When I first read these lines, I was perplexed. Dante always envisions the punishments on the Mountain of Purgatory as purifying and transformative, and I could not see how the downward gaze of the greedy could cure them of their lust for worldly good. Should they not be purified by the upward vision of God? Then, when I thought of *memento mori,* I recognized Dante's genius. The avaricious sin because they love too much the finite beauty of worldly

7. See *Sir Gawain and the Green Knight,* lines 2374-75.

things. A pious soul — the person who explains the punishment is a long-dead pope who meant well — can become a slave to Mammon when he makes an idol of worldly wealth and power. The eyes are forced downward in punishment so that the penitent soul can watch the objects of worldly greed rust and molder. To see the truth about Mammon's kingdom releases one from his thrall.

In our own time and place, we do well to fix our eyes downward and on the affairs of the world. Go to funerals, and be reminded that from dust we have come and to dust we shall return. Attend city council meetings, and learn that while the meek may inherit the earth, it is currently run by the real estate developers, lobbyists, and ill-informed elected officials. Read the *Wall Street Journal,* and enjoy the absurdity of current efforts to ensure that stock analysts are not influenced by the investment bankers who pay their salaries. This is not to say that love, dignity, and honesty do not shine through worldly affairs. Dante's poetic image of the punishment of the avaricious does not breed contempt for humanity or a hatred of finite existence. Rather, the point of contemplating the world is to recognize the utter absurdity of imagining that anyone other than God himself could fashion it into a heavenly kingdom. God may call us to become doctors and fight to snatch a few more years out of death's grip. He may call us to political action or economic responsibility. But anyone who imagines that such vocations are intrinsically divine, and that one's successes and failures are freighted with transcendent significance, will fall victim to avarice and will serve Mammon in order to serve God — something Jesus refused to do when tempted by Satan in the wilderness with the offer of worldly power.

I must leave off the path of contemplation and turn to the way of action. The old writers consistently advocate charity as the great bulwark against greed. Langland again and again emphasizes that giving money to the poor is the direct route to defeating the dominance of Meed the Maiden. She may rule society, but she need not rule our hearts. We must part with something in order to drive a wedge in our hearts between God and Mammon. Giving away money is a crucial step in breaking off our adulterous romance with wealth.

Exhortations to charity are common in our churches. Yet, in my experience, most contemporary Christians, especially sensible and responsible American Christians, fail to understand and practice the ancient idea of charity. Christian writers have long urged the wealthy and powerful to take responsibility for the common good. We are called to support projects and programs that ameliorate poverty, promote education, and support public institutions. These forms of charity may reflect a proper Christian concern for civic responsibility and social justice, but they do not adequately address the temptations of avarice. For this reason, one consistently finds that the old writers endorse forms of "irresponsible" charity. The nobleman is not just to set up a poorhouse. He is to throw a springtime banquet for all. The former involves an attempt to work within the constraints of worldly affairs, because it seeks to do a good that will endure. The latter is an act of contempt for the world, for the celebration cares not for the morrow.

We should take up a discipline of "foolish" charity. Give and do not try to control the outcome of your giving. Give with a careless attitude that trusts in the providence of God rather than the ways of the world. Do not say, "He will use the money only to buy another bottle of booze." Do not say, "Why throw good money after bad?" Do not say, "How can I be sure the resources are being used well?" Show contempt for the world with an act of charity that does not simply take from the right hand of Mammon to give to the left, from your mutual fund to a foundation's endowment. For a well-meaning and philanthropic American Christian, an act of charity that has no promise of bearing worldly fruit may be a very important way of escaping from the subtle insinuations of avarice.

I have briefly developed two strategies for overcoming the temptation to worship Mammon: contempt for the world and wanton charity. I wish to end with a third, for we cannot overcome sin by recognizing its ugliness and perversity. We can free ourselves from lower loves only by a higher love. Contemplation of the rusting and moldering structures of worldly life frees us from fantasies about our lower loves. Foolish acts of charity help us free our souls for the foolishness of the gospel. But to escape from Mammon we must turn our eyes upward. We can resist a finite beauty only if we allow ourselves to be ravished by infinite beauty. Only if we nourish a love for the kingdom of God can we develop and sustain a contempt for the world that does not decay into despair or cynicism.

This exchange of loves is endorsed by Saint Augustine as the cure for avarice. Commenting on the final verses of Psalm 90, he urges us, "If we are greedy, we should be greedy for eternal life. Yearn for the life that has no end. That is where our greed should stretch. Do you covet endless money? Then desire eternal, endless life. Do you hope for possessions unlimited? Seek eternal life."[8] Concretely, Augustine's advice entails developing a greedy love of prayer. The discipline of prayer is a stick in the eye of worldly necessity. The morning and evening offices are pure and perfect opportunities to waste time. Daily mass is a lovely extravagance that frees us from the reign of Mammon because a sacrifice of praise and thanksgiving involves a spiritual contempt for the world. It snatches our lips and hands from the maw of Mammon and redirects them toward God.

The absorptive worldly waste of worship holds for the study of Scripture. It is not a curse that the languages are ancient, the idiom foreign, and the content hopelessly complex. God has blessed us with a word that is such a puzzle and challenge that one must give over one's entire life to trying to understand it. Take this blessing to heart. Pile up the commentaries and lexicons. If we will exhaust ourselves in the study of Scripture, *then nothing is left to be consumed by Mammon.* Thus does the psalmist petition God: "Incline my heart to thy testimonies, and not to gain" (Ps. 119:36). The psalmist is confident that contempt for the world will not evacuate us and leave us with a thin whisper of mere spiritual existence. A contempt for gain does not impoverish. It frees us to be filled with far more than we can ever digest or understand, for the Lord promises, "Open your mouth wide and I will fill it" (Ps. 81:10).

If we turn toward the beauty of holiness, then we can see how Jesus' law is also a promise. His moral demands are a species of his gospel, always circling back to the first commandment, which is itself more declaration of truth than moral imperative. This is clearly evident in Jesus' teaching on wealth. We cannot, as he tells us, serve God and Mammon. The logic of the disjunction is pure grace. If we will but serve God, then we *cannot* serve Mammon. The sword that divides us from the world is the sword that delivers us from our own grasping desire to hold on to the many finite loves that cannot save us. The first commandment tears us from the grasp of all the other false gods of this world, and in so doing, sets us free. Our jealous God, his consuming love, leaves nothing to be subjugated in the rusting, rotting kingdom of Mammon.

8. Augustine, *Exposition of the Psalms,* Exposition 2 of Psalm 90, 12.

Response

Shalom Carmy

"How Much Land Does a Man Need?" asks Tolstoy in one of his late stories. Pahom has heard of a fabled region where land is plentiful. For a
thousand rubles he can own all the land he can circumnavigate in the
course of a day. If he fails to return by sundown to the spot he began from,
the money is forfeit. Tolstoy accompanies him through the appointed day,
as the buyer starts out with high hopes and just a bit too much appetite for
acquisition. Morning turns to afternoon and the sun, which waits for no
man, begins to sink. Pahom rushes to meet the deadline, casting away his
coat, his boots, his flask, and his cap. Alas, in his moment of triumph he
collapses and dies. Tolstoy concludes: "In the end, six feet, from head to
heels, is all he needed."

This unforgettable parable dramatizes greed. Pahom wants more than
he needs. He doesn't want what belongs to someone else. Coveting is always about "your brother's something" — his wife or home or ox or donkey. Though greed is a prominent vice, it is not the vice specifically proscribed in the Decalogue.

Is coveting, then, essentially an offense against others? If that is the
case, the covetous man's viciousness is akin to that of the thief or the rob-
ber. It is unlikely that desiring someone else's possession or spouse, without any external manifestation of that desire to the other, would qualify as
an offense against that person. What kind of nonmental act defines coveting? Jewish legal analysis (halakha) of covetousness must therefore distin-
guish precisely the legal act of coveting from other intrusions on the property of others. To the extent that the mere attitude of covetousness is
prohibited, this would be connected to its practical consequences: the covetous person is liable to harm his neighbor by coveting.

212

An alternative approach to coveting would emphasize the wrongness of the desire irrespective of the actions it leads to. From this perspective the sin of coveting is like the vice of greed, with the difference that coveting targets the possession of the desired object by another. It is the desire itself that is prohibited. On this reading, halakhic discourse devoted to the demarcation of tangible actions associated with coveting would be legal in nature. Its purpose would be to measure the degree of covetousness susceptible to legal proceedings.

However we define coveting, covetousness, as an attitude, is forbidden. This raises the educational problem: How can we train ourselves, not only to avoid intruding on other people's relations with what is theirs, but to avoid desiring to do so? One major focus of the Jewish doctrine of coveting is halakhic; another is moral and psychological. This second theme is identical with Professor Reno's primary concern. Like his essay, the sources I present on this question, while ostensibly addressing covetousness, also treat the more general question of greed.

In what follows I will try to illustrate both the legal debate about the nature of coveting, by reference to the dispute between Maimonides (late twelfth-century Egypt) and his older contemporary from Provence, R. Abraham b. David (= Ravad), and medieval and modern edifying reflections on the psychological problem of covetousness.

Coveting: Act or Attitude?

Maimonides' most important treatment of coveting (*Mishneh Torah*, Laws of Robbery and Loss 1:9-12) states:

> 9. Whoever covets his neighbor's male or female servant or his home and utensils or anything that he can purchase, and he pressed him through friends and importuned him until he acquired it — even though he paid him a substantial sum, he transgresses . . . "thou shalt not covet"; there is no [criminal penalty] because no act is involved. He does not violate this commandment until he acquires the object. . . . 10. Whoever desires the home or wife or utensils of his neighbor or any other thing that can be bought from him — once he considered in his heart how to buy it and was tempted in his heart, he has transgressed "thou shalt not desire. . . ." 11. Desire

leads to coveting; coveting leads to robbery. For if the owner did not wish to sell, even though the sum offered was substantial and he was pressed through friends, [the buyer] will resort to robbery. . . .
12. Hence you learn that he who desires violates one negative commandment, and he who bought the things he desired by pressuring the owner or pleading with him violates two, and if he took it by robbery he violates three.[1]

One distinctive feature of this approach is the enumeration of coveting and desiring as two separate commandments, reflecting the Decalogue recorded in Exodus 20 and Deuteronomy 5 respectively.[2] My concern, however, is with the orientation of both prohibitions. Maimonides' rationale (in section 11) appears to categorize coveting and desiring as offenses against one's neighbor: the "offer you can't refuse" is one step from robbery; the covetous person is one step from refusing to take no for an answer.

Ravad disagrees with Maimonides at two points. He maintains that one does not violate the transgression unless the owner parts with the object unwillingly, after all attempts to appease him have failed. He also rejects Maimonides' explanation of the lack of criminal penalty. For Maimonides the reason is that no action has been done by the coveter. For Ravad, by contrast, a criminal act has been performed, but the halakhic principle of monetary remedy, namely, returning the wrongfully procured object, renders such penalty inappropriate.

Now the question before us is whether Maimonides regards desiring or coveting as an offense against others, like robbery, or as a psychological vice akin to greed. Influential medieval commentators, like the *Maggid Mishneh,* seem to adopt the first alternative, following the argument of section 11. According to this interpretation, Maimonides agrees with Ravad that coveting is defined by a set of external actions. They disagree only about the threshold of transgression: for Maimonides it is enough to pressure the owner for the object; for Ravad the pressure must ultimately be

1. For earlier formulations of Maimonides' position, see his *Sefer ha-Mitzvot,* Negative Commandments 265-266. The act of coveting one's neighbor's wife, on this analysis, is to promote the possibility of divorce, upon which the coveter could press his suit on the woman.

2. For criticisms of this distinction by later exegetes on linguistic grounds, see Nehama Leibowitz, *Studies in Shemot* (Jerusalem, 1983), pp. 342-51.

successful. Thus Maimonides is vulnerable to Ravad's objection: the offender cannot be exempt from criminal penalty on the grounds that he has done no action. Another rationale for this law is necessary.

My colleague Rabbi Michael Rosensweig has championed the alternative approach to Maimonides.[3] He proposes that the essence of the transgression, according to Maimonides, is the psychological attitude, not the manipulation of the other person. For that reason it does not count as an "external" prohibition. The application of pressure and wheedling to the seller is not what is forbidden: these are only external manifestations of the forbidden attitude, which measure the intensity of covetousness that defines the transgression. Ravad, however, holds that coveting is indeed an act allied to extortion and robbery. Therefore his standard for coveting is higher (the pressure must bear fruit), and this achievement defines the violation rather than the attitude motivating it.[4]

Interpreted narrowly, the prohibition of coveting condemns a fairly specific kind of activity. It is not a very common activity in my immediate circles. We are rarely tempted to induce others to sell us their personal possessions. Most of the things we desire are readily available, in generic form, on the commodity market, the only obvious exception being the quest for perfect housing at the optimal location. Insisting on having a particular object belonging to another, and then plotting to acquire it, seems largely confined to gangsters, collectors, and small children. From the viewpoint of everyday morality, the approach that assimilates coveting to robbery or exploitation may nevertheless remind us of the nasty, quasi-coercive element in many personal and professional transactions. In this spirit, my colleague Rabbi Aaron Levine has suggested that intrusive sales tactics, where the seller aggressively pressures the buyer, may constitute a technical violation of the law against coveting.[5]

---

3. Michael Rosensweig, "On Coveting" (in Hebrew), *Bet Yitzhak* 19 (1987): 215-27.

4. This analysis would also explain Maimonides' omission of the coveter from the list of individuals disqualified as witnesses because they violate the property of others (Laws of Testimony 10:4).

5. Aaron Levine, "Ethical Dilemmas in the Telemarketing Industry," *Tradition* 38, no. 3 (Fall 2004): 1-39.

Coveting as Envy and/or Greed

In the nonhalakhic literature, the educational challenge comes to the fore. Medieval and modern commentators and moralists recognize that the prohibition of coveting entails control over one's thoughts and desires and that this is a difficult undertaking. Discussions of coveting from this vantage point inevitably offer guidance with respect to envy and greed as well.

Perhaps the most famous of these treatments is Rabbi Abraham Ibn Ezra's in his commentary on Exodus (twelfth-century Spain). The habit of putting one's trust in God, for Ibn Ezra, is the great prophylactic to covetousness and to greed. A villager does not aspire to marry a princess, despite her attractiveness, nor is a man tempted to lust after his mother. So too the wise individual knows that our possessions are meted out by the deity. Adultery is "more sublime" a prohibition than the villager's lack of desire for the princess: the former is divinely established, while the latter merely reflects the social order. The wise person therefore rejoices in the portion allotted him by God; he trusts the Creator and eschews plots and stratagems.

The great educator Nehama Leibowitz states that the fundamental idea — training can mold our imagination — survives the feudal associations of Ibn Ezra's parable of the villager and the princess that "cannot appeal to us in this democratic age." To the extent that we accept the moral judgments about what we ought to aspire to and what we ought to leave to God, this remains true. Thus we acknowledge that our neighbor's spouse is off limits or, as the saying goes: "don't even think about it!" The problem for many of us is that, because we believe that our horizons of possessiveness are not rigidly deduced from our original social station, we do not believe in any natural moral limits to our desire for more.

In a democratic age, we can still derive constraints from a sense of the inherent inviolability of other people's property, but this would rule out covetousness, not greed or even envy. Though we should surely rejoice in the portion God has appointed for us, in the absence of stratified social-economic classes, why should we accept our lot passively? Isn't God's will for us dependent on our own efforts? Why not set our sights as high as we can, and strenuously strive to meet our goals? The society we live in has come closer than any in history to removing the shamefulness in envy and transforming it into a peculiar egalitarian virtue. Ibn Ezra's parable would effectively motivate us to dismiss greed and envy only if it were conjoined to some insight about our worthwhile needs and aspirations growing out of our self-discovery as individuals standing before God.

Rabbi Jacob Mecklenburg served the Konigsberg Jewish community in the nineteenth century. In his commentary *Ha-Ketav ve-ha-Kabbala,* after citing Ibn Ezra approvingly, he offers a further exploration of the motivational question. Drawing on an earlier author, he notes that the Shema section recited twice daily during worship (Deut. 6:4-9) calls upon us to love God with *all* our heart. He takes this as a demand for wholehearted love. The heart must overflow; it must be completely filled with the love of God. The person who loves God in this way has no room, so to speak, for covetous desires. Without such love, it is difficult to expel covetous, greedy, or envious feelings, even when the believer is intellectually convinced that such desires are immoral and ought to be resisted. The joy that accompanies wholehearted engagement with God precludes obsession with "this man's gift and this man's scope," as Eliot put it, and with others' material possessions and achievements as well. If Ibn Ezra recommended the satisfied joy that grows out of trust in God, R. Jacob preaches to his modern reader the consuming joy that is the passion for God and his service.

The sources and methods of my analysis are very different from Professor Reno's. Our practical conclusions converge. We confront the same society, deeply confused about how many possessions a man needs, and deeply disturbed at the human cost of our disordered desires and dreams, both the manipulation of others and the cheapening of ourselves. Our response to the acquisitiveness, be it covetousness, greed, or envy, is to confront it with the knowledge that all we own is in truth not ours, and valuable as an instrument to serve him. Our response to the passion of acquisitiveness, in all its forms, is the passion of love that sets the right value on our worldly ambitions.

Afterword

Richard John Neuhaus

I have long had a problem with the Ten Commandments. Of course, we all do. But I don't mean a problem with observing one or another of them. I mean a problem with the very idea of commandments. It undoubtedly has everything to do with my being reared and theologically formed as a Lutheran.

The critical distinction in my training was that between law and gospel. As it was commonly put, the law is the bad news of what God requires of us, the gospel is the good news of what God has done for us. In the Lutheran Church–Missouri Synod of which I was part, this theme, in all its detailed implications, was magisterially set forth in a book by the nineteenth-century founder of the Missouri Synod, C. F. W. Walther, *The Proper Distinction between Law and Gospel.* It is a rigorously theo-*logical* book and has provided for many a satisfyingly coherent "system" for understanding the Christian faith. I, too, was quite taken with it as a Lutheran seminarian.

In addition to its satisfying logic, Walther's system is also, I came to believe many years ago, thoroughly wrongheaded. Meaning no disrespect for Dr. Walther, who was a great man in many ways, his understanding of law and gospel puts one in mind of G. K. Chesterton's observation that the problem with some people is not that they aren't logical but that they are *only* logical. Of course, the system was designed for the assiduous defense of the sixteenth-century Reformation's insistence upon *sola gratia* and *sola fides* — grace alone and faith alone.

In the Missouri Synod of the time there were heated and endless debates about "the third use of the law." Everybody agreed on the first use of the law: it is a "mirror" in which we see our sins, leading us to flee to God

218

for forgiveness. And almost everybody had no difficulty with the second use of the law: it is a "curb" against the ways of the wicked, and also against our own fallen and unruly human nature. But most rejected what some proposed as the third use of the law: it is a "guide" for leading a life pleasing to God. That third use, it was said, smacked of "works righteousness" and compromised the utter gratuitousness of God's love.

In that world, it was clear that the chief difference between Lutheranism and Roman Catholicism was that the former is premised upon grace and the latter upon fulfilling the demands of the law. Even more dramatically different — so dramatically different as to warrant only passing mention — is true Christianity from Judaism. Employing Luther's employment of Paul, and wrapping the whole package in Walther's "proper distinction," Judaism was portrayed as a deadeningly legalistic religion that was discredited, rejected, and superseded by the coming of Christ. The biblical story is the triumph of gospel over law.

I first began to question this account of Judaism when Rabbi Sol Bernards, then working for the Anti-Defamation League and now well into his nineties, came to the campus of Concordia Theological Seminary, St. Louis. He was something of a circuit rider, tirelessly traveling the country to alert people to a new thing called the Jewish-Christian dialogue. I was hooked from the start, and it has never let me go. Most critical to my subsequent understanding, however, was Rabbi Abraham Joshua Heschel. He helped me to see how it was possible and necessary to join the psalmist in saying, "I rejoice in the law of the Lord." Put differently, he helped me to understand the law as grace. Even, if you will, the law as gospel.

I first met Heschel in 1965. It was in connection with our shared concern about the war in Vietnam. We hit it off in a big way, and ours became an intense intellectual and spiritual friendship that ended with his death in December 1972. We both loved to argue, and mainly we argued about the connections and conflicts between the Jewish and Christian ways of being children of Abraham. I thought he was too given to an easy pluralism, and he thought I was too insistent in my Christian particularism. "Why must Christ be the absolute center of everything?" he persistently protested. I, just as persistently, tried to explain. So far as I know, to no avail. For hours upon end, the two of us went back and forth, often in his book-crammed office high in the tower of the Jewish Theological Seminary, he smoking his cannon-sized cigars and I puffing my pipe until the air was so thick we had to open the window even in the dead of winter. I expect that I learned much more than he did from our conversations. He was a very learned man, and a great soul.

Heschel's books are still widely read. For instance, *The Earth Is the Lord's*, *The Sabbath*, *Man Is Not Alone*, and *God in Search of Man*. In Jewish-Christian conferences over the years, I have had many occasions to recall his maxim that "Interfaith dialogue begins with faith." It perhaps does not need saying that much of what is called interfaith dialogue operates by the rule that faith — or at least articles of faith suggesting tension or conflict between believing Christians and Jews — must be checked at the door. That is not the case with the present book. I think Heschel would have liked this book. I know I do, and not least because, among many other things, it explores the ways in which the flourishing of the truly human depends upon our rejoicing in, and observing, the law of the Lord.

Contributors

Authors of Essays

#1 — James A. Diamond, Joseph and Wolf Lebovic Chair of Jewish Studies, University of Waterloo

#2 — Daniel Polish, Rabbi of Congregation Shir Chadash of the Hudson Valley, Poughkeepsie, New York; author of *Bringing the Psalms to Life*

#3 — R. Kendall Soulen, Professor of Systematic Theology, Wesley Theological Seminary, Washington, D.C.

#4 — David Novak, J. Richard and Dorothy Shiff Chair of Jewish Studies, University of Toronto

#5 — Byron L. Sherwin, Distinguished Service Professor of Jewish Philosophy and Mysticism, Spertus College, Chicago

#6 — John K. Roth, Edward J. Sexton Professor of Philosophy; Director, Center for the Study of the Holocaust, Genocide, and Human Rights, Claremont McKenna College, Claremont, California

#7 — Carl E. Braaten, Executive Director of the Center for Catholic and Evangelical Theology, Sun City West, Arizona

#8 — Allen Verhey, Professor of Theological Studies, Duke Divinity School, Durham, North Carolina

#9 — Miroslav Volf, Henry B. Wright Professor of Systematic Theology, Yale Divinity School, New Haven, Connecticut, with student Linn Tonstad

#10 — R. R. Reno, Professor of Systematic Theology, Creighton University, Omaha, Nebraska

Respondents

#1 — Calvin P. Van Reken, Professor of Moral Theology, Calvin Theological Seminary, Grand Rapids, Michigan

#2 — Leanne Van Dyk, Professor of Reformed Theology and Dean of the Faculty, Western Theological Seminary, Holland, Michigan

#3 — Rochelle L. Millen, Professor of Religion, Wittenberg University, Springfield, Ohio

#4 — Marguerite Shuster, Professor of Preaching, Fuller Theological Seminary, Pasadena, California

#5 — Anathea E. Portier-Young, Assistant Professor of Old Testament, Duke Divinity School, Durham, North Carolina

#6 — Roger Brooks, Elie Wiesel Professsor of Judaic Studies, Department of Religious Studies, Connecticut College, New London, Connecticut

#6 — Jean Bethke Elshtain, Laura Spelman Rockefeller Professor of Social and Political Ethics at the University of Chicago

#7 — Elliot N. Dorff, Rector and Professor of Philosophy, University of Judaism, Bel-Air, California

#8 — Sue Ann Wasserman, Director, Department of Worship, Music, and Religious Living, Union for Reform Judaism

#9 — David Patterson, Professor of Judaic Studies, University of Memphis

#10 — Shalom Carmy, Professor of Jewish Studies and Philosophy, Yeshiva University, New York City

Foreword

Peter W. Ochs, Edgar M. Bronfman Professor of Modern Judaic Studies, University of Virginia

Afterword

Richard John Neuhaus, editor in chief of *First Things* and president of Religion and Public Life